Grammar for Written English

DAVID A. CONLIN · *Arizona State University*

HOUGHTON MIFFLIN COMPANY · BOSTON

05988

Contents

Preface

THE AIM OF THIS TEXT is twofold. First, it is to synthesize the most useful elements of the traditional and the linguistic viewpoints, in order to make grammar a more practical tool for students in their writing. Second, it is to give students the widest possible experience with the structures of written English in building sentences.

Clearly, then, this book is grounded in the belief that a knowledge of grammatical principles, and practice with them, is related to skill in composition. Traditional grammar, it is true, has failed to the extent that it does not provide an accurate description of our language. Structural grammar has provided valuable correctives — new insights into the structure of English and a more accurate description of it. But the grammar of the structuralists has been largely a "pure science." Except by uncompromising devotees, there have been few attempts to infuse its findings into the composition class, and fewer still in manageable form. To teachers and students traditionally trained, the host of new concepts and terms is bewildering, and *the relative lack of concern with improvement* seems alien and irrelevant to their needs. This is a real misfortune, for structural grammar has a great deal to offer in the composition class, if only it can by some process of apperception be made to buttress and inform what teachers and students know already. That is what this book seeks to do: to harmonize the achievements of linguistic research with the grammar of the schools and apply the most helpful parts of both to the improvement of writing. Because the nomenclature of traditional grammar is so firmly embedded in the language, we are retaining as many of the old terms as possible, introducing new ones only for new concepts.

But a mere description of the English language, however complete and simple, does not much help the student to better writing habits, no matter how well he may understand it or how glibly he may discuss it. Practice with the great variety of language forms is essential. Without such experience the student tends to fix in habits of writing the limited structures and patterns of speech. One learns to write only by writing, and the student must *use* the language forms with which he becomes familiar. He will master the various grammatical devices for building sentences only by using them to build sentences of his own. He will learn to handle co-ordination and subordination by constructing many compound and complex sentences within the context of his own writing. He will learn to make his meaning more explicit through modifiers, both single words and word groups. He will explore the potentialities of verbals and verbal phrases. He will learn to avoid structural ambiguity by using signals to identify function. He will benefit by reading widely, discussing what he has read, and imitating the language forms of various writers. Through all this he will develop skill in handling a multiplicity of language patterns for more effective communication. Facility in writing will come when he no longer must make a conscious effort to select the appropriate structures of standard written English — in other words, when his use of these structures has become habitual, much as are the language forms of his speech. This, then, is the second aim of the text: to provide the opportunity, through extensive exercise materials, for practice in the use of grammatical resources in building sentences.

Since this description of the language is for the *writer*, it is focused on the sentence. We begin with the physical characteristics and basic patterns of the sentence, then examine it for its constituent word groups — subject-predicate and modifier. The principles of subordination and co-ordination are explained and illustrated in relation to subject-predicate word groups. The study of modifier word groups includes prepositional phrases, participial phrases, infinitive phrases, and the variety of head-words about which the modifiers may cluster. Nouns, verbs, adjectives, and adverbs are studied not as parts of speech but as elements in the communication pattern of the sentence, with stress on formal characteristics and environment. A special chapter on structure words explains and illustrates their importance to the language. The problem of form and function is next considered, followed by a study of functional shift. This is logically succeeded by a discussion of the importance and use of verbals in our communication patterns. Chapters on agreement, substitution, and appositives and absolutes conclude the discussion of syntactical structures and principles as related to the writer's problems and needs. From the sentence, we move to the study of the word in a chapter on compounding and affixation, followed by one on problems of spelling in relation to the significant sounds of the language — the phonemes. The two final chapters deal with practical problems of punctuation and sentence building.

In abundant exercise materials throughout, the student is given practice in identifying and using grammatical structures and language categories in their various forms and functions; and the problems and practice materials of the final chapter provide him with an opportunity to synthesize his knowledge of grammar and apply it to an intensive study of sentence building.

The writer wishes to acknowledge his debt to the linguists who have so patiently studied the language and have written of their craft. He is particularly grateful to John B. Carroll, Charles C. Fries, Donald J. Lloyd, Harry R. Warfel, Paul Roberts, and Harold Whitehall. And to L. M. Myers, Division Head, Division of Language and Literature, Arizona State University, go his thanks for the priceless ingredient of motivation.

DAVID A. CONLIN

Grammar, Old and New

To SOME PEOPLE grammar means the study of "correct English." To others it means the definition and identification of parts of speech. To still others it means sentence analysis, often with diagrams.

Modern grammar is none of these things, exactly. It is the study and description of the *structure* of language. Not much concerned with definitions and rules, modern grammar deals mainly with *morphology*, the study of the formation of words and the changes in word forms; with *syntax*, the study of the relationship of words and word groups within the sentence; and with *phonology*, the study of the sounds of language, particularly those significant to meaning.

Modern grammar grows out of the study of linguistics, the science of language. It has developed rapidly in the past twenty-five years through the work of anthropologists, philologists, psychologists, and students of social science, many of whom have perceived dynamic relationships between their disciplines and linguistic science. Indeed, the study of structural linguistics has produced such swift and extensive changes in grammatical concepts that it has been referred to as a "revolution in grammar." And, according to the linguists, this development places our "traditional grammar" in the same category as four-element chemistry or Ptolemaic astronomy.

Limitations of Traditional Grammar

In the light of the modern study of language structure, students of linguistics have examined the older grammar very critically. They have pointed to a number of limitations.

1. The description of the English language in conventional grammar has developed largely from the study of Greek and Latin. The adaptation of Latin grammar to English has not been adequate, since English is largely an uninflected language dependent mostly on word order for clues to meaning, whereas Latin is a highly inflected language dependent on changes in word forms for clues to meaning. The structural difference between English and Latin is denoted in language study by designating English as an analytic language and Latin as a synthetic language.

2. Definitions in the older grammar often depend on meaning and are therefore ambiguous. A noun is defined as the "name of a person, place, or thing," yet the meaning of *thing* may vary from one person to another. The linguist, on the other hand, maintains that we identify a noun in communication (as we must) not because it is a *thing*, but because of the structural clues or signals present.

3. In conventional grammar there is inconsistency in method of definition. The older grammarian defines some of the "parts of speech" according to meaning and some according to function. The noun is defined according to *what it is*, but the adjective is defined according to *what it does*, as a word which modifies a noun or pronoun.

4. In conventional grammar the classifications are unnecessarily complex. We have many kinds of complements — direct objects,

indirect objects, predicate complements, objective complements, and adverbial objects. Subjects have been classified as grammatical, notional, elliptical, and appositive, as phrase subjects, clause subjects, and subjects of verbals. We have declarative, imperative, and interrogative sentences as well as simple, complex, compound, and compound-complex sentences, to say nothing of balanced and periodic sentences.

5. The older grammar often includes in its subject matter the study of usage, thus confusing the *description* of the language as it is used with the *evaluation* of linguistic forms in terms of social appropriateness. Hence has grown the formulation of rules to prescribe how the language *ought to be used*. This, the linguists say, assumes the existence of universal, unchanging language truths and denies the concept of language as a changing social convention.

6. Conventional grammar lacks uniformity. First, there is variation in nomenclature. Verbals are also called verbids. Linking verbs are sometimes called copulative verbs. Predicate complements are also called subjective complements. The possessive case is often referred to as the genitive case. Second, there is variation in definition. According to Charles C. Fries, the sentence has been defined in over two hundred different ways. Third, there is variation in classification. The expression *Get out!* has been called both a sentence and a non-sentence. In the sentence *Freddy is a fraternity man*, the word *fraternity* might be classified by some as an adjective and by others as a noun. In *Put the cat out*, the word *out* might be considered part of the verb, or it might be called an adverb. *There* in *There is a good show tonight* has been called both an adverb and an expletive.

Some Basic Linguistic Principles

Those who read carefully in the literature of structural linguistics will discover a number of basic principles which may throw some light on the nature of the new grammar.

1. The linguist defines language as communication by sequence of speech sounds. He is interested in the basic significant sounds made by the speaker; in the patterns in which these sounds are uttered; and in the aspects of stress, pitch, and juncture which

he calls *intonation.* He views writing as a derivative form of language, a separate symbolism which has to be learned after the language itself has been mastered. Linguistics is primarily directed to the study of the speech of a language community.

2. The linguist is mainly concerned with a language *system,* not with the content of communication. His chief aim is to describe the form or structure of the language, and he is interested in meaning only as it is related to structure. This kind of meaning is called *structural* meaning in contrast to the meaning of words, which is called *lexical* meaning. For example, word order is an important structural characteristic of our language. Meaning may be a function of word order.

> Joe ate the fish.
> The fish ate Joe.

In these sentences, the words are identical, but the order is changed. The different meanings arise from the difference in word order, a structural difference.

3. The linguist is not concerned with rules of right and wrong. He does not evaluate language as correct or incorrect; he is interested only in how the language is used in various speech communities. Of course, he studies dialect and the usage of educated and uneducated classes. But he does not evaluate; he merely reports and describes. Unlike the traditional grammarian, he does not tell others how the language *should* be used.

4. The linguist is concerned with a rigorous analysis of a language in order to achieve a structural description in terms of its elements from the smallest unit of sound, the phoneme, to the largest element, the sentence. Structure is concerned with patterned contrasts — in sounds, in inflections, in syntactical arrangements, and in the meaning of linguistic forms.

5. The linguist has developed a new terminology of description. He has felt that much of the traditional nomenclature is ambiguous and that the new concepts require new words precisely defined. The new terminology includes such words as *phoneme,* *morpheme,* and *immediate constituent.*

The phoneme is the unit of sound which differentiates meaning. The words *ton* and *son,* different in meaning, contrast only in the initial sounds of *t* and *s.* The *t* sound and the *s* sound are distinctive sounds, therefore, and are phonemes. The English language is said to have 45 phonemes: 9 vowels, 3 semi-vowels, 21 consonants, 4 degrees of pitch, 4 degrees of loudness, and 4 kinds of juncture. To record phonemic analysis, the linguists have developed a rather elaborate symbolism, some of it derived from the International Phonetic Alphabet.

The morpheme is the unit of form. It is not necessarily a word. For example, the word *peaches* consists of two morphemes, *peach* and *es*.

Immediate constituents (IC's) are the component parts of a structure on its highest level of organization, the parts into which a structure is divided at the first step of analysis. The IC's of "People who live in glass houses shouldn't throw stones" are *People who live in glass houses* and *shouldn't throw stones*. The IC's of *shouldn't throw stones* are *shouldn't throw* and *stones*.

Some linguists have abandoned the concept of *parts of speech* and have developed that of *form classes*. Instead of eight parts of speech there are usually four form classes: noun, verb, adjective, and adverb. These are sometimes called simply Class 1 words, Class 2 words, Class 3 words, and Class 4 words, abandoning the traditional names. The remaining word forms are called structure words or function words.

6. The linguist is concerned also with the cultural aspects of language. Many linguists are anthropologists. The study of a language is part of the study of the culture itself, a phenomenon of a human society.

Practical Applications of Linguistics

Many linguists are interested in more than the pure science of language. The question of what the new grammar has to offer the English teacher has become important to a number of them. A survey of reports indicates some of the directions in which applied linguistics may take the teacher of English language arts.

1. Emphasis on the primacy of the spoken language has focused attention on the differences between the sound symbolism and the graphic symbolism. Whereas speech is variable in different parts of the English-speaking world, with several accepted dialects in the United States alone, written English is highly standardized.

Speech is often fragmentary, whereas writing is developed mainly
with the structure of the sentence. Young men and women of
college age have attained a high degree of mastery of the spoken
language, but have usually not achieved a comparable skill with
standard written English. A knowledge of his mastery of speech
patterns may give the student confidence in his ability to use
language. A knowledge of the importance of the sentence in
writing may motivate him to study the variety of structures used
in sentence development and to practice with them for more
effective written communication.

2. Developing from emphasis on the spoken language, the study
of intonation provides clues to syntax. By intonation the speaker
groups his words into meaningful patterns. Pitch and juncture
are important signals to the listener in helping him to perceive
language in word groups — a noun with its modifiers, a verb
with its modifiers, a prepositional phrase, a verb phrase, a participial phrase, a subject-predicate word group, and so on. Similarly the reader in responding to written language tries to group
the words into approximately the same patterns he would use if
speaking them himself. The perception of word groups is the key
to syntax and therefore to meaning.

3. The writer may use intonation as a rough guide in punc-
tuating. Since written communication is not reinforced by
rhythms of sound, punctuation serves instead to provide the
reader with clues to syntactical relationships. But the correspondence of intonation and punctuation is only approximate. For
example, a pause and a rising pitch may call for a question mark,
a comma, or even a period. A pause with a falling pitch may
indicate a period, a comma, or even a question mark. A pause
with no change of pitch may or may not require punctuation. A
change of pitch with a pause, however, usually signals to the writer
that a problem of punctuation must be faced, and he will solve
it according to his knowledge of syntax and the conventions of
punctuation.

4. Linguists have emphasized objective signals of form as clues
to syntax and therefore to meaning. These include word order,
inflections, characteristic suffixes and other contrasting forms,
and structure words.

Word order is one of the most important clues to meaning.

> Is it a boy?
> It is a boy.

The response of the listener to each of the above sentences is quite different; that is, the meanings are quite different. The word order in each case plays an important part in determining this response or meaning.

In the following sentences a slight change in form (inflection) alters the meaning:

> She is my girl friend.
> She is my girl's friend.

In the next pair of sentences the use of a characteristic adjectival suffix changes the meaning entirely:

> Manfred is a child actor.
> Manfred is a childish actor.

Structure words are words which are relatively empty of meaning themselves, but which serve to give coherence to the language, to relate words and word groups, to provide totality of meaning. They include such words as *a, an, the, when, where, in, of, why, who, which, that, should, would, and, but, yet,* and many more. They constitute a very small percentage of our total vocabulary, but almost one word in four in our spoken and written language is a structure word. Almost fifty per cent of the words in the last sentence are structure words.

We identify the noun in communication because it is usually preceded by one of the characteristic structure words *a, an,* or *the.* The verb is often preceded by such words as *should have, will be, was, has been, may,* and so forth; these are the "helping verbs."

> *The* speaker *will be* introduced *by a* student.

In the above sentence the structure words *the, will be, by,* and *a* are important signals of meaning.

In the following sentences, the structure words *when, who,* and *if* are signals of subordination.

> The child came *when* she was called.
> He likes a man *who* can fight.
> He will go *if* it doesn't rain.

Familiarity with the structural devices which signal meaning will help the student of composition to avoid reliance on subjective definitions and give him insight into the syntactical relationships of the words and word groups in the sentences he reads and writes.

5. The study of phonemics provides an opportunity to become familiar with the basic significant sounds of English, and with their relationship — or lack of relationship — to the spelling of words. For example, while the *th* sound in *bath* has only one spelling, the *e* sound in *me* has at least twelve different spellings.

e	be	ey	monkey
ee	keen	oe	Phoenix
ei	perceive	eo	people
ie	relieve	i	machine
ea	team	ay	quay
ae	Caesar	y	soliloquy

From lists built upon the variant spellings of a single sound, the student will learn how a sound may be spelled and the words which illustrate these different spellings. In this way he will tend to become more sensitive to sound and spelling. Word lists may also be developed with words in which a "silent" letter is found, words in which there is a lack of relationship between sound and spelling; for example, a word with a silent *g* such as *phlegm*. Thus phonemics offers a method for the study of spelling and for improvement in this skill.

Summary

In this chapter we have discussed some of the limitations of the old grammar and some of the characteristics of the new, with a few suggestions for its application to the art of written discourse. We are now ready to examine the formal characteristics of a sentence, the functional unit of written communication.

Students and teachers who are interested in the scientific study of language should explore the extensive literature which has been developed in the field. A selected bibliography follows.

BIBLIOGRAPHY

Allen, Harold B., ed. *Readings in Applied Linguistics*. New York: Appleton-Century-Crofts, 1958.

Bloomfield, Leonard. *Language*. New York: Henry Holt, 1933.

Carroll, John B. *The Study of Language*. Cambridge: Harvard University Press, 1955.

Fries, Charles Carpenter. *The Structure of English*. New York: Harcourt, Brace, 1952.

Hockett, Charles F. *A Course in Modern Linguistics*. New York: Macmillan, 1958.

Lloyd, Donald J., and Harry R. Warfel. *American English in Its Cultural Setting*. New York: Alfred A. Knopf, 1956.

Roberts, Paul. *Patterns of English*. New York: Harcourt, Brace, 1956.

Sapir, Edward. *Language*. New York: Harcourt, Brace, (Harvest Book No. 7).

Whitehall, Harold. *Structural Essentials of English*. New York: Harcourt, Brace, 1956.

2

What Is a Sentence?

THE SENTENCE is the basic structure of standard written English. Since effective writing depends largely on skill in using its varied designs, a clear understanding of its essential forms is of first importance.

Many grammarians have attempted to define the sentence, and though they have done so in a great variety of ways, the most common single criterion is that a sentence must express a complete thought. But what is a complete thought? Each of the following expressions could be considered a complete thought, but none of them could be described as a sentence according to conventional definition.

> What a beautiful morning!
> Some dinner.
> Never again!
> Down the hatch.
> Hands up!

10

Because the expression "complete thought'" means different things to different people, it is not suitable as a criterion. A more precise description is needed. Rather than add a new definition to the long list we already have, let us examine the physical characteristics of the standard sentence so that we may have objective means of identifying and describing it. Perhaps it is too complex a structure to be defined in a single statement.

There are a number of formal signals by which one may identify a sentence. They are: (1) Punctuation; (2) Subject-Predicate Structure; (3) Finite Verb; (4) No Signal of Subordination; (5) Word Order; (6) Intonation. Let us examine these in turn.

Punctuation

The sentences in a paragraph of written or printed material can be quite closely identified and counted by merely observing the elements which begin with a capital letter and end with a period or question mark. The count may go wrong because punctuation alone is not a sufficient criterion; there may be non-sentences or even sentence fragments in the group. But punctuation is an approximate guide to sentence structure. Certainly it is of tremendous value in helping the reader separate the elements of communication. One can easily verify the importance of end punctuation by reproducing a paragraph without capitals or periods; the difficulty in reading is immediately apparent. Again, if one reads a stanza of poetry aloud, stressing complete sentences rather than lines, the greater ease of comprehension is surprising.

The student proofreading his own theme for complete sentences, however, cannot be guided solely by his punctuation. Failure to perceive other signals of sentence structure may have led him to punctuate incorrectly. Let us consider an example.

The man tripped and fell down, he injured his ankle.

The above expression separates two sentences by a comma instead of a period, indicating by punctuation that this is a single free utterance and so violating a convention of standard written English. Since the reader habitually responds to conventional usage, he is apt to be confused by this expression. Hence as written it is not acceptable and is condemned as a "comma fault."

Punctuation, then, is useful in sentence identification only so far as we can assume that the conventional signals of relationship or coherence have been used.

Subject-Predicate Structure

A second important characteristic of the standard sentence is its subject-predicate structure. English is basically a subject-predicate language, describing to us reality as we see it, a world of entities, isolates, "things." We live in an environment of houses, cars, trees, people, books, chairs, stones. We perceive collections or masses such as clouds, oceans, audiences, mountains, the air, a river, the lawn, all designated with names and belonging to our world of entities. We have names for "things" which do not exist in the ordinary sense but which seem necessary to our thinking: intelligence, conscience, pride, love, honesty, and so on. In our description of the language we have called all these names *nouns*. These are the elements of experience we think about, talk about, and write about. We consider these elements as the "subjects" in our discourse.

The world of entities which our language describes is an active world. Houses *burn*. Horses *run*. Trees *grow*. Men *work*. Children *play*. Clouds *move*. An audience *applauds*. A jury *disagrees*. The river *flows*. Our world is also one of being and becoming. The girl *is* pretty. The weather *is* hot. Men *grow* old. Father *seems* mad. We thus have words to describe the action, existence, and change of the entities or subjects of our "thing" world. These words are verbs. Verbs with their complements and their modifiers make up what is thought of as the predicate of a sentence. The subject of the sentence will be the noun (or substitute), together with its modifiers, which is used in a bound relationship with the verb. English is a bipolar language. The subject and predicate of a sentence express this bipolarity — actor and action, entity and movement, isolate and change, individual and being.

> Father / painted the house.
>
> The horse / ran away.
>
> The sky / is blue.
>
> My cousin / has pneumonia.

I / must go home now.

The man across the street / works in the factory.

The house that Washington slept in / was torn down.

The book which you gave me / is a gift I will always keep.

What I say / won't hurt you.

To go to school in this weather / would be very foolish.

Finite Verb

Another clue to identifying a sentence is the presence of a finite verb, one which is not an infinitive or a participle. An infinitive is generally preceded by *to: to go, to come, to play, to save.* Participles are verb forms which end (usually) in *-ing, -ed,* and sometimes *-en, -d,* or *-t.* For example, *seeing, running, dressed, fallen, lined, swept* are participles. An expression which does not have a finite verb is not a sentence.

> The women brought their pitchers to the well. The pitchers to hold the water.

The first expression is a sentence using the finite verb *brought.* The second is not a sentence, since the infinitive *to hold* is not a finite verb.

> John Smith is president of the class. John being so popular with the girls.

The first expression is a sentence with the finite verb *is.* The second is not a sentence, since the participle *being* is not a finite verb.

If a participle is used with a helping verb it becomes a finite verb.

> The car *was towed* to the garage.

> Henry *has been going* to the doctor for weeks.

Both of these expressions are sentences. Both contain finite verbs, since the participles are used with helping verbs.

As will be shown in a later chapter, infinitives may be used in a variety of ways in a sentence. For example,

> I want *to hold* the baby.

This expression is a perfectly good sentence with a finite verb *want*. The infinitive *to hold* is used here as the complement of the verb.

No Signal of Subordination

In English, subordination is an important structural device. It enables us to express many relationships between ideas, and makes our language a flexible, supple instrument of communication.

> I will come *when* you call me.
> I will go *if* you will come with me.
> I wonder *where* she put the scissors.
> *Unless* you wear your coat, you will catch cold.
> The man was injured *because* he was careless.

When, if, where, unless, because, and many other words connect dependent or subordinate clauses to the main part of the sentence. Like a sentence, a subordinate clause is a subject-predicate word group, with a finite verb, but *it is always included as part of a sentence.* The signal of inclusion, or subordination, is the connective, followed, of course, by normal subject-verb-complement word order. A partial list of subordinating connectives follows.

SUBORDINATE CONJUNCTIONS

if	why	whether
though	since	that
while	because	how
as	before	whoever
when	until	whatever
where	unless	wherever
what	after	whenever
which	although	whichever
who		

A subordinate clause not included in a complete sentence is not a sentence by itself. For example,

> We drove forty miles to the mountains and stopped at Horizon Lake. Where we unpacked our tent and made camp.

The second expression is not a sentence. The word *where* signals a subordinate clause which, in this case, is not included in a complete sentence.

A question is often begun with one of the words listed above as subordinate conjunctions. The question is easy to recognize by inverted word order.

> Where are you going?
> Why did you sell your house?
> Which day of the week is it?

Here both the introductory words and the inverted word order signal the questions.

Word Order

Word order as a signal of meaning is useful in identifying the sentence. In statements (declarative sentences) the word order is subject, verb, complement. In questions (interrogative sentences) the order is usually inverted; that is, the verb may precede the subject, or the subject may come between parts of the verb.

> Have you a garage for your car?
> Do you have a garage for your car?
> When will you change the tire?

The above expressions are all good sentences (interrogative). The word order signals the question.

Knowledge of word order will help the writer detect sentence fragments he has written when these begin with a subordinate conjunction.

> I will send you a statement at the end of the month. When I expect you to pay in full.

The second expression is recognized as a sentence fragment because *when*, followed by the normal word order of subject-verb-complement, is a signal of subordination.

Intonation

Intonation, our final clue to the sentence, is achieved by changes in stress, variations in pitch, and the ways in which word groupings are joined.

> I want to go *home* to my *mother.*

The word *home* and the first syllable of *mother* are stressed. We unconsciously respond to these signals of stress.

> I didn't say *you* stole the money.
> I didn't say you *stole* the money.
> I didn't *say* you stole the money.

These three sentences mean three quite different things to us. Stress is thus a grammatical signal of meaning, a part of the rhythm of language to which we have learned to respond.

Changes in pitch occur when the tone of voice rises or falls. For example,

> You are going to college.
> You are going to college?

At the end of the first sentence, the voice drops and fades off. The response of the listener is one of agreement or understanding. At the end of the second sentence, the voice rises and stops abruptly. The listener recognizes the signal and responds with an answer to what he knows is a question.

The term *juncture* indicates the joining of words and word groups. In speech recordings, we observe minute intervals separating words, word groups, and sentences. Sometimes these junctures are accompanied by changes in pitch. For example,

> I want to go home to my mother. I am very tired and sick.

There is a short pause after *home* and a slightly longer pause after *mother*. The pauses mark off the word groups into syntactical units. These junctures or joinings are aids to comprehension.

Intonation or rhythm, then, is a useful signal of sentence structure. A student proofreading his paper may note all the long pauses accompanied by falling pitch and fading sound, or rising pitch and sudden cessation of sound. He may use these intonation patterns as a rough guide to sentence structure. By applying his knowledge of the other characteristics of a sentence, he may avoid many comma faults and sentence fragments.

Summary

Since standard written English is based on sentence structure, the student of composition must learn at the outset to identify a sentence. Six useful tests may be applied to this identification:

1. Punctuation.
2. Subject-predicate structure.
3. Requirement of the finite verb.
4. No signal of subordination before the subject-predicate word group.
5. Normal pattern of word order for a statement, and inverted pattern for questions signaled by words such as *when* and *where* or forms of *to be, have, do* and helping verbs such as *will* and *would*.
6. Signals of intonation.

EXERCISE A

Applying the six tests discussed in this chapter, identify the sentences in the following list of utterances.

1. He was a sober man, rarely laughing or even smiling.
2. Then we were fortunate in finding the bus terminal.
3. After all that research, not to find the information I wanted.
4. Apparently not observing that half the audience was alseep.
5. Being actual life size, the statue looked almost human.
6. Hoping but not expecting to meet Jane there.
7. Reformers come and go, but the poor are always with us.
8. To quit school now would be to disappoint my parents.
9. He was tall and awkward, and the girls were not impressed.
10. As I did not want him to know that I had a hundred dollars.
11. To destroy the faith they had in me.
12. We hiked on ahead to make the trail that others were to follow.
13. After that, Jim wanted me to go to the movies with him.
14. Emerging a few minutes later only to be confronted by her.
15. No matter what he says, you must keep your temper.
16. To help needy students take advantage of the educational opportunities they might otherwise be denied.
17. I have an electric clock which turns on my radio in the morning which wakes me up.
18. As we walked down the muddy lane, the birds were singing and the sun was shining.
19. The dog is so cross that it is dangerous to tease him.

20. Because it is here that I almost drowned last year when on my vacation.
21. Pulling his hat down over his eyes, he braved the crowd.
22. What is the use of working so late?
23. What the difference is between humor and wit.
24. Having been caught in a storm, the plane was forced down.
25. As the twilight wind gently swayed the summits of the trees.
26. The house in which his family had lived for fourteen years.
27. When, like a flash, I saw a way out.
28. There being no reason to remain.
29. Increased means and increased culture are the two civilizers of man.
30. Honest men esteem and value nothing so much in this world as a real friend.
31. Clever men are good, but they are not always the best.
32. War seemed inevitable; consequently we made haste to leave the country.
33. Only a rude hut made of split logs filled in with clay.
34. Taking life easy is one way of making poor grades.
35. When I look upon the tombs of the great, every emotion of envy dies within me.
36. Not knowing what courses I would be required to take.
37. Empires and kingdoms rise, flourish, and decay.
38. Because I was not familiar with the processes of registration.
39. "Reading maketh a full man; conference a ready man; and writing an exact man." (Bacon)
40. How small the attendance is.
41. How much money do you have?
42. Here are the papers you requested.
43. The kind of cake that Mother used to bake.

Exercise B

Identify the subject and predicate of each of the following sentences. (See pages 12–13.)

1. Mark Twain was the pen name of Samuel Clemens.
2. Five employees in the plant's history have received such awards.
3. The quiet, brown-eyed man likes to read such books as you have given him, about travel and adventure.

4. The woman who lives in the world of business and finance often longs for the peace and quiet of a fragrant kitchen.

5. The teacher of social problems or current events will testify to this.

6. In the preface to his speech, the president sharply pointed out the truth that learning to write is a highly important process for the college student.

7. There is another argument to support this opinion.

8. Business letters and book reports were included in the work of the English class.

9. It is raining.

10. Here is your supper.

11. To help the student advance more rapidly in her music, the teacher advised more practice.

12. Baudelaire is the French poet who wrote *Fleurs du Mal*.

13. One day I received a letter inquiring whether I had ever paid the money.

14. The horses raced into the pasture and frolicked about for a long time.

15. The assignment to be read was a chapter on motivation in learning.

16. The three children became very happy when their mother returned home.

17. The freshman students soon got into the spirit of the campus.

18. The American people, spurred by the desire for material wealth, made tremendous gains in production.

19. The change of hydrogen to helium with its enormous release of energy is a very intricate process which involves several intermediate changes.

20. My other good friend was also English, a good singer, whom I had met in London.

21. If we Americans had had the same experience in World War II as the British, we would probably feel much the same as they do now.

22. Too much teaching in American universities is just plain dull.

23. The school is so overcrowded that the students have to attend in two sessions.

24. Children are accepted in school at the age of six.

25. What the people say is not necessarily what the people believe.

26. To show a substantial profit year after year is the normal desire of the average businessman.

27. After being discharged from the Army, Kelly went to New York and looked for a job.

28. Singing in a night club was no job for Mary.

29. What you want and what you're going to get are two different things.
30. In the long run, developments in transportation, housing, optimum size of plant, etc., might tend to induce an industrial and demographic pattern similar to the one that consciousness of vulnerability would dictate.[1]

Exercise C

The following paragraph is to be read aloud by the instructor, with normal intonation, and the students are to write it down and punctuate it. An interesting comparison may be made of the number of sentences which different students have indicated.

Behind all of them lay two fundamental causes, which most Germans have persistently refused to admit. One was the failure of the will to do; the other was the almost organized abandonment of the currency to its fate. This is why I have all along maintained that there has never been anything vitally wrong with the country itself. Her soil is as productive as ever. The bosom of her earth is still a treasure house of coal and iron. The people have not lost their craft or cunning. The country escaped war ravage. The only concrete thing that went to pot was the currency.[2]

[1] Samuel T. Williamson, "How to Write Like a Social Scientist," *The Saturday Review of Literature*, October, 1947.

[2] Charles C. Fries, *The Structure of English* (New York: Harcourt, Brace, 1952), p. 11.

3

Basic Sentence Structures

THERE ARE relatively few basic sentence patterns in English, but it is important to know them well, since all sentences, however complex, are built upon them. The most commonly used patterns are illustrated here.

Basic Patterns

1. Children run.
Noun   Verb

Any number of verbs may be used or substituted for *run.*

Children *play.*
Children *sing.*
Children *cry.*

Any number of nouns may be substituted for *children*.

> *Horses* run.
>
> *Men* run.
>
> *People* run.

Verb phrases may be substituted for *run* in the first sentence.

> Children *are running*.
>
> Children *have been running*.
>
> Children *might have been running*.

This sentence pattern (Noun–Verb) is the simplest structure in our language. The classic example is from the Bible:

> Jesus wept.

2. Horses eat hay.
Noun Verb Noun

In this pattern (Noun–Verb–Noun complement) there may be endless substitution.

> Horses eat corn.
>
> Cows eat corn.
>
> Children eat candy.
>
> Children like ice cream.
>
> Men build houses.
>
> Women buy hats.

Verb forms (verbals) may be substituted for either noun in this pattern. For example, in the sentence

> John likes spinach.

you may have

> John likes *to eat*.
>
> John likes *swimming*.

In the sentence

> Birds build houses.

you may have

> *Walking* builds health.
>
> *To exercise* builds strength.

Subject-predicate word groups (subordinate clauses) may be substituted for the noun complement in the pattern N–V–N. For example,

> Children eat candy.
>   N   V   N
> Children eat *what they like.*
> Dogs chew bones.
> N   V   N
> Dogs chew *whatever they can find.*

We may also substitute a subject-predicate word group for the subject noun in this pattern.

> Men may cause trouble.
> N   V   N
> *What you are saying* may cause trouble.
> Mary helps Mother.
> N   V   N
> *What you are doing* helps Mother.

3(a). Flowers are beautiful.
>   N   V(l)   Adj   (Noun — Linking verb — Adjective)

Again, we may substitute freely in this pattern.

> Mary is pretty.
> Boys are rough.
> Men are funny.
> Boys become angry.
> Men grow old.
> Mother is growing old.
> Cities are becoming obsolete.
> Joseph is getting sick.

The linking verbs in English are verbs which couple the subject and the complement. The most frequently used linking verbs are forms of *to be, become, appear, seem, look, taste, feel.*

In this pattern, verbals may be substituted for the subject noun or for the adjective complement.

> *Walking* is difficult.
> *To speak* would be cruel.
> Teachers become *annoyed.*
> Books are *to be enjoyed.*

Subject-predicate word groups may be substituted for the noun subject.

> *What I hear* is beautiful.
>
> *What I see* is lovely.
>
> *Why he did it* is evident.
>
> *What you are telling me* is becoming obvious.

3(b). Bread is food.

N   V(l)   N   (Noun — Linking verb — Noun)

Roses are flowers.

Alcohol may be poison.

Miss Smith is my teacher.

Boys will be boys.

Some men become criminals.

Children will become adults.

Soldiers may become heroes.

A verbal may be substituted for the noun subject in this pattern.

> *Understanding* is a necessity.
>
> *Reading* is a great pleasure.
>
> *Smoking* becomes a habit.
>
> *To paint* is an art.
>
> *To go* back would be a great sacrifice.
>
> *To witness* this scene is a real pleasure.

Subject-predicate word groups can be substituted for the noun subject, for the noun complement, or for both.

> *What you learn here* is a help.
>
> *Whatever you carry* becomes a burden.
>
> *That you will help me* is a great satisfaction.
>
> I am *what you think.*
>
> Your gift will be *what you want.*
>
> The order is *that you will be transferred.*
>
> *What you learn here* will be *what you want to learn.*
>
> *What you are saying* is *that I am to blame.*
>
> *Where you are going* is *what I want to know.*

4(a). Boys give girls flowers.
N   V   N   N

In this sentence there are two complements. We may call *girls* the indirect object and *flowers* the direct object, or from the viewpoint of basic structure, we may call them the inner complement and the outer complement.

> Teachers give children books.
> Teachers ask children questions.
> Parents tell boys stories.
> Mother handed me the shovel.
> Father passed the minister the roast chicken.
> The experience taught me a lesson.

A verbal may be substituted for the outer complement, the direct object.

> The instructor taught him *swimming*.

A subject-predicate word group may be substituted for the outer complement, the direct object.

> Teachers give children *what they need*.
> John tells his mother *what he likes*.
> Mary asked me *why I came*.

4(b). Mother named the baby John.
N   V   N   N

In this sentence we again have two complements. The structure of this pattern looks the same as that described in 4(a). However, there are important differences between the two. In 4(b) the inner complement is the direct object and the outer complement is called an objective complement. The outer complement and the direct object have the same referent. This contrasts with 4(a) in which the two complements have different referents. Expressed in symbols, the two sentences become:

4(a) N_1 V N_2 N_3
4(b) N_1 V N_2 N_2

Other illustrations of 4(b) are:

> Voters elected Roosevelt President.
> They appointed Mary secretary.
> The people called him a scoundrel.
> The team named Paul captain.
> The committee selected him chairman.

We might examine one additional contrast between 4(a) and 4(b), the pattern with an indirect object and the pattern with an objective complement. Let us take two illustrations:

> 4(a)   They gave him a new watch.
> 4(b)   They elected him president.

In 4(a) the statement may be restated in two ways using what is called the passive form or passive voice.

> 4(a).   He was given a new watch.
>   A new watch was given to him.

Either the indirect object or the direct object of the original statement may be used as the subject when the passive voice is employed.

> 4(b)   He was elected president.

In 4(b) only the direct object may be used as the subject. We cannot restate the sentence using the objective complement as the subject in the passive form.

4(c). Men call boys lazy.
$$N \quad V \quad N \quad Adj$$

The outer complement or objective complement in this sentence is an adjective. More illustrations follow.

> Mother called Mary pretty.
> Father thought John strong.
> People believe him good.
> Agatha considers herself beautiful.

In this pattern a verbal may be substituted for the adjective complement.

Father thought John amusing.
People believe the actress entertaining.
Folks consider Mr. Brown boring.
The students felt the warning undeserved.
The girl kept the children amused.
The noise made the baby frightened.

A subject-predicate word group may be substituted for the inner complement, the direct object.

Students find what they read dull.
Father considered what I said funny.
The spectators thought what he did foolhardy.

Inverted Statements

In modern English, there are two common types of declarative sentences in which the word order of subject and verb is inverted.

There is a good show on television tonight.
There is a vacant apartment on Eighth Street.
There is a storm coming up.
There are my parents getting off the plane.

Here is a dollar for you.
Here are the keys to the car.
Here is my sister coming to meet me.

Questions

Simple question patterns may be introduced by such words as *when, where, why, how, which,* and *who.*

When are you going?
Where are the men working?
Why was this door locked?
What did the people say?
How did you get the cover off?

In this pattern the word order is inverted. The subject comes after the helping verb and before the main verb.

Questions are signaled when introduced by helping verbs such as *have, can, may, will, could, would, do,* and forms of *to be.*

Can you go tonight?

May I have the bread, please?

Would you help me with the lesson?

Are you having a good time?

Do the lights hurt your eyes?

In this pattern also, the word order is inverted. The subject of the sentence follows the helping verb and is followed by the main verb.

Any of the basic sentence patterns may express a question if the sentence ends in a rising pitch and a sudden stop.

The children are sleeping?

You have had supper?

This is your book?

Father is angry?

You gave him the money?

They elected him chairman?

You call her beautiful?

Building Sentences — Headwords and Modifiers

Extended English sentences are built upon the simple sentence patterns we have been considering. In the process of elaboration, nouns and verbs serve as nuclei or headwords to which modifiers are added to develop the meaning of an utterance. A variety of modifying structures gives the language flexibility and makes it possible to communicate a vast range of ideas with considerable finesse. The following paragraphs will show how modifiers are built into the simple sentence patterns. The patterns will be given the same numbers as in earlier paragraphs of this chapter.

1. Roosters crow.
N   V

The roosters crow.

The old roosters crow.

The old roosters in our yard crow.

The old roosters in our yard which wake up early crow.

The noun *roosters* is used as a headword for modifiers. In the last sentence a whole cluster of modifiers has been built upon this headword. These modifiers include single word modifiers such as *the* and *old*, and the word groups *in our yard* and *which wake up early*. The word group *in our yard* is called a phrase, and the second word group *which wake up early* is a subordinate clause.

> Roosters *crow proudly.*
> Roosters *crow proudly in the morning.*
> Roosters *crow proudly in the morning when the sun rises.*

This time the verb *crow* has been used as the headword or nucleus for modifiers, both single words and word groups. *Proudly* is called an adverb. The word group modifiers include *in the morning*, a phrase, and *when the sun rises*, a subordinate clause.

From the simple pattern

> Roosters crow.

we may thus construct a rather complicated sentence simply by building modifiers about the subject noun and the verb.

> The old *roosters* in our yard which wake up early *crow* proudly in the morning when the sun rises.

When one considers that modifiers may cluster about each noun and verb in a sentence, and about adjectives, adverbs, and even function words; that the modifiers may include verbal phrases as well as prepositional phrases; that other structures such as appositives and absolutes may be used; and that there may be compounding of various elements and structures — one may then well appreciate the complexity and flexibility of our language.

2. Boys play games.
N   V   N

The little boys who live here play games.

boys	HEADWORD
the	
little	} MODIFIERS
who live here	

Boys *joyfully play* games *in the morning when they are young.*

play	HEADWORD
joyfully in the morning when they are young	MODIFIERS

Boys play *the rough games which they like.*

games	HEADWORD
the rough which they like	MODIFIERS

3(a). Children are happy.
　　　　　　　N　　　V(l)　　Adj

Good children are happy.
The good children are happy.
The good children in the village are happy.
The good children in the village who obey their parents are happy.

children	HEADWORD
the good in the village who obey their parents	MODIFIERS

Children are *always happy.*
Children are *always happy in the winter.*
Children are *always happy in the winter when Christmas comes*

happy	HEADWORD
always in the winter when Christmas comes	MODIFIERS

3(b). Roses are flowers.
　　　　　　　N　　　V(l)　　　N

Red roses are flowers.
The red roses are flowers.

The red roses in our garden are flowers.
The red roses in our garden which Mother planted are flowers.

roses   HEADWORD

the
red   ⎫
in our garden   ⎬ MODIFIERS
which Mother planted   ⎭

Roses are *beautiful flowers.*
Roses are *beautiful flowers in the summer.*
Roses are *beautiful flowers in the summer when they bloom.*

flowers   HEADWORD

beautiful   ⎫
in the summer   ⎬ MODIFIERS
when they bloom   ⎭

4(a). Mothers give children toys.
N   V   N   N

In this pattern, the subject noun, the verb, the inner complement, or the outer complement may serve as the headword of a word group, a nucleus with modifiers.

Mothers give children toys.
Kind mothers give children toys.
The kind mothers give children toys.
The kind mothers in our town give children toys.
The kind mothers in our town who love their families give children
   toys.

mothers   HEADWORD

the
kind   ⎫
in our town   ⎬ MODIFIERS
who love their families   ⎭

Mothers *usually give* children toys,
Mothers *usually give* children toys *at Christmas.*
Mothers *usually give* children toys *at Christmas if they behave.*

give   HEADWORD

usually
at Christmas   } MODIFIERS
if they behave

Mothers give *the children* toys.
Mothers give *the little children* toys.
Mothers give *the little children in the neighborhood* toys.

children   HEADWORD

the
little   } MODIFIERS
in the neighborhood

Mothers give children *pretty toys*.
Mothers give children *the pretty toys*.
Mothers give children *the pretty toys which they buy*.

toys   HEADWORD

the
pretty   } MODIFIERS
which they buy

Summary: Sentence Patterns

English sentences are built on simple sentence patterns. The patterns used most frequently are:

N V
N V N
N V(linking) Adj
N V(linking) N
N V N N

Inverted sentences are frequently used which begin with the words *there* and *here*. The verb is usually some form of the verb *to be*.

Questions are constructed (a) by introducing the utterance with such a word as *when, where, why, how,* etc., followed by inverted word order; (b) by introducing the utterance with a helping verb such as *do, have, will, can,* etc., followed by inverted word order. Questions may have normal word order if the utterance is terminated with a rising pitch.

Sentences are developed by the use of modifiers built chiefly upon nouns and verbs, usually the nouns and verbs that are the essential parts of the sentence pattern. These nouns and verbs are thought of as headwords of word groups. The word group in this case is the noun, or verb, with its modifiers. In a word group headed by a noun, the modifiers are thought of as *adjectival* modifiers. In a word group headed by a verb, the modifiers are thought of as *adverbial* modifiers.

Word Order

The essential parts of a sentence in English follow a pattern of fixed word order. For example,

> Horses run.

We cannot communicate this fact if we write

> Run horses.

Let us take the sentence

> Men build houses.

We are communicating something entirely different if we say

> Houses build men.

When we say

> Mary gave John a present.

we communicate a unique fact. Changing the order to

> John gave Mary a present.

tells the listener something else indeed. The five words in the sentence may be arranged in many different ways. Only *one* word order will communicate the fact which we wish to relate.

Fixed word order of the essential elements (subject, verb, complement) of a sentence is a very important grammatical principle in English. We have grown so accustomed to this aspect of our language structure that we have developed unconscious automatic responses to the position of words (just as we respond to the rhythm of language).

> John hit Joseph.

The position of the words *John* and *Joseph* in the above sentence is very significant, and our response is immediate and certain. We know who delivered the blow and who received the blow, and we appraise the situation accordingly.

> The whale swallowed Jonah.

There is no doubt in our minds who rests in whose stomach. Our response is determined by the order of the words in the sentence. It would be entirely different if the subject and complement were interchanged.

Fixed word order of the essential sentence elements gives the language stability. It virtually eliminates the need for other grammatical devices, such as inflection (to be discussed later), to supply the necessary clues to meaning. To be sure, we still use inflected forms of some words, such as personal pronouns, but we do so more from custom than from structural necessity. For example,

> John hit him.
> not
> John hit he.

The second expression would communicate the same fact as the first, since fixed word order eliminates the need for inflection as far as meaning is concerned. We do not inflect (change the form of) nouns in the object position, and we still communicate our meaning perfectly without the signal of inflection.

Nonessential elements of a sentence (modifiers) are often the movable parts. This situation can be very helpful since it gives flexibility to the language. But it can also cause trouble, since a careless or unskilled speaker or writer may fall into ambiguity or even communicate a ridiculous misstatement of fact.

> I will not go *unless you come with me.*

The word group *unless you come with me* is a dependent or subordinate clause, a modifier of the verb *will go.* Technically, it is a modifier in a verb-headed word group. Its function, then, is adverbial.

> Unless you come with me, I will not go.

In this sentence, the position of the adverbial clause has been changed. It now comes before the subject and there is a change of emphasis: attention is now drawn to the condition stated in the subordinate clause.

> People live crowded together in tenements in a large city.
>
> In a large city, people live crowded together in tenements.

Again a shift in the position of an adverbial modifier, this time a prepositional phrase, creates a shift in emphasis, and to that extent in meaning.

> Having just graduated from college, I was eager to find a suitable position.
>
> I was eager to find a suitable position, having just graduated from college.

In this illustration a word group modifier, a participial phrase, is shifted from proximity to the word it modifies (*I* in this sentence) to the end of the sentence, where it assumes secondary importance.

Let us examine a sentence to determine which parts may be moved.

> The energetic Mr. Holdback from New York, who represented Smith Brothers, willingly gave the teacher a book, although it was very expensive.
>
> Mr. Holdback gave teacher book.
>
> N   V   N   N

These are the essential parts of the sentence and cannot be re-arranged without changing the content, or meaning. However, we may shift some of the modifiers.

> The energetic Mr. Holdback from New York, who represented Smith Brothers, gave the teacher a book *willingly*, although it was very expensive.
>
> *Although it was very expensive*, the energetic Mr. Holdback from New York, who represented Smith Brothers, willingly gave the teacher a book.

In both cases here, the modifiers shifted are adverbial. One is the single word, *willingly*, and the other is a dependent clause. Adverbial modifiers are the most movable of all. Adjectives are sometimes placed after the nouns they modify, but this is not usual in prose.

> The house *beautiful*
> The forest *primeval*
> The throne *perilous*
> The fighter, *beaten* and *bruised*
> The salesman, *energetic* and *forceful*

Fixed word order is again illustrated by the relative positions of a prepositional phrase and a dependent clause when they each modify the same noun. In the sentence given above, the adjective clause *who represented Smith Brothers* follows the prepositional phrase *from New York*. And both phrase and clause follow the noun *Mr. Holdback* which they modify.

Summary: Word Order

The grammatical device of word order is an important structural clue to meaning. The writer who is familiar with it may exploit it to his advantage. We may perceive the subtleties of this device when we examine the sentence from the Bible,

> In my Father's house are many mansions.

How different would be the emphasis and hence the meaning and our own response if the verse read

> Many mansions are in my Father's house.

EXERCISE A

Throughout this and similar exercises, give attention to vocabulary building.

1. Write ten sentences substituting other nouns for *horses* in the sentence:
   > Horses run.

   Try not to use commonplace words. Select as many words as you can find which will help you build your writing vocabulary. (For example, mares, colts, mavericks, etc.)

2. Write ten sentences substituting other verbs for *run* in the same sentence. Try to use unusual verbs as far as possible.

3. Write ten sentences substituting verb phrases for *run* in the sentence pattern of item 1. (For example: Horses *will be running*. Boys *have been quarreling*. Freshmen *should have been studying*.)

4. Write five sentences substituting nouns for *men* in the sentence:

Men build houses.

5. Write five sentences substituting verbs for *build* in the same sentence.

6. Write five sentences substituting nouns for *houses* in the same sentence.

7. Write six sentences substituting a verbal (gerund, a verb form ending in *-ing*) for *candy* in the sentence:

Ruth likes candy.

(For example: Ruth likes *swimming*. Ruth likes *fencing*.)

8. Write six sentences substituting a verbal (infinitive, a verb form preceded by *to*) for *candy* in the same sentence. (For example: Ruth likes *to ride*. Ruth likes *to embroider*.)

9. Write six sentences substituting a verbal (gerund) for *John* in the sentence:

John will cause trouble.

(For example: *Arguing* will cause trouble. *Teasing* will cause trouble.)

10. Write six sentences substituting a verbal (infinitive) for *John* in the same sentence.

11. Write six sentences substituting a subject-predicate word group (subordinate clause) for *John* in the same sentence. (For example: *What you did last night* will cause trouble.)

12. Write five sentences substituting nouns for *flowers*, five substituting verbs for *are*, and five substituting adjectives for *beautiful* in the sentence:

Flowers are beautiful.

13. Write ten sentences substituting gerund phrases and infinitive phrases for *mathematics* in the sentence:

Mathematics is difficult.

(For example: *Solving algebraic problems* is difficult. *To ride water skis* is difficult.)

14. Write six sentences substituting a subject-predicate word group for *the statement* in the sentence:

The statement is true.

15. Write six sentences substituting nouns for *mother* in the sentence:
> She is my mother.

16. Write ten sentences substituting verbals for *a command* in the sentence:
> The reply was a command.

17. Write ten sentences substituting a subject-predicate word group for *a lie* in the sentence:
> This is a lie.

18. Write six sentences substituting nouns for *girl* in the sentence:
> He gave the girl candy.

19. Write six sentences substituting nouns for *chairman* in the sentence:
> They named him chairman.

20. Write six sentences substituting verbs for *named* in the same sentence.

21. Write six sentences substituting a subject-predicate word group for *a question* in the sentence:
> Father asked me a question.

(For example: Father asked me *what I wanted for my birthday.*)

22. Write six sentences substituting a verbal for *funny* in the sentence:
> They thought John funny.

23. Write ten questions beginning with the function words *when, where, why, what, how, who,* etc.

24. Write ten sentences beginning with forms of the helping verbs *can, will, would, do, may,* etc.

25. Write ten inverted sentences beginning with the words *there* and *here.*

Exercise B

1. Write five sentences with adjectival modifiers built about the noun *ships* as a headword in the sentence:
> The ships sailed.

(For example: *The old fishing ships* sailed. *The ships of the Vikings* sailed. *The ships built of steel* sailed. *The ships that had been repaired* sailed. *The great ships of the British which had been hiding in the fog* sailed to the attack.) Use as many different types of modifying structures as you can in a variety of combinations. Identify the different structures which you use.

2. Write five sentences with adverbial modifiers built about the verb *sailed* as a headword, using the basic sentence of item 1. Use as many types of modifying structures as you can, identifying them in each case.

3. Write five sentences with adjectival modifiers built about the noun *Marines* as a headword in the sentence:

   The Marines won the battle.

4. Write a sentence with adverbial modifiers built about the verb *won* as a headword in the same sentence.

5. Write a sentence with adjectival modifiers built about the noun *battle* as a headword in the same sentence.

6. Write a sentence with adjectival modifiers built about the noun *teacher* as a headword in the sentence:

   Miss Brown is a teacher.

7. Write five sentences with adverbial modifiers built about the verb *sent* as a headword in the sentence:

   John sent his mother a letter.

8. Write five sentences with adjectival modifiers built about the noun *mother* as a headword in the same sentence.

9. Write five sentences with adjectival modifiers built about the noun *letter* as a headword in the same sentence.

10. Write a sentence with modifiers built about the three main sentence elements in:

    The mariner shot the albatross.

Exercise C

In the following selection, identify the simple sentence patterns of the sentences in the passage (N V, N V N, etc.). Place in brackets for further discussion all sentences whose basic structure you do not recognize.

American officialdom is notoriously rough on the dedicated man with a cause, especially in the armed services. Brig. General Billy Mitchell's crusade for air power only got recognition years after he had been court-martialled by his Army superiors. Alfred Thayer Mahan, whose strategy made the U.S. a great sea power, had his heaviest sailing inside the Navy Department. Matthew Fontaine Maury, the founder of modern Navy charting and meteorology, was forced out of active service as a lieutenant, although later reinstated. The man with a gleam in his eye seems to be a recurring near-casualty of our system. His society, and especially his superiors, find him too persistent for comfort.

Lieut. General James M. Gavin, whose second *Life* article appears on page 106, got further along in the service than either Mitchell or Mahan.

But in the end he resigned in order to fight for what he believes is the only sound military strategy. Gavin's views still have to have their proper hearing in Washington — both his tactical plans for sky-cavalry and mobile ground forces, and his strategic insistence that we are unprepared for limited or space war. But besides listening to him the country should also profit by his uphill struggle to get his views discussed. We may live in an age of adjustment, where the committee is king and the best-modulated opinion generally wins out. The fact remains that the U.S. is still a military power to be reckoned with, largely due to a small group of enlightened, cantankerous ax grinders like Gavin.

One of them is his co-worker in Army space projects, Dr. Wernher von Braun, whose Explorer satellites would never have got into space when they did without his combination of designing genius and unremitting heckling powers. Another such zealot is Rear Admiral Hyman Rickover, whom the Navy is now ponderously considering for another overdue promotion. Rickover not only fought through the nuclear submarine — the only modern weapon in which the U.S. is probably still ahead of the Russians. He also got the nuclear power plant at Shippingport, Pa. going, the pioneer project in large-scale commercial atomic power.[1]

Exercise D

The following selection is an excerpt from a student theme. Identify the simple sentence patterns.

I recently read an article in a magazine which completely damned the school system as we know it now. It said that the teachers taught as little as they possibly could; that the students could get away with anything; that the courses tended to overemphasize extracurricular activities; and that the schools themselves were very demoralizing.

I went through three years of private schooling and nine years of public schooling. I learned a lot during the first three years, but I learned much more in my public schooling.

The most important thing about the public school today is that it helps you learn to get along with your fellow students and citizens. The whole school system is based on this, and I think it's good. But that isn't all the schools do. The five public schools I went to each wanted to help me get an education. I have found that any teacher living is willing to help a student if he will show a particle of interest. The whole system depends on the student — if he wants an education, there will be always someone to help him.

[1] From "The Value of Zealousness," Editorial in *Life* Magazine, August 11, 1958, p. 24. Copr. 1958 Time Inc.

Each school offers a wide variety of courses, as well as extracurricular activities. It is up to the student to choose wisely. If he wants a good education, he will pick the necessary courses; if he doesn't want to learn, he will choose courses such as woodshop, metal shop, photography, gardening, and library training.

The magazine article was wrong in many of its assumptions. True, the school system is not perfect, but each school wants to help the student if the student wants to learn. Even the most perfect school in the world cannot teach a person science or mathematics if he doesn't want to learn these subjects. Everything depends on the individual. If he wants an education badly enough, he can get it.

Exercise E

In the following sentences, identify the words or word groups which may be moved. Rewrite the sentences in as many different ways as possible by changing only positions. Explain in each case what the change in position does to the total meaning of the statement.

1. The army of George Washington suffered from cold and hunger during the winter at Valley Forge.

2. The prisoner paced nervously up and down his cell waiting for the warden to arrive.

3. When the hot summer sun rises over the vast desert, all animal life moves quietly into the protective cover of rocks and bushes.

4. The old minister, quiet and serene in his black robes, rose to deliver the address.

5. The hound sensing the nearness of his prey moved gracefully forward.

6. Realizing that he was risking his own life, the boy bravely dived into the swiftly running stream just as a child swept past him close to the shore.

7. Henry James was born in New York City, in 1843, the son of Henry James, Sr., and the brother of William James, the psychologist.

8. When Mark Twain was eighteen, he left Hannibal, Missouri, to earn his living as a printer, working for newspapers in New York, Pennsylvania, and Ohio.

9. In the old deserted house was dust, cobwebs, silent rooms, and memories.

10. The cracked and ancient bell tolled sadly as the news of the defeat spread swiftly through the village.

4

Subject-Predicate Word Groups

WE SAW in Chapter 3 that quite complex sentence structures may
be built upon simple sentence patterns by adding, substituting,
and manipulating various kinds of word groups. In this chapter,
we will observe more closely the subject-predicate word group
— the basis of all English sentences — and illustrate many of
the kinds of sentences which may be developed by co-ordination
and subordination.

Co-ordination

Many devices give flexibility to the language. One of these is
compounding. This, very simply, is the device of *adding on*.
Almost all kinds of language structures may be compounded.
When subject-predicate word groups are added to each other, a

compound sentence is formed and the grammatical principle of co-ordination is applied.

One of the best-known illustrations of the use of this device is in the New Testament.

> And Satan entered into Judas, who was named Iscariot, one of the twelve.
>
> And he went and discoursed with the chief priests and the magistrates, how he might betray him to them.
>
> And they were glad and covenanted to give him money.
>
> And he promised. And he sought opportunity to betray him in the absence of the multitude.
>
> And the day of the unleavened bread came, on which it was necessary that the pasch should be killed.
>
> And he sent Peter and John, saying: Go and prepare for us the pasch, that we may eat.[1]

In modern English, compound sentences are formed by joining two or more subject-predicate word groups with appropriate connectives. These connectives may be drawn from the following list of words known as co-ordinate conjunctions.

and	nor
but	so
for	yet
or	

It is very important to memorize these connectives.

The following are compound sentences using co-ordinate conjunctions to join two or more subject-predicate word groups.

1. The river / overflowed its banks, *and* the flood / destroyed the village.
2. I / have been waiting for you for an hour, *and* I / am tired *and* I / want to go home.
3. The car / was badly damaged, *but* fortunately nobody / was hurt.
4. The spirit / is willing, *but* the flesh / is weak.
5. The Indians / attacked the settlers, *for* they / knew of the shortage of ammunition.
6. The boy / was unwilling to go home, *for* he / was afraid to tell his parents of the accident.
7. I / must catch the last bus, *or* I / will have to stay here all night.
8. The old car / can be used for local transportation, *or* it / can be sold.

---

[1] Luke 22:3–8

9. The old lady / cannot read English, *nor* can / she / even write her own name.
10. I / do not want to eat anything, *nor* do / I / even wish to speak of food.
11. Mr. Brown / has been working for five years, *yet* he / has not saved a dollar.
12. The football team / has not won a single game, *yet* the boys / are not discouraged.
13. The rain / had stopped, *so* we / decided to continue our trip over the mountain.
14. The ties / cost only one dollar, *so* I / bought two of them.

In speech, the connectives most frequently used from the above list are *and, but, or,* and *so.* Indeed, *and* and *so* are often overused. Students with little experience of written composition carry over their speech habits to writing and neglect to use the connectives *nor, for,* and *yet.*

Sentences 1–14 above are compound sentences. In each there are at least two subject-predicate word groups. These are called co-ordinate or independent clauses. They are not *included* word groups in the main sentence; they are *added on* to the main sentence. The student familiar with the co-ordinate conjunctions may employ them as signals of co-ordination when they precede a subject-predicate word group.

When a co-ordinate conjunction is used as a connective between clauses in a compound sentence, it is usually preceded by a comma. The chief exception to this generalization is with short independent clauses connected by *and.*

I am tired and I want to go home.

A second group of connectives may be used to link subject-predicate word groups in compound sentences. These connectives are somewhat different from co-ordinate conjunctions in their function. The main connectives in this group, called conjunctive adverbs, are:

however	else
therefore	otherwise
moreover	nevertheless
furthermore	hence
also	then
besides	accordingly
consequently	likewise

The following compound sentences employ conjunctive adverbs.

15. I / am planning to go to Chicago; *however*, I / do not know how long I will stay.
16. You / have overspent your allowance; *therefore* I / will not give you any more money.
17. Your brother / is completely tired out; *moreover*, it / is your fault for keeping him up so late.
18. Oxygen / supports combustion; *furthermore* it / is necessary to all animal life.
19. The woman / is a very competent musician; *also* she / is an excellent cook and housekeeper.
20. We / were very tired when we reached Phoenix; *besides* we / were hungry and dirty.
21. The accused / has been convicted of armed robbery; *consequently* he / will have to spend many years in prison.
22. Judy / will have to wash her face; *else* she / can't go.
23. This product / is made with cheap materials; *otherwise* it / would cost much more money.
24. The Colonial Army / was without proper food and clothing at Valley Forge; *nevertheless* it / was able to carry on and win the war.
25. The two triangles / have their three sides respectively equal; *hence* they / are congruent.
26. I / will remain in college four years; *then* I / expect to graduate.
27. He / shows a desire to reform; *accordingly* the judge / will give him another chance.
28. Chicago / was destroyed by a great fire; *likewise* San Francisco / was ruined by similar destruction following the earthquake.

The connectives used in sentences 15–28 to join the subject-predicate word groups and form compound structures have an adverbial function in the clause which they introduce, and may be shifted in position in their clause. The connectives used in sentences 1–14 cannot be so shifted.

> You have overspent your allowance; I, *therefore*, will not give you any more money.
>
> You have overspent your allowance; I will not, *therefore*, give you any more money.

We may substitute an adverb for *therefore* in either of the two preceding sentences.

> You have overspent your allowance; I *naturally* will not give you any more money.

> You have overspent your allowance; I will not, *naturally*, give
> you any more money.

We cannot change the position of a co-ordinate conjunction in
this way.

> You have overspent your allowance, *and* I will not give you any
> more money.

The punctuation of compound sentences in which conjunctive
adverbs are used as connectives should be noted and learned.[2]
Standard written English requires a semicolon between the
clauses. Sentences 15–28 and their variants illustrate this punctuation. The comma is used to separate the clauses of a compound
sentence only when a co-ordinate conjunction is used as a connective.

Subordination

Whereas co-ordination *adds on* subject-predicate word groups
to the main sentence, subordination *includes* such word groups
within the main sentence. The sentence thus formed is called
complex.

A number of important connectives are used to include subject-
predicate word groups in the main sentence, or, as it is more
frequently said, to introduce subordinate clauses. A list of the
more common ones follows.

because	where
unless	why
if	who, whose, whom
although	that
while	which
though	until
as	whether
when	how

These words are used as connectives to signal subordination.
They are sometimes called subordinate conjunctions.

> I will not go *unless you drive the car.*

The italicized word group is a subordinate clause. It is included
within the main sentence *I will not go*, and the connective used
for this inclusion is the word *unless*.

[2] Refer also to pages 44–45

Noun Clauses

A subordinate clause may be substituted for a noun in any position in the sentence. It is then called a noun clause.

1. Subject of the sentence

> This *information* is none of your business.
> *What I know of this case* is none of your business.

2. Complement (direct object)

> I bought a new *coat*.
> I bought *what you told me to buy*.

3. Complement (predicate complement)

> This is the *place*.
> This is *where I came in*.

4. Object of a preposition

> He argued about the *money*.
> He argued about *how much he knew*.

5. Complement (indirect object)

> The director gave *them* the assignments.
> The director gave *whoever was there* the assignments.

6. Appositive

> This fact, your *divorce*, may keep you from getting the position.
> This fact, *that you are divorced*, may keep you from getting the position.

7. Complement (objective complement)

> They called him *leader*.
> They called him *whatever they liked*.

8. Object of a participle

> Knowing your *preference*, I have ordered roast beef for dinner.
> Knowing *what you like*, I have ordered roast beef for dinner.

9. Object of an infinitive

> I was told to buy some *clothing*.
>
> I was told to buy *what I needed*.

The subject-predicate word group which is substituted for a noun (the noun clause) is, like a noun, fixed in position in the sentence. Because it permits the speaker or writer to elaborate more fully — to be more explicit — it is a very useful grammatical structure.

In speech, the noun clause is used mainly as the object of a verb.

> I know *what you want*.
>
> I heard *what she said*.
>
> She said *that he was angry*.

Very often in such sentences the connective *that* is omitted.

> She said [that] he was angry.
>
> I know [that] I'm to blame.
>
> I heard [that] you were sick.

Adverbial Clauses

A subject-predicate word group may be substituted for an adverb in any of its functions. It is then called an adverbial clause.

1. Modifying a verb

> She arrived at the airport *early*.
>
> She arrived at the airport *before the sun was up*.
>
> She arrived at the airport *after the plane had departed*.
>
> She arrived at the airport *when it was crowded with busy travelers*.

2. Modifying an adjective

> The decision of the jury made him *intensely* angry.
>
> The decision of the jury made him more angry *than we had expected*.
>
> The little boy was *really* sorry.
>
> The little boy was sorry *that he hit his brother*.

3. Modifying an infinitive

> I told him to wait *patiently*.
>
> I told him to wait *until we arrived*.

4. Modifying a participle

I found him breathing *heavily*.

I found him breathing *as if he were about to choke*.

5. Modifying an adverb

His death came *very* suddenly.

His death came more suddenly *than we had thought*.

Adverbial clauses do not occupy a fixed position in the sentence but, like adverbs, are movable. Often they are placed before the subject instead of after the verb (the most common position of an adverbial modifier).

Since it was early in the morning and we had plenty of time, we decided to relax for a while.

(Note the comma used to separate the adverbial clause from the subject of the sentence.)

In writing, an adverbial clause introducing a sentence is often an effective device of transition.

We were up at sunrise our first day out. Since it was so early in the morning and we had plenty of time, we decided to relax for a while.

The adverbial clause at the beginning of the second sentence looks back to the first, for the words *early in the morning* are linked in meaning to *sunrise* in the first sentence. This transition from *sunrise* to *early in the morning* secures coherence, the relatedness of ideas.

You finish, and *the copy goes to the printer. When it gets into print* a reader sees it.[3]

The great man makes the great thing. *Wherever Macdonald sits,* there is the head of the table.[4]

Many people look to *poetry* today as an illumination of *religious* and *philosophic* problems. *Although poetry is not and cannot be a substitute for religion and philosophy,* nevertheless it may lead people to think seriously about such things.[5]

[3] Charles A. Dana, "Words that Laugh and Cry."
[4] Ralph Waldo Emerson, "The American Scholar."
[5] Stephen Spender, "On Teaching Modern Poetry."

The adverbial clause introducing a sentence may also place emphasis on the idea it expresses.

> *Unless he gives me a good raise next month,* I'm going to quit.
>
> *When you go to see your mother,* perhaps you will ask her for those old pictures.

Perhaps the commonest reason for putting an adverbial clause at the beginning of a sentence is to gain variety in rhythm.

> *In the brightness of the wintry sun next morning as it streamed over the breakfast table* Herbert laughed at his fears. There was an air of prosaic wholesomeness about the room which it lacked on the previous night, and the dirty shriveled little paw was pitched on the sideboard with a carelessness which betokened no great belief in its virtues.[6]

Adjective Clauses

A subject-predicate word group may be substituted for an adjectival modifier. It is called an adjective clause.

> The *wicked* man killed his stepfather.
>
> The man *who was wicked* killed his stepfather.
>
> This is the *new* house.
>
> This is the house *that Jack built.*

Whereas an adjective precedes the noun it modifies (its headword), an adjective clause follows its noun.

> We bought the car *which the salesman showed us.*
>
> Tom met a girl *whose name was Rose.*
>
> The man *that you sent for* is in the office.
>
> He spoke of the past *which he had almost forgotten.*
>
> Arizona is a state *where the sun shines every day.*

Adjective clauses are usually connected by the relative pronouns *who, whose, whom, which,* and *that.* The relative pronoun has a function in its clause besides that of connective: It may be the subject of the clause, a complement, the object of a preposition, or a possessive adjective.

[6] W. W. Jacobs, "The Monkey's Paw."

1. Subject of subordinate clause

  Geoffrey Chaucer, *who* wrote *The Canterbury Tales*, died in 1400.

2. Complement

  My oldest son, *whom* you have never met, has just been married.

3. Object of a preposition

  The house *that* you talked about is out in the country.

4. Possessive adjective

  This is the boy *whose* brother won the prize.

NOTE: Students should not confuse a noun clause used as an appositive with an adjective clause introduced by *that*. When introducing a noun clause, *that* is used purely as a connective and has no other function in its word group.

  The news *that Germany had declared war* shocked the world.
  The news *that was revealed in the newspaper* shocked the world.

The italicized subordinate clause in the first sentence is a noun clause in apposition with the noun *news*. The connective *that* has no other function in its word group. The italicized clause in the second sentence is an adjective clause modifying the noun *news*. The connective *that* does have a function within its word group. It is the subject of *was revealed*.

The connective *that* when used with an adjective clause could also function within its word group as the complement of the verb or as the object of a preposition.

1. As complement

  The news *that* you mentioned surprised me also.

2. Object of a preposition

  The book *that* you are looking for has been lost.

Adjective clauses may be connected by *when*, *where*, and *why*.

  The year *when the exposition was held* . . .
  The ruins *where the excavation was made* . . .
  The reasons *why the Constitution was adopted* . . .

As with noun clauses, the connective is sometimes omitted.

> The man [that] I love . . .
> The house [which] he built . . .
> The girl [whom] I met . . .
> The boy [whom] I spoke to . . .

Summary

The subject-predicate word group or clause is the basic structure of the English sentence. Series of clauses may be *added* or co-ordinated by such connectives as *and, but, for, yet, nevertheless, however,* and others. In this way additional meaning is communicated.

> This is my son, and I love him, and I won't let you hurt him in any way.
>
> I warned you not to go there; nevertheless you ignored me and now you see your mistake.

Subject-predicate word groups may be *included within* sentences either as modifiers or as substitutes for nouns. Such inclusions are called subordinate clauses.

> The storm *which had done so much damage* subsided almost as quickly *as it had begun.*

Subordination too is a way of adding meaning, but it is more than that. It is a way of communicating relationships and inter-relationships among the elements of communication.

Exercise A

1. From your reading, prepare a list of compound sentences in which each of the co-ordinate conjunctions is used.
2. From your own themes, prepare a list of compound sentences in which you have used co-ordinate conjunctions.
3. Check the frequency of the co-ordinate conjunctions in your writing. Which ones do you use most frequently, seldom, never?
4. Write a series of compound sentences using the co-ordinate conjunctions which you seldom or never use. Prepare five sentences for each connective.

5. Discuss the rhetorical importance of each of the co-ordinate conjunctions.

6. From your reading, prepare a list of compound sentences in which each of the conjunctive adverbs is used.

7. From your own themes, prepare a list of compound sentences in which conjunctive adverbs have been used.

8. Check the frequency of the conjunctive adverbs in your writing. How does your use of them compare with your use of the co-ordinate conjunctions?

9. Write a series of compound sentences using conjunctive adverbs which you seldom or never use. Prepare three sentences for each connective.

10. Discuss the value of the conjunctive adverb as a connective in the development of compound sentences.

EXERCISE B

1. The following sentence contains a noun clause used as object of a verb. Write five sentences substituting other noun clauses for the one in the sentence:

   Abraham Lincoln believed *that the Union should be preserved.*

2. Write five sentences of your own in which a noun clause is used as object of a verb.

3. The following sentence contains a noun clause used as subject. Write five sentences substituting other noun clauses for this one:

   What the scientists observed during the experiment created tremendous excitement.

4. Write five sentences of your own in which a noun clause is used as subject.

5. The following sentence contains a noun clause used as predicate complement. Write five sentences substituting other noun clauses:

   The prisoner's only hope was *that the governor might commute his sentence.*

6. Write five sentences of your own in which a noun clause is used as a predicate complement.

7. The following sentence contains a noun clause used as object of a preposition. Write five sentences substituting other noun clauses:

   The old man always talked about *what he had done as a boy.*

8. Write five sentences of your own in which a noun clause is used as object of a preposition.

9. The following sentence contains a noun clause used as an appositive. Write five sentences substituting other noun clauses:

> The thought *that he might be able to graduate with his class* encouraged the young man.

10. Write five sentences of your own in which a noun clause is used as an appositive.

11. The following sentence contains a noun clause used as object of a participle. Write five sentences substituting other noun clauses:

> Believing *that the lost fliers might have landed in the immediate vicinity*, the party made its way through the thick woods.

12. Write five sentences of your own in which a noun clause is used as object of a participle.

13. The following sentence contains a noun clause used as object of an infinitive. Write five sentences substituting other noun clauses:

> The engineer wanted to determine *what the cost of the bridge would be.*

14. Write five sentences of your own in which a noun clause is used as object of an infinitive.

Exercise C

1. The following sentence contains an adverbial clause used as a modifier of a verb. Write six sentences substituting other adverbial clauses for this one. Use a variety of appropriate connectives.

> The fugitive surrendered *when he found that he was trapped in the canyon.*

2. Write five sentences of your own in which an adverbial clause modifies a verb. Use a variety of connectives.

3. Rewrite the sentences of item 2, shifting the position of the adverbial clause in each sentence.

4. The following sentence contains an adverbial clause used as modifier of an adjective. Write five sentences substituting other adverbial clauses:

> The team was ready *when the whistle blew for the beginning of the game.*

5. Write five sentences of your own in which an adverbial clause modifies an adjective.

6. The following sentence contains an adverbial clause used as modifier of an adverb. Write five sentences substituting other adverbial clauses:

The troops advanced cautiously *because the field had been planted with deadly mines.*

7. Write five sentences of your own in which an adverbial clause modifies an adverb.

8. The following sentence contains an adverbial clause used as modifier of a participle. Write five sentences substituting other adverbial clauses:

Mrs. Smith was very entertaining *when she attended a party.*

9. Write five sentences of your own in which an adverbial clause modifies a participle. Use a variety of subordinate connectives. If possible, use a variety of participial constructions.

10. The following sentence contains an adverbial clause used as modifier of an infinitive. Write five sentences substituting other adverbial clauses:

I like to eat *when I am hungry.*

11. Write five sentences of your own in which an adverbial clause modifies an infinitive. If possible, use a variety of constructions.

12. Construct five sentences with adjective clauses introduced by the relative pronoun *who.* Use a variety of structures so that the noun which the adjective clause modifies serves different functions within the sentence — subject, complement, object of a preposition, etc.

13. Repeat item 12 using the relative pronouns *whom, whose, which,* and *that.*

14. Construct six sentences with adjective clauses introduced by the connectives *where, when,* and *why.*

15. Construct six complex sentences with two or more subordinate clauses fulfilling different functions.

16. Construct six compound sentences with one of the co-ordinate clauses including a subordinate clause. Use a variety of subordinate functions.

EXERCISE D

In the following selection, study the sentence structure carefully. Observe the use of co-ordination and subordination in each sentence. Identify the function of each subordinate clause. Observe the variety of sentence structures used. Be prepared to comment on the writer's purpose in using this or that particular grammatical device.

The longest undefended border in the world has lately grown quite a crop of thistles. That is why President Eisenhower went to Ottawa to address the Canadian parliament, and confer with Prime Minister Diefenbaker last week.

Canadians don't like our wheat-dumping policy, which seems to them to put free or bartered U.S. wheat into some of their normal export markets. Ike assured his audience that "the basis of these objections has been largely removed," and promised continuing consultation. Canadians also fear a resurgence of U.S. protectionism which threatens their U.S. market for oil, aluminum, lead, and zinc. Ike tried to rationalize our "voluntary" oil quotas as necessary to hemisphere defense and promised that U.S. trade policy, reciprocal since 1934, would stay liberal. Canadians welcome, but also fear the huge influx of U.S. private capital which has sparked their recent expansion, but which has also put some 25% of the control of Canadian industry in U.S. hands. Ike reminded them that subsidiaries of U.S. firms "are of course subject to Canadian law," and virtually invited them to pass more laws if they really feel dominated.

If this flat, frank speech chopped few thistles, that is because most of the thistles sprang not from U.S. seeds but from profound changes within Canada. Of these changes the U.S. should be much more aware.

Canada is not only bigger in area than the U.S., it is the fourth or fifth industrial power in the world, though its population is only one tenth of our own. Canada would dominate almost any part of the earth except the one it is in. It is muscular, prosperous, expansive and self-confident in every direction — except when it looks south. It fears U.S. economic and cultural penetration all the more since these are so unintentional on our part. U.S. negligence is what Canadians hate most.[7]

EXERCISE E

One of the important problems of composition is to express related facts in coherent statements by using the principles of co-ordination and subordination. Five related facts are given here. Students had been given these separate facts to express in one or more coherent statements. Below are listed some of the expressions used in response to this assignment.

Evaluate and discuss these statements. What devices of subordination have been used? Identify them and note their functions. Which sentences express the facts clearly and effectively, and which do not? Explain.

[7] "From "Cutting Thistles in Canada," an Editorial in *Life* Magazine, July 21, 1958, p. 24. Copr. 1958 Time Inc.

William Dean Howells wrote *The Rise of Silas Lapham.*
The book was published in 1885.
The book deals with the moral problem of a successful businessman.
Howells was the literary authority of his day.
The Rise of Silas Lapham is considered one of Howells' best novels.

1. William Dean Howells, who was the literary authority of his day, published *The Rise of Silas Lapham* in 1885. Considered to be one of Howells' best novels, the book deals with the moral problem of the American businessman.

2. *The Rise of Silas Lapham,* which was published in 1885, was written by William Dean Howells who was considered the literary authority of his day. The book, which is considered one of Howells' best novels, deals with the moral problems of a successful businessman.

3. William Dean Howells was the literary authority of his day when he wrote *The Rise of Silas Lapham* in 1885. One of the reasons that this book is considered his best novel is that it deals with the moral problems of a successful businessman.

4. The book that is considered William Dean Howells' best work is *The Rise of Silas Lapham.* In 1885 when the book was published, Howells was considered the literary authority of his day. The moral problems that confront a successful businessman are the theme of his book.

5. That William Dean Howells was the literary authority of his day was derived partly from the reputation of that novel which was considered one of his best, *The Rise of Silas Lapham.* It is interesting to note that the book dealing with the question, "What is morality for the successful businessman?" was published in 1885.

6. In 1885 William Dean Howells, the literary authority of his day, published what is considered one of his best works, *The Rise of Silas Lapham,* which deals with the moral problems of a successful businessman.

5

Modifier Word Groups

We saw in Chapter 4 how subject-predicate word groups may be *added on* to the main sentence to form co-ordinate clauses, or *included within* the main sentence to form subordinate clauses. In this chapter we shall see how groups of modifiers are *built about* the nouns and verbs, as well as the modifiers of nouns and verbs — the adjectives and adverbs.

Noun-headed Word Groups

When modifiers are *built about* a noun as a nucleus, the word group is called a noun-headed word group, or a noun cluster. For example:

The WOLF

The wicked WOLF

The wicked WOLF in Wyoming

The wicked WOLF in Wyoming who roams the forest

Here is a noun-headed word group with the noun as nucleus and modifiers built about it. Each modifier adds meaning to the noun. We know a number of facts about the wolf:

The wolf is wicked.

The wolf is in Wyoming.

The wolf roams the forest.

The noun-headed word group expresses these meanings compactly and coherently. Each modifier in the word group has an adjectival function (modifier of a noun).

The adjectival modifier may be a single word such as *wicked*, which is called an adjective. (We will discuss adjectives in Chapter 8.) Or it may be a word group such as *in Wyoming* or *who roams the forest*. We immediately recognize *who roams the forest* as a subject-predicate word group, a subordinate clause, in this case an adjective clause. The word group *in Wyoming* is called a prepositional phrase.

Prepositional Phrases

A prepositional phrase is a modifier word group signaled by a connective called a preposition. This is followed by a noun, or a noun with its modifiers (a noun-headed word group). The following list includes the prepositions most frequently used to signal prepositional phrases.

in	from	above	beneath
on	through	across	beside
to	out	toward	among
by	up	under	against
at	off	beyond	after
down	with	over	about

There are also double prepositions such as *inside* and *within* and group prepositions such as *in back of* and *on top of*.

Some prepositional phrases modifying nouns in noun-headed word groups are:

The WATER *in the well* . . .

The APPLES *on the tree* . . .

The HOUSE *by the hill* . . .

The MAN *from old Virginia* . . .
The PATH *through the quiet woods* . . .
The GIRL *across the street* . . .
The ROAD *over the mountain* . . .

Participial Phrases

Another word group frequently used to modify a noun is the participial phrase, a modifier word group used in an adjectival function. It is signaled by a verbal (verb form) ending, usually, in *-ing* or *-ed* or *-en*. Verbals will be discussed more fully in Chapter 12.

Some participial phrases are:

The WOLF *roaming the forest* . . .
The BIRDS *singing so sweetly* . . .
The MEN *tilling the fields* . . .
The RAIN *soaking the ground* . . .
The WIND *scattering the leaves* . . .
The CHILDREN *riding their bicycles* . . .

Here again we have noun-headed word groups in which one of the adjectival modifiers is itself a word group. The participial phrase contrasts with the prepositional phrase in that it is signaled by a participle, in these cases, the verb form ending in *-ing*. This form is called the present participle of the verb. *Roaming, singing, tilling, soaking, scattering,* and *riding* are inflected forms of their respective verbs.

Participial phrases may also be signaled by the inflected verb form called the past participle, usually the *-ed* or *-en* form. For example,

The FIGHTER *backed against the ropes* struggled to keep on his feet.
The cook served SALMON *fried in butter.*
The CAR *driven at a fast rate* skidded on the pavement.
They found the MONEY *hidden in the old trunk.*

The italicized word groups in the above sentences are participial phrases. The noun in small capitals in each sentence is the head-word of a noun-headed word group in which the participial phrase is an adjectival modifier. The participle which signals each phrase is the inflected verb form known as the past participle (the *-ed* or *-en* form).

The following are examples of sentences in which a modifier word group is a participial phrase.

> The SAILOR, *lashed to the wheel of the storm-tossed ship*, guided it through the gale.

The noun headword is *sailor*. The participial phrase, *lashed to the wheel of the storm-tossed ship*, is an adjectival modifier of the noun *sailor*.

> I saw the BOY *studying his lesson*.

The noun headword is *boy*. The participial phrase, *studying his lesson*, is an adjectival modifier of the noun *boy*.

> The wild HORSES *galloping swiftly from the desert* raced into the corral.

The noun *horses* is the headword of the noun-headed word group *The wild horses galloping swiftly from the desert*. The participial phrase, *galloping swiftly from the desert*, is an adjectival modifier of the noun *horses*.

Participial phrases are often placed at the beginning of a sentence, before the subject.

> *Walking into the library*, I was surprised to meet Mr. Brown.
>
> *Jutting out into the sea*, the cliffs looked dark and somber in the moonlight.
>
> *Pickled in vinegar*, the onions were served with cold ham and potato salad.
>
> *Walking slowly down the street*, we saw many new automobiles.

In such cases, the modifying participial phrase must immediately precede the noun it modifies. If the participial phrase does not introduce the sentence, it is best placed immediately after the word it modifies. Otherwise ambiguity may result.

> 1. The boy *reaching for the book* stumbled against his brother.
> 2. The boy stumbled against his brother *reaching for the book*.

In sentence 1 the meaning is perfectly clear. In sentence 2 we are not certain who is reaching for the book.

Another common kind of ambiguity results when a participial phrase begins a sentence but does not modify the subject of the sentence.

> *Pickled in spiced vinegar,* we thought the peaches were delicious with the roast beef.

> *Moving swiftly across the sky,* we saw the dark threatening clouds.

Such constructions, called dangling participial phrases, fail to communicate clearly.

To sum up, then, a participial phrase may introduce a sentence if the noun it modifies follows it immediately. If the participial phrase does not introduce the sentence, it should follow the noun which it modifies to avoid possible ambiguity.

Infinitive Phrases

Another common modifier word group, the infinitive phrase, may be part of a noun-headed word group. That is, like the participial phrase and the prepositional phrase, it may serve as the adjectival modifier of a noun. In each of the following sentences the italicized infinitive phrase modifies a noun headword.

> He is the MAN *to watch closely in this election.*

> The PERSON *to tell the story* is your father.

> He told of a PLAN *to sell his estate.*

> My mother gave me a BOOK *to read while she was away.*

> This is the PLAY *to be given next season.*

> The only HOUSE *to be rented at a fair price* was on the outskirts of the city.

> I gave him the name of the APPLICANT *to be interviewed for the position.*

> The doctor gave me MEDICINE *to be taken every night.*

Verb-headed Word Groups

As a noun may serve as the nucleus of a word group about which different kinds of modifiers may be built, so may a verb. When modifiers are built about a verb, a verb-headed word group is developed. The modifiers may be single words, phrases, or clauses and are called adverbial modifiers. For example,

> Mr. Smith RAN *quickly.*
> Mr. Smith RAN *quickly into the house.*
> Mr. Smith RAN *quickly into the house when the storm broke.*

Here is a verb-headed word group consisting of the verb *ran* as the headword and its modifiers. The modifiers — *quickly, into the house,* and *when the storm broke* — add meaning to the verb. Besides knowing that "Mr. Smith ran," we know also three additional facts:

> Mr. Smith ran quickly.
> Mr. Smith ran into the house.
> Mr. Smith ran when the storm broke.

The verb-headed word group expresses these meanings compactly and coherently. Each modifier in it has an adverbial function (modifier of a verb).

Again, the modifiers may be *single words* (*quickly,* an adverb), or *word groups* such as the prepositional phrase *into the house* and the subject-predicate word group *when the storm broke.*

Some prepositional phrases modifying verbs are:

> The excited man RAN *up the street.*
> The leaves BLEW *across the lawn.*
> The guests ARRIVED *in great numbers.*
> The president SPOKE *to the point.*
> The sun SHONE *during the afternoon.*
> The boys SWAM *across the lake.*

Infinitive phrases are word groups which also may modify verbs.

> The salesman CAME *to see me.*
> The woman RAN *to escape the fire.*
> The boy JUMPED *to get across the ditch.*
> The children STAYED *to see the second show.*
> The senator WAS ELECTED *to represent the people.*
> The soldiers WAITED *to attack the advancing enemy.*

Adjective- and Adverb-headed Word Groups

Although modifying words and word groups are built mainly on nouns and verbs, other word classes (parts of speech) may serve as headwords for modification. Both adjectives and adverbs often have modifiers in conventional English sentences.

ADJECTIVES AS HEADWORDS

1. With single word modifiers:

> The woman bought *strictly* FRESH eggs.
> The sky had a *dark* RED color.
> The material was a *yard* WIDE.
> The water was *boiling* HOT.

2. With word groups as modifiers:

> The young man is ELIGIBLE *for promotion.*
> The boy was EAGER *to join the army.*
> The box was HEAVIER *than he could lift.*

ADVERBS AS HEADWORDS

1. With single word modifiers:

> He went *far* AWAY from his house.
> The boy arrived *an hour* EARLY.
> The child did not read *very* WELL.

2. With word groups as modifiers:

> The plane arrived EARLY *in the morning.*
> The boy ran FASTER *than he had ever run before.*

Summary

Nouns and verbs are the key words in the English language. As headwords they may be modified by single words (adjectives and adverbs) or by word groups (subordinate clauses, prepositional and verbal phrases). The clusters of modifiers developed about nouns and verbs together with headwords are called noun-headed word groups and verb-headed word groups.

In the illustrative sentences that follow, a partial analysis indicates the headwords and the modifiers.

> The most startling FACT about the young PEOPLE is their AMBITION to succeed quickly.

HEADWORDS — NOUN	MODIFIERS
fact	the
	most startling
	about young people
people	the
	young
ambition	their
	to succeed quickly

> The gay PARTY celebrating the ARRIVAL of the beautiful CO-ED *had begun* early in the AFTERNOON.

HEADWORDS — NOUN	MODIFIERS
party	the
	gay
	celebrating the arrival of the beautiful co-ed
arrival	the
	of the beautiful co-ed
co-ed	the
	beautiful
afternoon	the

HEADWORDS — VERB	MODIFIERS
had begun	early in the afternoon

> Recalling his early YEARS, the old MAN *fell* a deep LONGING to return home to his native LAND where he *had lived* when he *was* a little BOY.

HEADWORDS — NOUN	MODIFIERS
man	the
	old
	recalling his early years
years	his
	early

longing	to return home to his native land where he had lived when he was a little boy
land	his
	native
	where he had lived when he was a little boy
boy	a
	little

| HEADWORDS — VERB | MODIFIERS |
| had lived | when he was a little boy |

(*fell* and *was* are verbs without modifiers)

Groups of modifiers are also built up on the adjectives and adverbs that themselves modify nouns and verbs. In their great variety, modifiers and modifier word groups make up a rich resource of language. They create a wealth of forms and structures to provide the writer with communicative power and flexibility of style.

EXERCISE A

Indicate the noun-headed word groups in the following sentences. Identify the headword and each of the modifiers and modifying word groups.

1. We strolled along a dim-lit street of the Latin Quarter, silent and deserted.
2. Many students who attend college spend their free time in profitable employment.
3. The father of Matthew Arnold was a very famous schoolmaster.
4. On a bright, sunny Sunday afternoon in April, the President walked briskly down Pennsylvania Avenue.
5. We saw the young horses running swiftly across the pasture.
6. She took out of the oven a pan of biscuits stuffed with apples.
7. The sick young man who had worked so hard was obliged to give up his plan to go to college.
8. Lured by adventure and the desire to make money, the boy set out for the city.

9. With the greater knowledge of the world gained through these vivid experiences, Johnson began his new life as a writer.

10. The whole shelf of books had been scattered on the floor, where they were now trampled by the boots of the men who had never read in their lives.

11. The English test tomorrow will be related to the Victorian poetry which you have read.

12. Mr. Smith had never seen the house on Tenth Street where George had lived so many years.

EXERCISE B

Indicate the verb-headed word groups in the following sentences. Identify the headword and each of the modifiers and modifying word groups.

1. He will buy the material where he can find the best price.

2. As he walked along, Mr. James realized that he would get to the theater quickly.

3. Suddenly the wind lashed the small boat and it rocked wildly in the rough water.

4. When he comes tomorrow, he will bring with him all of the books which you ordered.

5. The conversation ended quickly with a cry that indicated that the man had been struck violently from the rear.

6. I was told the story by an old man who came here yesterday.

7. He ran quickly to catch the ball sailing high in the air.

8. Uncle Joe stood by the fence while they were running across the field to catch the horses.

9. It was noon when the box was delivered suddenly at the rear door of the hotel by the old driver.

10. I have suddenly now, after all these years, remembered what she said to me when she was a little girl.

11. If you will go quietly into the house you will find her there where I just left her.

12. He went to college to study law, and when he graduated he soon became one of the great lawyers of the state.

EXERCISE C

Indicate the noun-headed word groups and the verb-headed word groups in the following selection, and identify each of the modifiers and modifying word groups.

Man is a passing sunshower blessed with the power to dream. While his primal forebear blazes daylight overhead, he lives through a different burning: hurting and crying, laughing and playing, hoping and wishing, loving and wondering. Sometimes he pauses to write down his wonderment about the still mysterious broth of creation that in the beginning bubbled and boiled up from the splash of the Sun on the bare raw face of Earth. For a billion or two years the splashing fermented before it cooked out anything like a cabbage, and for almost three billion more years before it burbled the first rough makings of a king.

We have breathed the bottom currents of this air ocean ever since man first stood up at the edge of the sea a million years ago. We have been washed about the planet by its tides, and have evolved as thinking animals in order to continue to enjoy its evolving environment. We have had no choice. Should the Earth's atmosphere dissipate into space tomorrow, the subsequent interval of our survival would be precipitately short.

The photograph at our masthead above gives a fleeting glimpse into the mysterious depths of the atmosphere's workings. There we see smog rising from the hand of a scientist at the California Institute of Technology. Cupped in that palm are a few hydrocarbon particles. Blowing across them is a breath of ozone: the death-dealing three-atomed form of oxygen. Until we can explain simply and completely how this mixture occurs in the open air, weather control is idle talk. Yet, if we are to avert the risk of being overwhelmed — perhaps a quarter century hence — by sudden discovery that weather can be made to order and visited upon us for unpleasant purposes, we must learn enough about the air meanwhile to decide whether control is in fact possible and if so how it can be exercised economically and constructively.[1]

EXERCISE D

1. In the following sentence the prepositional phrase is an adjectival modifier of a noun headword. Write six sentences substituting other prepositional phrases. Use a variety of prepositions.

    The man *in the blue suit* bought Grandfather's farm.

[1] From "The Mysterious Broth of Life: Earth's Atmosphere — I," *Saturday Review*, October 4, 1958, p. 39 (Science and Humanity Section); reprinted by permission of John Lear, Science Editor.

2. Construct six sentences with prepositional phrases modifying noun headwords. Develop sentences in which nouns are used in a variety of functions.

3. In the following sentence a participial phrase is used as an adjectival modifier of a noun headword. Write six sentences substituting other participial phrases:

> The football player *standing on the fifty-yard line* just made a touchdown.

4. Construct six sentences with participial phrases modifying noun headwords. If possible, vary the position of the participial phrases.

5. In the following sentence an infinitive phrase modifies a noun headword. Write six sentences substituting other infinitive phrases:

> Father employed a man *to paint the barn.*

6. Construct six sentences each containing an infinitive phrase used as an adjectival modifier of a noun headword. Develop sentences in which nouns are used in a variety of functions.

7. In the following sentence a prepositional phrase is an adverbial modifier of a verb headword. Write six sentences substituting other prepositional phrases:

> The sweet, little old lady walked quietly *down the street.*

8. Construct six sentences each containing a prepositional phrase used as an adverbial modifier of a verb headword. Use a variety of prepositions and verb forms.

9. In the following sentence an infinitive phrase is used as an adverbial modifier of a verb headword. Write six sentences substituting other infinitive phrases:

> Mr. Plumkin was surprised *to see his son mowing the lawn.*

10. Construct six sentences each containing an infinitive phrase used as an adverbial modifier of a verb headword.

11. Construct four sentences each having single word modifiers built about an adjective as headword.

12. In the following sentence a prepositional phrase is used as the modifier of an adjective headword. Write four sentences substituting other prepositional phrases:

> Cassidy was usually nervous *in the morning.*

13. Construct four sentences each containing a prepositional phrase used as a modifier of an adjective headword.

14. In the following sentence an infinitive phrase is used as the modifier of an adjective headword. Write four sentences substituting other infinitive phrases:

> The old witch was eager *to push the little children into the oven.*

15. Construct four sentences each containing an infinitive phrase used as the modifier of an adjective headword.

16. Construct four sentences with single word modifiers built about an adverb as a headword.

17. In the following sentence a prepositional phrase is used as the modifier of an adverb headword. Write four sentences substituting other prepositional phrases:

   Charlie Hartneck played formerly *with the Sing Sing Tigers.*

18. Construct four sentences each containing a prepositional phrase used as the modifier of an adverb headword.

Nouns

6

LANGUAGE is a set of stimuli to which we have learned to respond. Learning to respond to language in a satisfactory way consists not only in becoming familiar with its separate symbols (words), but in mastering the structures which serve as instruments of meaning. These structures enable us to describe the world as we see and experience it and to communicate our perception to others.

The universe, as we see it in the Western world, is a creation of *separate* entities or things which exist, change, and move. We have developed names for the things that are in our universe, or that we think are there, for we cannot always experience them through our senses. In our grammatical description of our language, we classify these names as nouns. And the words which describe the being, the change, the movement of the entities in our world, we call verbs.

In order to respond appropriately to language stimuli, we must be able to identify and differentiate the nouns and the verbs. To do this we need not consciously name the word a noun or a verb.

Even very young children are able to discriminate between the two in terms of responding satisfactorily to them. But because the business of grammar is to describe the structure of language, it is our purpose now to study and identify the signals of language which enable us to communicate and respond.

Structural Signals of Meaning

Let us consider an easy sentence in order to observe some of the elementary signals of language.

The boys eat the fish with their forks.

First of all we have several signals to tell us that there is more than one boy. We note the "s" on *boys*, the pronoun *their*, and the "s" on *forks*. Also the verb *eat* instead of *eats* helps to let us know that there is more than one boy. The verb form *eat*, instead of *ate* or some other combination of verb forms, gives a time sense to the action. The order of the words themselves signals in a very decided way the nature of the action. We know that the fish did not eat the boys. Words like *the* and *their* come before the names, the nouns.

The structural signals of meaning in our language are essentially four in number:

1. Word order,
2. Inflection,
3. Structure words (*the, this, and, to, which,* etc.),
4. Word grouping.

We shall see as we develop this discussion how these signals aid us in responding to words as nouns or verbs or adjectives or adverbs, thereby insuring adequate behavior.

Determiners as Signals of Nouns

For the identification of nouns, the most important signals are words which the linguists call determiners. They include such words as *a, an, the, this, that, these, those, my, their, several, many, each, one, two, all, some, few,* and so on.

Few *people* came to the *party*.

Many *children* go to this *school*.

Several *paintings* will be sold at his *store*.

These *houses* need many *repairs*.

A *fool* and his *money* are soon parted.

Two *dollars* was too much to pay for one *admission*.

The importance of determiners as signals for the identification of nouns in communication may be shown by the ambiguity which results when these little words are left out. For example,

Cook scraps Monday.

We do not know how to respond since we cannot surely identify the noun or the verb. This may be a statement of fact, that the cook is going to fight on Monday. If so, *cook* is a noun and *scraps* is a verb. There is no signal to determine this interpretation. On the other hand, the communication may be an order to cook the leftovers on Monday, with *cook* a verb and *scraps* a noun. The use of a determiner would signal the intended meaning.

If we place the word *the* before *cook* or before *scraps* the noun will be identified and the noun-verb relationship established.

The cook scraps Monday.

Cook the scraps Monday.

Prepositions as Signals of Nouns

A second signal for the identification of nouns is the preposition. Nouns follow prepositions. If we have learned the prepositions, and if we can recognize the preposition as a connective in a sentence, then we can perceive the noun which follows it. In the use of spoken language we have all learned to do this while very young.

I will go home in the *morning*.

The man drove swiftly up *Morningside Avenue*.

The robbery took place between *dawn* and *daylight*.

The great plane flew across many *states*.

Simpson got into *trouble* over *money*.

Agatha fell in love with *Plumkin*.

The preposition is a connective which serves to include a word group within a sentence — the prepositional phrase. The noun has a definite place in this word group. We have always found it there, and we have learned to respond habitually to it as a noun in this position. The little child responds quickly to the question,

> Where's Mama?

by the answer

> In the house.

If he asks the question, and the answer is given as above, he is ready to respond with appropriate behavior.

Position of Nouns

The identification of nouns and of words that function as nouns, together with the appropriate response to them as language stimuli, results largely from the normal fixed positions of nouns in the English sentence patterns. In Chapter 3 we discussed these elementary sentence patterns. We may recall them now.

1. N V
2. N V N
3. N V(linking) Adj
4. N V(linking) N
5. N V N N

Besides these simple sentence patterns, there are questions and inverted sentences, as well as patterns in which nouns are used as appositives.

We have all mastered these sentence patterns in speech and have learned to use them in communicating and responding. The word order of the main sentence elements is fixed. The nouns come before the verbs as subjects, or after the verbs as complements. We shall observe later the signals which help us identify and respond to verbs. The identification of verbs, of course, further helps us in identifying the nouns by virtue of their position relative to the verb in the fixed sentence pattern.

1. *Lillian* graduated.
2. The old *man* caught the *tarpon*.

3. Mad *dogs* are dangerous.

4. *Cyclotrons* are atom *smashers*.

5. The *voters* elected *Mr. Plumkin mayor*.

Some confusion in grammatical classification has resulted from the fact that words which we do not think of as nouns (for a number of reasons to be discussed later) often are used in positions in the sentence where nouns are used. For example,

1. *Nobody* contributed.

2. *He* caught a tarpon.

3. *These* are dangerous.

4. *Everyone* is a winner.

5. He won't give *anybody* a break.

These words, *nobody, he, these, everyone, anybody,* used in place of nouns, are substitute words but they function in the sentence just like nouns. Substitution is an important grammatical principle, as we shall see. Words which usually substitute for nouns have been called pronouns in many textbooks of grammar, and they have been subclassified in various ways. It is sufficient here to think of these words, which function like nouns in a sentence, as noun-words. From the standpoint of function, they are nouns; from the standpoint of form, they are not.

Our discussion of the identification of nouns in a sentence has related principally to function (syntax), the position of words in a sentence and their relation to other words and word groups, and the resultant signals of communication. There are, however, certain characteristics of form, formal signals, which serve to aid in the identification of nouns. These formal signals result usually from inflection and affixation.

Inflection

Inflection is a grammatical signal of meaning. It involves some change in the form of the word. For example, *man* becomes *men* to show plurality, or we change *boy* to *boy's* to indicate a possessive relationship between two words such as the *boy's hat.* The English language, however, does not depend very much on inflectional changes for its structural signals. We say that English, therefore, is not a highly inflected language. It uses word order, structure words, and word groupings to signal grammatical meaning more than it uses inflectional endings. In English we prefer to say "the color of the wall" rather than "the wall's color." In German, if an indirect object is used, the article corresponding to *the* in English changes its form to show the dative case, as it is called. In English we merely say, "I gave *the girl* the book." We rely entirely on the word order to indicate that *girl* is the indirect object. In some languages, such as Latin, inflection is the chief signal of grammatical meaning. Latin, therefore, is called a synthetic language. English, which is not a highly inflected language and which relies on other types of structural signals of meaning, is called an analytic language.

Inflection is used to signal several different kinds of grammatical meaning. It may indicate number, the contrast between singular and plural: for example, *dog* and *dogs*. It may indicate case, a syntactical or relationship signal: for example, the possessive, "the *boy's* hat"; or the objective (with pronouns), "I gave *her* the book," where *her* contrasts with the subject form *she*. Nouns are not inflected for the object relationship, only for the possessive, and relatively few nouns for that. Inflection may also indicate sex, or gender. A few English nouns have contrasting forms for the masculine and the feminine: *count* and *countess*, *aviator* and *aviatrix*. The personal pronouns *he*, *she*, and *it* afford the unique illustration in English of inflection for masculine, feminine, and neuter gender. In German all nouns are classified as masculine, feminine, or neuter, and the appropriate article, *der*, *die*, or *das*, is used to show this distinction. The classification is not necessarily made on the basis of sex. For example, though *man* is masculine, *wife* is neuter. The nearest we come to such a practice in English is the habit of referring to some objects as *he* or *she*. Speaking of a *boat*, we may say, "Isn't *she* a beauty?" We would not dream of referring to the boat as *he*.

Although we are mainly concerned in this chapter with inflection as a formal signal for identifying nouns, we should note here that adjectives, adverbs, and verbs are also inflected. With adjectives and adverbs we may by this means indicate comparison or show contrasting degrees of quality.

ADJECTIVES

The *tall* boy is my brother; the *taller* boy is my cousin.

ADVERBS

The children came in *quietly*.
The children came in *more quietly* than before.

The old man walked *slow* on his way to church.
The old man walked *slower* than he had ever walked before.

Changes in the forms of verbs to indicate tense or time are among the most important ways in which inflection shows structural meaning in our language. For example, contrasting verb forms distinguish between the present and the past.

I *am* a citizen of the United States.
I *was* a citizen of England.

The child *wants* a train for Christmas.
The child *wanted* a train for Christmas.

In this chapter, since we are discussing the noun, we shall describe in some detail the inflection of nouns. Our problem will be related mainly to the discussion and illustration of variant plural forms, and the limited use of possessives. For convenience of reference, nouns will be grouped arbitrarily in terms of the variety of ways in which they are inflected.

1. Nouns which have four forms, singular, plural, singular possessive, and plural possessive. The plural is formed by adding *s* to the singular.

girl	girls	girl's	girls'
boy	boys	boy's	boys'
aunt	aunts	aunt's	aunts'
uncle	uncles	uncle's	uncles'
dog	dogs	dog's	dogs'
chair	chairs	chair's	chairs'

In this group we find mostly words which refer to living things, although words like *chair* and *table* may be included. The inflected possessive form for inanimate objects, however, has largely fallen into disuse. Thus we say "the leg of the table," not "the table's leg."

2. Nouns which form the plural by adding *es* instead of *s*. These words end in the sounds *sh*, *ch* (as in chur*ch*), *s*, and *x*. Words that end in *z* also add *es* for the plural, but they double the final *z*. Only the singular and plural forms are given here since conventional usage does not include possessives for most words of this kind.

church	churches
crutch	crutches
crash	crashes
bus	buses
gas	gases
box	boxes
quiz	quizzes
fez	fezzes

3. Nouns which end in *y* preceded by a consonant. In forming the plural, the writer changes the *y* to *i* and adds *es*. These words may or may not be inflected for the possessive.

ally	allies	ally's	allies'
jelly	jellies		
army	armies	army's	armies'
city	cities	city's	cities'
lady	ladies	lady's	ladies'

Words ending in *quy* are also included in this group, although they are exceptions, since *u* precedes *y* and *u* is a vowel.

colloquy	colloquies
soliloquy	soliloquies

4. Nouns ending in *o* which add *es* to form the plural. (Nouns ending in *o* that form their plurals by adding only *s* belong in Group 1.)

potato	potatoes		
tomato	tomatoes		
hero	heroes	hero's	heroes'
Negro	Negroes	Negro's	Negroes'
torpedo	torpedoes		
tornado	tornadoes		

It is true that many words ending in *o* may form the plural by adding either *s* or *es*. However, since one or the other form is usually preferable, and since some words such as those listed above use only the *es* inflection for the plural, the student should consult a recent dictionary when in doubt. When dictionaries differ, as they sometimes do, the student may be permitted a variant spelling.

5. Nouns ending in *f* or *fe* which form the plural by changing the *f* or *fe* to *ves*.

loaf	loaves		
leaf	leaves		
half	halves		
wolf	wolves	wolf's	wolves'
wife	wives	wife's	wives'
knife	knives		

There are some words such as *beef* and *wharf* which form their plurals either by adding *s* or by changing the *f* to *ves*.

beef	beeves or beefs
wharf	wharves or wharfs

6. Nouns which form their plurals by means of an internal vowel change.

man	men	man's	men's
woman	women	woman's	women's
foot	feet		
mouse	mice		
tooth	teeth		
goose	geese		

When compounds are formed from words of this group, variant usage in plural inflection is found.

policeman	policemen
mongoose	mongooses

7. Nouns which form their plurals by adding *en* to the singular form.

child	children	child's	children's
ox	oxen		

It is interesting to note that *brethren* is the variant plural of *brother*, and *kine* of *cow*, although both are now considered archaic.

8. Nouns adopted into the English language which retain their foreign plurals.

alumnus	alumni
alumna	alumnae
analysis	analyses
hypothesis	hypotheses
datum	data
larva	larvae
stimulus	stimuli

Some words in this group have developed variant English plurals.

curriculum	curricula or curriculums
appendix	appendices or appendixes

9. Nouns which have the same form in both the singular and the plural. They are not inflected for the plural sense, although they may take a plural verb form.

deer
moose
salmon
trout
species
sheep
Japanese
Portuguese

10. Nouns used only in the singular. They have been called "uncountables."

anger
information
intelligence
arithmetic
gold
magnetism

11. Nouns which are plural in form but are singular in meaning and take a singular verb form.

mathematics
physics
economics

measles
news
summons

12. Nouns which are plural in form and plural in meaning.
They take a plural verb form.

pliers
wages
scissors
trousers
clothes
thanks

13. Nouns, sometimes called "mass" nouns, which have a plural
sense in the singular form and add *s* for a secondary plural.

people	peoples
fish	fishes
fruit	fruits
hundred	hundreds
ton	tons
money	moneys

14. Compound nouns which form the plural by adding *s* to or
otherwise changing a word other than the last word.

brother-in-law	brothers-in-law
editor-in-chief	editors-in-chief
passer-by	passers-by
man-of-war	men-of-war
court-martial	courts-martial

Most compound nouns, however, now form the plural by adding
s at the end (Group 1).

Finally, though nouns in English do not as a rule change their
form to show difference in gender, a few are inflected to distinguish
between masculine and feminine.

hero	heroine
alumnus	alumna
man	woman
duke	duchess

prince	princess
host	hostess
waiter	waitress

The fourteen lists of representative nouns showing variations in the ways in which the plural is formed and illustrating in a limited way inflection for the possessive case, together with the listing of some nouns which inflect for gender, give the student some idea of the complexity of inflected forms which we have inherited in our language. He should find it interesting to search for other words in his own vocabulary and in his reading to make these partial lists more nearly complete. It is important to be familiar with the inflected forms of nouns, not only for the advantage of using the appropriate forms of standard written English, but for the recognition value of inflectional endings and changes as signals in communication. Inflectional endings and changes are important markers of nouns, and we are very sensitive to these stimuli. As a matter of fact, we are prone to give words permanent classifications on the basis of inflected forms rather than consider their function within the sentence in which they are used. We think of *cow* as a noun with the plural *cows* and the singular possessive *cow's*. Yet *cow* may be used appropriately and effectively as a verb.

The sergeant *cowed* the new recruits into submission.

Since we have indicated some inflected forms of nouns for the possessive case, it may be useful to elaborate more fully on the problem and to summarize the important considerations. The term *genitive* is sometimes used instead of *possessive*, but neither word precisely describes the grammatical function involved.

The possessive case is a grammatical device which fulfills a number of functions in communication. Examples of its usefulness are given here.

1. Arthur's hat does not fit him very well.
2. Hemingway's novel *The Old Man and the Sea* is an epic story of human fortitude.
3. The young man's ambition was to become a successful lawyer.
4. The capable secretary was given a month's vacation.
5. Brown and Brown are having a sale of ladies' shoes.

6. Willie drank the lemonade to his heart's content.
7. Wickenburg's finest paraded down Main Street.
8. Clara May is a dear friend of my mother's.
9. Cassidy's punting won the football game.

Very frequently grammarians classify the different kinds of possessives, but the multiple classifications would seem to be of little practical value to the student writer. It is enough for him to be familiar with the range of usefulness of this grammatical device and to exploit this knowledge in his writing.

Sentence 8, above, is worth special mention as an example of the *double possessive*, a combination of the inflected possessive and the *of* phrase which is often substituted for it. This form is used only in referring to persons.

He is my brother's friend.
He is a friend of my brother.
He is a friend of my brother's.

The possessive case is used mostly with nouns referring to human beings and animals. To communicate equivalent meaning related to plants and inanimate objects, the *of* phrase is used.

They placed a bridle on the *horse's head*.
Where MacDonald sits, there is the *head of the table*.
The *patient's color* is very bad this morning.
She had cheeks like the *color of the rose*.

There is a tendency in modern usage to substitute a noun modifier for the possessive in many situations.

She is a family friend.

instead of

She is the family's friend.
Clara May is very fond of the Gilligan baby.

instead of

Clara May is very fond of the Gilligans' baby.

In naming organizations and buildings the possessive inflection is usually ignored.

We received a grant from the Ford Foundation.

Bill heard yesterday from the Veterans Administration.

The books are carefully preserved in Matthews Library.

The use of the apostrophe in forming possessives often proves troublesome. Here are some suggestions that may be helpful.

1. If the singular does not end in an *s* sound, add apostrophe and *s*.

> boy's   man's   dog's   crowd's   father's

2. If the plural form of the noun ends in *s* or *es*, simply add an apostrophe.

> boys'   girls'   families'   sisters'

3. If the singular form of the noun ends in *s*, simply add an apostrophe to form the possessive.

> boss'   Thomas'   Jones'   Socrates'

4. If the plural form of the noun does not end in *s*, add an apostrophe and *s* to form the possessive.

> children's   men's   women's   oxen's

Full agreement on suggestion 3 will not be found in handbooks and manuals of style, but current usage seems to be tending in this direction. Moreover, the alternative rules to this practice are so complicated that most students will ignore them or misinterpret them. If you write for publication and your editor does not like *boss'*, he will be quick to change it to *boss's*. Both forms communicate the same idea.

Affixation

We have discussed in some detail the nature and importance of inflectional changes to communicate meaning and to mark the inflected word as a noun in a sentence. Another grammatical device useful in establishing the identity of nouns and in providing contrasts with other word classes in the sentence is the identifying suffix. The signals provided by affixation, as by inflection, are formal ones; they inhere, that is, in the form of the word rather than its position or relationships in the sentence. There are a number of characteristic suffixes, most of them adapted from the Latin and the Greek, which serve as markers of nouns and distinguish them from verbs and adjectives. Following is a list of some of the more common noun suffixes and two examples of nouns formed with each.

-acy	aristocracy, democracy
-age	marriage, carriage
-al	burial, survival
-ant	claimant, entrant
-ance	remembrance, resistance
-dom	freedom, kingdom
-eer	engineer, auctioneer
-er	adviser, farmer
-ery	bindery, brewery
-ful	cupful, mouthful
-hood	manhood, boyhood
-ior	behavior, savior
-ism	socialism, baptism
-ist	novelist, humanist
-ity	vanity, insanity
-ing	meaning, calling
-ment	inducement, refinement
-ness	ugliness, holiness
-ship	friendship, penmanship
-sion	admission, permission
-tion	attention, construction
-ure	procedure, failure
-y	jealousy, accuracy

Proper Nouns

In German, all nouns are capitalized; in English, only certain nouns are capitalized, usually the ones customarily regarded as most important. A capital letter is an eye-catching device. When a word within a sentence is capitalized, it takes on added significance to the reader. Capitalization, then, in a sense, is a reading device. Nouns which are capitalized are called proper nouns. Usage varies from time to time; however, standard written

English currently requires that the following classes of nouns
be capitalized.

1. Geographical names and names of political units

>   Philadelphia, North Carolina, Lake Erie, Africa, County Wicklow

2. Personal names

>   George Washington, Franklin Delano Roosevelt, Dwight D.
>   Eisenhower, Robert Frost

3. Organizational names

>   General Motors Corporation, Boy Scouts of America, Ancient
>   Order of Hibernians

4. Institutional names

>   Arizona State Hospital, Syracuse University, Scottsdale High
>   School, Seaman's Institute

5. Names of ships, trains, Pullman cars, etc.

>   *Lusitania, Twentieth Century Limited, Eldorado*

6. Names of days of the week, the months, holidays

>   Tuesday, July, Memorial Day

7. Trade names

>   Coca Cola, Lucky Strikes, Hillman Minx, Socony

8. Titles when used before individual names

>   Captain Kidd, General Dawes, President Smith

9. Names related to deification

>   God, the Almighty, Jehovah, the Deity, Allah

10. Names of historical periods and events

>   the Dark Ages, the Renaissance, the Louisiana Purchase

11. Names of areas of the United States derived from points of
    the compass.

>   the Southwest, the North, the deep South

Summary

Nouns are important words in communication. The listener and the reader must be able to identify them, consciously or unconsciously, in order to make appropriate responses. The writer must know and use effectively those structural signals by means of which the reader identifies nouns, in order to communicate clearly and avoid ambiguity.

Nouns are signaled in a number of different ways. They may be identified by means of their accompanying structure words: the determiners (words like *a, an, the, this, some, few,* and many others), which precede nouns and serve as noun markers; and the prepositions, which also may serve as signals for nouns to follow. Or nouns may be identified by their fixed positions in the sentence as subject or complement. Finally, they may be identified by their form, either because of inflection or because of characteristic suffixes. Usually several signals co-operate in the context of a sentence to point out the nouns.

The candidates directed their attention to Wisconsin.

We know that *candidates* is a noun because of its position as the subject of the sentence, because it is inflected like a noun, and because it is preceded by the determiner *the.* We know that *attention* is a noun because of its position as complement, because it is preceded by *their,* and because of the noun suffix *-tion.* We know that Wisconsin is a noun because it follows a preposition, *to.* We may further identify it as a proper noun, capitalized according to the usage of standard written English.

EXERCISE A

Identify the nouns in the following paragraph.

Perhaps more than any of its predecessors, this generation wants a good, secure job. This does not mean that it specifically fears a depression, as some aging New Dealers claim. The feeling is widespread that anyone who wants to work can find a decent job; the facts confirm that feeling (and starting pay is better than ever). But youth's ambitions have shrunk.

Few youngsters today want to mine diamonds in South Africa, ranch in Paraguay, climb Mount Everest, find a cure for cancer, sail around the world, or build an industrial empire. Some would like to own a small business, but most want a good job with a big firm, and with it a kind of suburban idyll.[1]

EXERCISE B

This exercise in grammar may also be a vocabulary lesson if the student will search for unusual or colorful terms or will substitute a more specific word for the noun given.

1. Rewrite the following sentence six times, substituting other nouns for the noun subject:

> The *bird* flew over the great tree screaming wildly as it glided out over the bay.

2. Rewrite the following sentence six times, substituting other nouns for the noun used as the direct object:

> We saw the *vessel* in the harbor belching out great clouds of black smoke.

3. Rewrite the following sentence six times, substituting other nouns for the noun used as the object of a preposition:

> The vintner poured the wine into dark red *bottles*.

4. Rewrite the following sentence six times, substituting other nouns for the nouns used as a predicate complement:

> The play was a *comedy* in three acts.

5. Rewrite the following sentence six times, substituting other nouns for the noun used as an objective complement:

> The class elected Fred the *senior* most likely to succeed.

6. Rewrite the following sentence six times, substituting other nouns for the noun used as the indirect object:

> The nurse gave the *patient* aspirin.

7. Rewrite the following sentence six times, substituting other nouns for the noun used as an appositive to the subject:

> Thomas Dooley, a *fellow* at Harvill College, has just published a book on English grammar.

8. Rewrite the following sentence six times, substituting other nouns for the noun used as the modifier of a noun (a noun adjunct):

> My brother has been selected *department* supervisor.

[1] "The Younger Generation," *Time*, November 5, 1951.

Exercise C

Write all the inflected forms of the following nouns.

1. mouse
2. family
3. Filipino
4. valley
5. alumnus
6. child
7. mathematics
8. deer
9. information
10. quiz

For each of the nouns in the following list, write a sentence containing the plural form.

11. ox
12. datum
13. alumna
14. ally
15. moose
16. criterion
17. potato
18. Japanese
19. fish
20. bus

Exercise D

In the blank spaces, supply nouns which are appropriate to the context of the following passage.

Across West Germany's 95,000 square _____, from the southern _____ of Bavaria to the salty _____ of the North Sea, this burgeoning _____ booms at you, in a crashing cacophony of drilling, blasting and hammering.

"What are you building now?" I asked a _____ in Munich.

"Who knows?" shrugged the _____. "First they build. Then they find out what for."

Dusseldorf, in rich North-Rhine-Westphalia, which cradles the roaring
_____ of the Ruhr, is traffic-jammed with Mercedes 300's, an $8000
_____ laughingly called the *Rheinische Volkswagen.* On the broad
_____ of Frankfurt, Hamburg, any big _____, you pick your way
around _____, old ones from bombs or new construction ones, to gape
into glittering plate-glass _____ at flashing diamonds and _____,
luxurious minks and _____, silky Oriental _____, sparkling chrome-
and-blond-wood _____. Every first-class restaurant lists fresh caviar
and *pate de foie gras* at several _____ a spoonful. For seekers after a
different kind of _____ there were 26 music festivals throughout West
Germany in the summer of 1956 and there will be 31 this summer.[2]

Exercise E

1. Look up the dictionary definitions of the suffix *-acy.* List ten nouns
   ending in *-acy* which illustrate these definitions. Write five sentences
   using the nouns in a variety of functions.

2. Look up the dictionary definitions of the noun suffix *-ant.* List ten
   nouns ending in *-ant* which illustrate these definitions. Write five
   sentences using the nouns in a variety of functions.

3. Look up the dictionary definitions of the suffix *-dom.* List ten nouns
   ending in *-dom* which illustrate these definitions. Write five sentences
   using the nouns in a variety of functions.

4. Look up the dictionary definitions of the suffix *-er.* List ten nouns
   ending in *-er* which illustrate these definitions. Write five sentences
   using the nouns in a variety of functions.

5. Look up the dictionary definitions of the suffix *-ery.* List ten nouns
   ending in *-ery* which illustrate these definitions. Write five sentences
   using the nouns in a variety of functions.

6. Look up the dictionary definitions of the suffix *-hood.* List ten nouns
   ending in *-hood* which illustrate these definitions. Write five sentences
   using the nouns in a variety of functions.

7. Look up the dictionary definitions of the suffix *-ism.* List ten nouns
   ending in *-ism* which illustrate these definitions. Write five sentences
   using the nouns in a variety of functions.

8. Look up the dictionary definitions of the suffix *-ment.* List ten nouns
   ending in *-ment* which illustrate these definitions. Write five sentences
   using the nouns in a variety of functions.

[2] Adapted from Lin Root, "Germany Bounces Back," *Reader's Digest,* June,
1957.

9. Look up the dictionary definitions of the suffix *-ness*. List ten nouns ending in *-ness* which illustrate these definitions. Write five sentences using the nouns in a variety of functions.

10. Look up the dictionary definitions of the suffix *-ship*. List ten nouns ending in *-ship* which illustrate these definitions. Write five sentences using the nouns in a variety of functions.

11. Look up the dictionary definitions of the suffix *-tion*. List ten nouns ending in *-tion* which illustrate these definitions. Write five sentences using the nouns in a variety of functions.

12. Look up the dictionary definitions of the suffix *-y*. List ten nouns ending in *-y* which illustrate these definitions. Write five sentences using the nouns in a variety of functions.

EXERCISE F

Rewrite the following paragraph, capitalizing all the proper nouns.

Officials of the hoca pola bottling company have announced the appointment of a new sales manager, james r. cranston of 195 lexington avenue, el paso, texas. Mr. cranston moved to the southwest five years ago and since his arrival here, he has been active in public affairs. At present he is president of the local rotary club. He has two sons, both of whom are members of the boy scouts of america. Mr. cranston has a summer home at lake windmere, in the northern part of omega county. This country place is the former property of colonel poffington, a well-known texan who served his country in world war I. Mr. cranston's daughter is a teacher in the east windham high school where she is a member of the physics department. Miss cranston has been associated actively in relief work for the people of the near east. The many friends and associates of mr. cranston have planned a dinner for Thursday evening, january 16, to extend to him their best wishes and congratulations.

— The west texas evening star

7

Verbs

ENGLISH, as we have noted, is a bipolar language, a noun-verb language, with the noun-verb structure the basis of communication. Modifiers are built about the noun and the verb to make communication more *explicit*. The structural devices of subordination and co-ordination are employed to include word groups within and add them onto the basic noun-verb structure to make communication more *extensive*. Structure words are used to bind our words and word groups together to make communication more *coherent*.

In oral communication, the child learns very early to distinguish between the noun and the verb.

>Daddy comes.
>Mama spanks.
>Baby sleeps.
>Doggy barks.

The child learns to separate the actor from the action, the doer from the deed, the agent from the process. His responses to the stimuli of language soon show that he has unconsciously mastered the structural signals of language which enable him to discriminate between nouns and verbs.

In Chapter 6 we have considered the structural signals which enable us to respond to nouns as nouns. In this chapter, we turn to the signals for the identification of verbs.

Position of Verbs

One of the most important clues to the identification of the verb is its position in the sentence or word group. In Chapter 3 we discussed the simple sentence patterns:

N V

N V N

N V (linking) Adj

N V (linking) N

N V N N

The simple sentence patterns show us the main elements of a sentence, the subject, the verb, and the complement or complements. We have learned from long usage that the main elements of a sentence are fixed in position. The fixed position of the verb is an important signal of its identity.

The great steamer *ploughed* wearily through the heavy sea.

The youthful cowboy *roped* the calf in thirteen seconds.

Agatha Ann *becomes* more beautiful year after year.

Dreams *are* the building stones of reality.

The Senator *nominated* Henry a candidate for West Point.

In questions and requests the characteristic word order and the position of the verb again provide the clue.

Will you *dance* with me?

Are you *going* to the game?

Have you *seen* Tom Pooley?

Buy me some candy, Mama.

Take the children for a walk.

Go to the store and *buy* a loaf of bread.

In extended utterances, sentences with subordinate clauses included in the main sentence or with co-ordinate clauses added to it, the position of the verb in each subject-predicate word group is an important clue to its identity.

> The family *moved* to Arizona because Father *was* ill with asthma.
>
> When Henry *goes* to town, he always *spends* all his money.
>
> Columbus *sailed* to the West because he *believed* that the world was round.
>
> The boilers *exploded* with a loud roar, and the ship *sank* quickly into the sea.
>
> Willie *wanted* an airplane for Christmas, but Santa *brought* him a tricycle.
>
> Joe *wants* to enter college in the fall; therefore he *is saving* his money.

The subject-predicate word group is the familiar structure of the simple sentence, of the included subordinate clause, and of the added co-ordinate clause. The verb has the same relative position in any subject-predicate word group irrespective of its particular function in an utterance. We have formed the habit of responding to this positional signal. The verb in context is a stimulus to which we are sensitive and to which we have learned to make appropriate responses.

Structure Words as Verb Markers

Word order and position are not the only factors in the identification of the verb. English has many structure words which serve as markers of verbs. These have been called auxiliary or helping verbs, though they are not really verbs at all, since they cannot be inflected like verbs, nor can they be used independently as finite verbs. These words are:

can	may
could	might
will	must
would	ought (ought to)
shall	
should	

Various forms of certain inflected verbs, used singly and in combination, also serve as structure words in the auxiliary function, and hence as identifying signals to the listener or reader. These include forms of the verbs *to be*, *have*, *do*, and the form *used* (*used to*).

> Mary can *go* to school today.
> John could *graduate* this year if he would *study*.
> The projectile will be *launched* in a few minutes.
> Your name should have been *called* before this.
> And the night shall be *turned* into music.
> I may be *going* with you on Saturday.
> Our candidate would have been *elected* if the people had *known* his ability.
> Your father must *know* all about this.
> The mechanic ought to *know* all about this kind of engine.
> The prisoner does *know* who committed the crime.
> My father used to *live* in Connecticut.

The structure words used with verbs are extremely important in communicating shades of meaning and attitude through a great variety of combinations which grammarians have not attempted to classify completely. Such classification would in any event be relatively unimportant for the practical purposes of improved communication. The effective speaker or writer must become familiar with these words in use and develop some skill with them through practice. For example, if one is thinking of going to the city tomorrow, one may express this idea in a number of ways and in each way express some slight difference in meaning.

> I am going to the city tomorrow.
> I will go to the city tomorrow.
> I may go to the city tomorrow.
> I should go to the city tomorrow.
> I must go to the city tomorrow.
> I ought to go to the city tomorrow.
> I might go to the city tomorrow.
> I have to go to the city tomorrow.
> I do go to the city tomorrow.

I shall go to the city tomorrow.
I would go to the city tomorrow.
I can go to the city tomorrow.
I was going to the city tomorrow.
I may be going to the city tomorrow.
I might be going to the city tomorrow.
I must be going to the city tomorrow.
I will be going to the city tomorrow.
I shall be going to the city tomorrow.
I should be going to the city tomorrow.
I ought to be going to the city tomorrow.

These twenty sentences do not exhaust all the possibilities of communicating the various aspects of going to the city tomorrow. They do illustrate, however, the flexibility of our language arising from the use of auxiliary verbs. The various combinations of helping verbs and verbs are sometimes called *verb phrases*.

Inflection of Verbs

One of the most important means of identifying verbs is through familiarity with the inflected forms. Inflectional endings and internal vowel changes provide significant cues for our responses to verbs in context.

He *goes* to church every Sunday.
They *go* to the University of California.
Mr. Smyth *went* to the fair.
Lucy is *going* to the party.
Little Joe has *gone* to bed.

The verb *go* has five inflected forms — the plain form *go* (or the infinitive when preceded by *to*), the singular form *goes*, the past form *went*, the present participle *going*, and the past participle *gone*. *Go* is called an irregular verb because of the variety of its inflected forms. Not all irregular verbs, however, have five inflected forms. L. M. Myers[1] states that there are approximately 140 irregular verbs, of which 45 have separate forms for the past and past participle.

[1] L. M. Myers, *Guide to American English* (Prentice-Hall, Inc., 1955), p. 138.

Examples of other five-part verbs (verbs, that is, with five inflected forms) are given below.

PLAIN FORM	PRESENT, SINGULAR	PAST	PRESENT PARTICIPLE	PAST PARTICIPLE
throw	throws	threw	throwing	thrown
break	breaks	broke	breaking	broken
begin	begins	began	beginning	begun
lie	lies	lay	lying	lain
grow	grows	grew	growing	grown
swim	swims	swam	swimming	swum
know	knows	knew	knowing	known
eat	eats	ate	eating	eaten
fly	flies	flew	flying	flown
slay	slays	slew	slaying	slain

In written work, students often use the wrong form for the past tense or for the past participle. When dealing with irregular verbs, the inexperienced writer should develop the habit of looking up the forms in a good collegiate dictionary, where he will find the past, the past participle, and the present participle listed after the plain form. Very often irregular verbs have dialectal or archaic forms which the dictionary lists and so labels (*Dial.* or *Archaic*); students should note these labels and avoid such forms in their own writing. In *Webster's New Collegiate Dictionary*, for example, the past form of *swim* is first given as *swam* and then as *swum*, but the latter form is labeled *Dial. & Archaic*. In standard English one does not use archaic or dialectal forms. Therefore one does not write or say, "I swum across the lake." Neither does one use the dialectal form for the past tense of *swing* and say, "Freddy Mize swang at the third ball pitched and struck out."

Some irregular verbs have four inflected forms, instead of five, because the past and past participle forms are the same. The verb *find* is an example.

> Plumkin *finds* college life very dull.
>
> The girls *find* their chemistry class exciting.
>
> Henry *found* his book where he had left it.
>
> Scientists are *finding* new uses for the drug each year.
>
> Our people have *found* that production is the source of wealth.

More four-part verbs are listed below.

PLAIN FORM	PRESENT, SINGULAR	PAST AND PAST PARTICIPLE	PRESENT PARTICIPLE
bind	binds	bound	binding
cling	clings	clung	clinging
shoot	shoots	shot	shooting
fight	fights	fought	fighting
hold	holds	held	holding

Some irregular verbs have only three inflected forms. The plain form or infinitive, the past form, and the past participle are all the same. The verb *set* is an illustration of this type of verb.

The mason *sets* the blocks in mortar.

The French modistes *set* the styles for American women.

Mother *set* the table long before the guests arrived.

Angela is *setting* her hair for the party.

Father has *set* the date for our vacation in July.

Still other verbs with only three inflected forms are given here.

PLAIN FORM; PAST; PAST PARTICIPLE	PRESENT, SINGULAR	PRESENT PARTICIPLE
bet	bets	betting
cast	casts	casting
burst	bursts	bursting
shed	shed	shedding
slit	slits	slitting

The study of the inflection of verbs is complicated by the fact that there are variant forms for certain verbs. For example, *bear* is a five-part verb with two forms for the past participle, *borne* and *born*. When the meaning is *carried*, the form *borne* is used. When the meaning intended is *brought into the world*, the form *born* is used.

Among other verbs with variant inflected forms are the following.

PLAIN FORM	PRESENT, SINGULAR	PAST	PRESENT PARTICIPLE	PAST PARTICIPLE
sink	sinks	sank	sinking	sunk
				sunken
shrink	shrinks	shrank	shrinking	shrunk
		shrunk		shrunken

PLAIN FORM	PRESENT, SINGULAR	PAST	PRESENT PARTICIPLE	PAST PARTICIPLE
spring	springs	sprang sprung	springing	sprung
forget	forgets	forgot	forgetting	forgot forgotten
get	gets	got	getting	got gotten
weave	weaves	wove	weaving	wove woven

Most verbs in the English language are inflected like the verb *walk*, as illustrated in the following sentences. They have four parts, and they are called *regular verbs*.

President Truman *walks* two miles every day.

Horses *walk* with a stately grace.

Plumkin *walked* home from church with Tom Pooley's sister.

Josephine is *walking* to school in order to get some exercise.

Father has *walked* to work for a whole year.

Regular verbs do not have an internal vowel change in the past and past participle forms. The past and past participles have the same form, the plain form with -*ed* as a suffix. Examples of four-part regular verbs are given in the list below.

PLAIN FORM	PRESENT, SINGULAR	PAST AND PAST PARTICIPLE	PRESENT PARTICIPLE
add	adds	added	adding
believe	believes	believed	believing
work	works	worked	working
borrow	borrows	borrowed	borrowing
flirt	flirts	flirted	flirting
move	moves	moved	moving
carry	carries	carried	carrying
worry	worries	worried	worrying
serve	serves	served	serving
watch	watches	watched	watching

Some verbs have variant inflected forms which might place them in the class of irregular verbs as well as in the class of regular verbs.

Plain Form	Present, Singular	Past and Past Participle	Present Participle	Past Participle
hang	hangs	hanged hung	hanging	
heave	heaves	heaved hove	heaving	
sew	sews	sewed	sewing	sewed sewn
spill	spills	spilled spilt	spilling	
speed	speeds	speeded sped	speeding	

The most exceptional verb in the English language, and the verb most frequently used, is *to be*. It has eight inflected forms.

be	am	was	being	been
are	is	were		

The form *am* is used only with the personal pronoun *I*. The form *is* is used with any singular noun or with the pronouns *he*, *she*, and *it*. The form *are* is used with any plural noun or with the pronouns *you*, *we*, and *they*. The past form *was* is used with any singular noun or with the pronouns *I*, *he*, *she*, and *it*. The past form *were* is used with any plural noun or with the pronouns *you*, *we*, and *they*. The following sentences illustrate the use of these inflected forms.

> I *am* the captain of this ship.
> He *is* the only witness to the accident.
> She *is* the widow of Major Brown.
> It *is* time to go to bed.
> This dog *is* my best friend.
> The men *are* in the garage.
> You *are* the speaker for the evening.
> You *are* the only true citizens.
> We *are* here to play ball.
> They *are* here to see the game.
> Children *are* happy at Christmas.
> I *was* very foolish to listen to his advice.
> He *was* a hero during the war.

She *was* an honor graduate.

It *was* a failure from the start.

The new shotgun *was* a gift from my mother-in-law.

The boys *were* ready to go before dawn.

You *were* my partner for many years.

You *were* good children all morning.

We *were* the first to leave the ship.

They *were* the first family to have a new car.

The two old gentlemen *were* there in the first row.

Fred is *being* promoted to the second grade.

Plumkin has *been* a bird watcher for two weeks.

Characteristic Verb Prefixes and Suffixes

A fourth structural device in the verb-signaling system is affixation, the use of prefixes and suffixes. The most common verb prefixes and suffixes are given below, with examples of verbs formed with them.

be-	befriend, bemoan
en-	enable, enrage
em-	embody, embroil
re-	react, redecorate
de-	derail, debunk
with-	withdraw, withhold
-ize	oxidize, sterilize
-ate	officiate, negotiate
-fy	falsify, classify
-en	quicken, frighten

In addition, certain structure words like *in, out, up, down, through, over, with,* and others may be used in a compound relationship with a verb.

Joe Louis *knocked out* his opponent in four rounds.

Henry James *batted in* four runs during the game.

The crowd *stood up* and cheered wildly.

The deal *fell through* because of lack of funds.

The robber *held up* the cashier and took the money.

The feature picture was *held over* for two weeks.

Plumkin *ran up* a big bill at the candy store.

The boy *set up* the pins in the third alley.

The teacher asked the boys to *sit down.*

This girl has nobody to *go around with.*

She will *put on* whatever you tell her.

Active and Passive Voice

The student should be familiar with that aspect of verbs known as "voice."

ACTIVE VOICE   Mr. Jones *painted* the house.

PASSIVE VOICE   The house *was painted* by Mr. Jones.

ACTIVE   The band *played* "God Save the King."

PASSIVE   "God Save the King" *was played* by the band.

ACTIVE   The whole class *read* the poem beautifully.

PASSIVE   The poem *was read* beautifully by the whole class.

ACTIVE   They *are closing* Route 128 for repairs.

PASSIVE   Route 128 *is being closed* for repairs.

The passive voice is constructed by using the past participle of the verb with some form of *to be.* Many combinations of verb phrases are possible within this structure, as the following examples show.

The concert *was played* in Carnegie Hall.

The concert *has been played* in Carnegie Hall.

The concert *had been played* in Carnegie Hall.

The concert *was to have been played* in Carnegie Hall.

The concert *is being played* in Carnegie Hall.

The concert *was being played* in Carnegie Hall.

The concert *will be played* in Carnegie Hall.

The concert *is to be played* in Carnegie Hall.

Ordinarily, a complement does not follow a verb in the passive form. There are, however, two notable exceptions to this generalization, and they both stem from the sentence pattern

N V N N.

Two representative sentences conforming to this pattern are

Henry gave *Alice* a present.   (Indirect object)
They elected Johnson *president*.   (Objective complement)

When these are expressed with verbs in the passive voice, we have

Alice was given a *present*.
Johnson was elected *president*.

Both of these sentences have complements, and this kind of complement is called a *retained object*.

Transitive and Intransitive Verbs

The following verbs are said to be transitive verbs.

The woman *lighted* a candle before she knelt.
The soldier *lowered* the flag at sunset.
Gertrude Ederle *swam* the English Channel.
Einstein *developed* the principle of relativity.
Plumkin *eats* apple pie for breakfast.

In each sentence the verb is followed by the direct object. The sentence conforms to the pattern

N V N.

The following sentences have intransitive verbs.

The horses *ran* swiftly across the pasture.
The child *lay* there for an hour.
The baby *slept* the whole night.
The old barn *burned* to the ground.
The giant rocket *is spinning* around the earth.

An intransitive verb is not followed by a direct object. The sentence in which it occurs conforms to the pattern

N V.

Tense

Time, in our culture, is thought of in terms of past, present, and future. However, as evidenced in our discussion earlier in this chapter, verbs in English use inflection to show time only for the past. Present and future time, and past time also, are communicated by a variety of verb phrases.

To express past time, we may have

> I *drove* to Chicago last week. (The inflected form)
> I *was driving* to Chicago when the storm broke.
> I *have driven* to Chicago many times.
> I *had driven* to Chicago for the last time.
> I *used to drive* to Chicago.

To express present time, we may have

> I *sympathize* with you in your difficulty.
> I *am sympathizing* with you in your difficulty.
> I *do sympathize* with you in your difficulty.

To express future time, we may have

> I *go* to Philadelphia tomorrow.
> I *will go* to Philadelphia tomorrow.
> I *am going* to Philadelphia tomorrow.
> I *will be going* to Philadelphia tomorrow.

The plain form of the verb, then, may express either present or future time in communication, whereas the past form expresses only past time. As demonstrated above, however, all three conventions may be expressed in various ways by means of verb phrases.

Summary

The verb is an important element of communication in the context of the sentence. From earliest childhood, we have developed a sensitivity to the structural signals which identify verbs. We have learned that they are often preceded by such helping words as *can, may, have, had, will, do, must;* have a constant fixed position in the familiar basic sentence patterns; are inflected (change their form) in certain characteristic ways; often have identifying prefixes and suffixes; and are sometimes used with such structure words as *in, out, down,* and *through.* Any or all of these structural signals serve as verb markers in the context of a sentence, preventing ambiguity and securing the appropriate response from the reader or the listener. There is, for example, no uncertainty of response to these two sentences:

> Duck the cook.
>
> Cook the duck.

The invariable position of the verb within the fixed word order of the sentence pattern identifies the verb and names the action.

The following sentence, however, is ambiguous:

> Light signals end.

We do not find enough formal clues to identify the verb and so we do not know what the action is. By placing a structure word *will* before *end*, we make the sentence clear.

> Light signals will end.

A full understanding of these and other structural signals of meaning is especially important to one who wishes to improve his skill in written communication. For in learning to use them effectively, he will become a better writer.

Exercise A

Identify the verbs in the following passage.

Yesterday afternoon the six-o'clock bus ran over Miss Bobbit. I'm not sure what there is to be said about it; after all she was only ten years old, still I know no one of us in this town will forget her. For one thing, nothing she ever did was ordinary, not from the first time that we saw her, and that was a year ago. Miss Bobbit and her mother, they arrived on that same six-o'clock bus, the one that comes through from Mobile. It happened to be my cousin Billy Bob's birthday, and so most of the children in town were here at our house. We were sprawled on the front porch having tutti-frutti and devil cake when the bus stormed around Deadman's curve. It was the summer that never rained; rusted dryness coated everything; sometimes when a car passed on the road, raised dust would hang in the still air an hour or more. Aunt El said if they didn't pave the highway soon she was going to move down to the seacoast; but she'd said that for such a long time. Anyway, we were sitting on the porch, tutti-frutti melting on our plates, when suddenly, just as we were wishing that something would happen, something did; for out of the red road dust

appeared Miss Bobbit. A wiry little girl in a starched, lemon-colored
party dress, she sassed along with a grownup mince, one hand on her hip,
the other supporting a spinsterish umbrella. Her mother, lugging two
cardboard valises and a wind-up victrola, trailed in the background. She
was a gaunt shaggy woman with silent eyes and a hungry smile.[2]

Exercise B

*Insert in each blank the inflected form of the verb which you
think is appropriate to the context of the passage.*

Jack Carson was a hunter of wide experience. As a matter of fact, he
had _____ up in these hills. His father had _____ a hunter before
him and had roamed about in this area for many years. Jack had not
_____ his father very well, since the older man had _____ while
Jack _____ a baby. Jack had been _____ up by his mother who
_____ good care of him. She taught him to _____ across the river
and to _____ a shelter for himself when camping out of doors.

Now Jack was a grown man. He had _____ many a river since
boyhood and had _____ on the ground under his shelter many nights.
He _____ how to trap and fish and to stalk wild game. On this night
he was _____ in the shelter of a thicket for deer to cross the slope to
a water hole. He _____ two large bucks come into the clearing. They
_____ and sniffed the air as if suspecting his presence. Jack aimed his
rifle carefully and _____ twice. One deer _____ to the ground and
the other _____ swiftly into the woods. The bullet had _____ the
deer in the leg and had _____ it, and the deer struggled, trying to get
to its feet. Another shot ended the struggle.

Carson skinned the animal, cleaned it, and _____ the carcass high
on two poles. He _____ a fire and made ready to cook a venison steak,
for he had _____ very little during the past two days. The dry wood
_____ into flame, the sun _____ below the horizon, and Jack
_____ down beside the warm fire waiting for his supper.

Exercise C

1. Write a sentence using the present participle of *go* with the structure
   words *should have been.*
2. Write a sentence using the plain form of *come.*
3. Write a sentence using the singular form of *run.*

[2] From Truman Capote, "Children on Their Birthdays," in *A Tree of
Night and Other Stories* (New York: Random House, 1949).

4. Write a sentence using the past participle of *slew* with the structure words *could be*.

5. Write a sentence using the present participle of *grow* with the structure words *ought to be*.

6. Write a sentence using the past form of *tear*.

7. Write a sentence using the past participle of *sting* with the structure words *might have been*.

8. Write a sentence using the past form of *lie*.

9. Write a sentence using the past participle of *set* with the structure words *has been*.

10. Write a sentence using the past participle of *hid* with the structure words *can have been*.

11. Write a sentence using the past form of *spin*.

12. Write a sentence using the singular form of the verb *lay*.

13. Write a sentence using the present participle of *steal* with the structure words *may be*.

14. Write a sentence using the past participle of *sling*.

15. Write a sentence using the plain form of *work* with the structure words *had been going to*.

16. Write a sentence using the past form of *fling*.

EXERCISE D

1. Make up a list of ten five-part verbs not given in this chapter. Write out all their inflected forms.

2. Make up a list of ten four-part irregular verbs not given in this chapter. Write out all their inflected forms.

3. Make up a list of ten three-part irregular verbs not given in this chapter. Write out all their inflected forms.

4. Make up a list of as many verbs as you can find which have variant inflected forms.

5. Make up a list of twenty regular verbs. Write out the inflected forms of ten of them.

6. Write sentences illustrating the uses of the inflected forms of the verb *to be*.

7. Make up a list of five verbs with the prefix *be-*. Write sentences illustrating three of them.

8. Write sentences using verbs with the prefixes *en-*, *em-*, *re-*, *de-*, and *with-*.

9. Make up a list of six verbs with the suffix *-ize*. Write sentences illustrating three of them.

10. Write sentences using verbs with the suffixes *-ate*, *-fy*, and *-en*.

11. Make up a list of ten verbs which are used in combination with structure words such as *down, up, out, through,* and *in.*

12. Write six sentences using verbs of the type listed in item 11.

Exercise E

Rewrite the following sentences, changing the verb from active to passive voice.

1. They lighted the tree on Christmas Eve.
2. Jack built this house.
3. You may see the pictures at the Brooklyn Art Museum.
4. They are playing the football game today in the Yankee Stadium.
5. Jack Spratt could eat no fat.
6. The government will pay a reward of one hundred dollars for the arrest and conviction of Willie the Kid.
7. They had crowned Elizabeth queen before a wildly cheering multitude.
8. Beat two eggs thoroughly and whip in a little cream.
9. The cows had eaten the hay.
10. The kids threw snowballs at the house and broke three windows.
11. Plumkin eats three lamb chops every night before he goes to bed.
12. They are going to show "Snow White" at the movies next week.

Rewrite the following sentences, changing the verb from passive to active voice.

13. Mistakes are made by most people.
14. George Wilson will be seen on television on Saturday night.
15. Many houses are being built in the northeast section of the city.
16. Tom Pooley will be hanged tomorrow morning.
17. The prize had been awarded to him before his death.
18. The committee is being appointed by the governor to study the problem of public transportation.
19. The documents were being studied by the German scholars seeking to find the origins of their language.

20. Adequate preparations for the journey would have been neglected by most people.
21. This law should have been passed by Congress long ago.
22. This book has been published by the Foundation in order to describe the nature of general education.
23. By this time next year a man-made satellite will have been propelled into outer space by the U.S. Air Forces.
24. Jean is to be named Rodeo Queen by the student body at the Home-coming party.

EXERCISE F

By using the structure words which are commonly called aux-iliary or helping verbs, we can construct a great variety of verb phrases to express shades of difference in attitude, condition, time, mood, reality. Read the following passage carefully, ob-serve the variety of verb phrases, and study their context. Dis-cuss the purpose of the writer in using these particular phrases. What has he communicated to you by means of them?

By his threat to put Berlin at the mercy of the Communist regime sur-rounding it, Khrushchev has permanently upset the *status quo* in Central Europe, and with it U.S. policy there. As long as West Berlin shone like a free beacon behind the Iron Curtain, attracting refugees and creating unrest, there was much to be said for this *status quo* from the Western standpoint. But there was nothing to be said for our having no alternate policy. Now the time has come to consider alternatives other than to let Berlin become "a concentration camp on the installment plan" or to fight for it.

Last week on this page we proposed the first step in a diplomatic counteroffensive against Khrushchev: that the capital of West Germany be moved at once from Bonn to West Berlin where it belongs. Not only would such a move re-emphasize the West's announced determination to hold Berlin; it would also stop the economic hemorrhage (capital flight, etc.) which Khrushchev's mere threat has started in that be-leaguered city.

But as Mayor Brandt has also said, "there is no isolated solution of the Berlin question." The West cannot even discuss it without raising larger issues, such as Germany as a whole — issues whose solution must pierce or relocate the Iron Curtain. Berlin was and is the West's most vul-nerable and exposed position in Europe. To strengthen that position we must ourselves proceed against Communism's vulnerable points.

None is more vulnerable than the European satellite situation. This has been amply demonstrated by the revolts in East Germany, Poland and, above all, Hungary in the last five years. Communism has been a political and economic fiasco in Eastern Europe, a fiasco which has been a neglected opportunity for the West.[3]

EXERCISE G

The following sentences are ambiguous because of insufficient structural signals. Rewrite each sentence twice: supply markers which will identify nouns or verbs, eliminating the ambiguity and taking two different meanings from the original sentence.

1. Black clouds issue.
2. Cooks ham tonight.
3. Cousins pitch wins.
4. Board ships tomorrow.
5. Police requests change.
6. Women can fish.
7. Work stops for an hour.
8. Man pumps today.
9. Break ends for Smith.
10. Drive nails dope.

The following statements are not ambiguous because structural signals make identification of nouns and verbs certain. Remove one grammatical marker in each sentence so that ambiguity will result.

11. The red colors run.
12. Will bill shops early.
15. Army wants a change.
14. Cook will fish Monday.
15. Russian ships will sink.
16. Philadelphia misses the fight.
17. Early copies are white.
18. American plans are upset.
19. A better show results.
20. Girls will study burns.

[3] From "The Berlin Opportunity," an Editorial in *Life* Magazine, December 15, 1958, p. 28. Copr. 1958 Time Inc.

8

Adjectives

THE CLASSIFICATION of words in the English language is complicated by the factors of form and function. If we say that an adjective is a word that modifies a noun, we shall be plagued by the facts. It may be very easily shown that words which have the formal characteristics of nouns may modify nouns, and that certain adverbs and structure words may also modify nouns. To define an adjective as a word which modifies a noun, then, leads to a dilemma. Either we shall have to call certain nouns and adverbs adjectives, or we shall have to admit that our definition is not exclusive.

If, on the other hand, we define an adjective in terms of form alone, by means of identifying suffixes and inflectional endings, we shall again be in trouble. It will turn out that certain words which have the formal characteristics of adjectives will be used adverbially in a sentence, that is, they will modify a verb.

In dealing with modifiers, we must remember that our language is essentially a noun-verb language. Nouns and verbs are primary

111

words, modifiers are secondary words, and structure words are of a lower rank. We have a language of great flexibility: words shift in function, and substitution is commonplace. It is difficult, if not impossible, to classify all words as they are used. In communication, however, it is highly important that we identify the words which modify the nouns, and that we identify the words which modify the verbs. The writer must do this so that his composition will not be ambiguous, and the reader or listener so that his response will be appropriate.

We turn, therefore, to the identifying characteristics of the noun modifiers which we call adjectives. We shall try to define them in terms of both form and function.

Let us first observe some adjectives in context as they perform their usual function of modifying nouns.

> The Boy Scout helped the *old* lady across the street.
>
> The *beautiful* sunset spread the *golden* light across the *western* sky.
>
> The *vicious* dog was tied with a *long* chain.
>
> This will be a *suitable* building for our purpose.
>
> The *careful* secretary put the papers in the safe.
>
> The *American* flag flew at the masthead.

The italicized words are adjectives. They have the formal characteristics of adjectives and they behave like adjectives, that is, they modify nouns. (This, as we shall see later, is not the only function of adjectives.)

Characteristic Adjective Suffixes

In examining some of the identifying signals of the adjective, we may begin with adjective suffixes. Following is a list of some characteristic adjective suffixes with three examples of adjectives in each case.

-ful	careful, plentiful, beautiful
-ish	boyish, childish, foolish
-able	workable, suitable, readable
-ive	constructive, protective, selective
-ary	honorary, dietary, visionary
-ic	scenic, historic, plastic

-some	handsome, quarrelsome, tiresome
-less	careless, needless, hopeless
-ate	collegiate, affectionate, fortunate
-al	personal, national, fraternal
-ous	religious, vicious, nervous
-en	rotten, wooden, woolen
-ar	muscular, molecular
-an	Armenian, Anglican, suburban
-y	dusty, frosty, misty
-ly	timely, costly, friendly
-like	lifelike, warlike, homelike
-ed	aged, ragged, abused
-ent	confident, urgent, excellent
-ant	reliant, observant, pleasant

These suffixes are common markers of adjectives. They serve as identifying signals to the reader or listener so that his response may be appropriate. Words formed with them will usually be modifiers of nouns, or possibly predicate adjectives. The suffix, then, is one formal characteristic of an adjective.

The student should note, however, that not all of these suffixes are enough in themselves to identify adjectives, since some are characteristic also of nouns (e.g., cup*ful*, surviv*al*, entr*ant*) and some of adverbs, as we shall see in Chapter 9.

Position of Adjectives as Modifiers

A second means of identifying the adjective is its position in the sentence. In each of the sentences on page 112 illustrating adjectives modifying nouns, the adjective comes before the noun, usually between a determiner and the noun.

the *old* lady
the *beautiful* sunset
the *golden* light
the *vicious* dog
a *suitable* building
a *long* chain
the *careful* secretary
this *happy* couple
one *last* look

The usual pattern of the adjective modifying a noun is
D Adj N.

Sometimes the adjective modifier comes after the noun, especially in poetry, and in prose in which the writer is trying to create a particular stylistic effect.

> This is the forest *primeval.*
> The blisses of her dream so *pure* and *deep.*
> The little lady, *pale* and *serene*, sat with her hands folded.
> Her favorite topic of conversation is the house *beautiful.*
> Plumkin, *shaken* and *nervous*, forgot his speech and fled from the stage.

Inflection of Adjectives

Another formal characteristic of many adjectives is the ability to add the suffixes -*er* and -*est.* Following is a list of some of the adjectives inflected in this way.

young	younger	youngest
old	older	oldest
poor	poorer	poorest
pretty	prettier	prettiest
shabby	shabbier	shabbiest
cruel	crueler	cruelest
sad	sadder	saddest
fine	finer	finest
kind	kinder	kindest
soft	softer	softest

This method of inflection is called comparison. The -*er* form is said to be the comparative and the -*est* form the superlative.

Many adjectives do not have characteristic suffixes, and many cannot be inflected into the -*er* and -*est* forms. All adjectives, however, may be preceded by structure words called intensifiers. These words include *more, most, less, least, rather, really, very,* and *quite.*

> This is a *more conservative* investment.
> The *most competent* salesman was promoted.
> The *less fortunate* people were given aid.

The *least desirable* students were permitted to drop out.

This is a *rather dull* subject.

This *really wonderful* buy is yours for only ten thousand dollars.

He is a *very intelligent* person.

He is a *quite decent* individual.

Intensifiers such as *more* and *most*, *less* and *least* perform the function of comparison particularly with adjectives of more than one syllable.

This is a *more difficult* problem than yours.

This is the *most difficult* problem of all.

Yours is the *less intelligent* choice.

Hers is the *least intelligent* choice of the three.

Some adjectives are irregular in that they change their form in the process of comparison.

good	better	best
bad	worse	worst
many	more	most
little	less	least
old	older	oldest
	elder	eldest
far	farther	farthest
	further	furthest

Predicate Adjectives

So far, we have considered only one function of the adjective, the modifying or attributive function. A second important function of the adjective is the predicate function.

In the predicate function, the adjective follows the verb, which in this case is called a linking or copulative verb.

ATTRIBUTIVE   The *good* boy . . .

PREDICATE   The boy is *good*.

The verbs most commonly used in this linking function are forms of *to be, seem, become, appear, look, sound, feel, taste,* and *smell*.

The man was *angry* when he heard the news.

The boy seems more *serious* about his work now.

The play became very *sad* in the third act.

She appears *happy* in her new job.

Plumkin looks *important* in his new derby hat.

The story may sound *foolish*, but it's true.

The teacher feels *satisfied* with the progress of the class.

The apple pie tastes *delicious*.

The flowers smell *sweet*.

The verb in each of the above sentences links the subject with the predicate adjective. In a sense, this device is more effective than simple modification since the communication is reinforced by the weight of the verb. But the position of the predicate adjective, after the verb, creates a situation which may develop ambiguity. Because the adverb normally follows the verb it modifies, we are accustomed to interpret words in this position as verb modifiers. For example,

Bill looked harder *t*han Joe.

We do not know from this sentence whether Bill looked tougher than Joe, or whether Bill looked for something with more effort. We shall discuss this problem more fully when we observe the characteristics of adverbs and their function in the sentence.

Adjectives and Noun Adjuncts

Some confusion arises over the classification and use of nouns which are apparently modifiers of other nouns. For example, let us consider the following sentence:

Mr. Brown is a science teacher.

The word *science* is a noun in form but it appears to be an adjective in function. *Science* is inflected like a noun and not like an adjective, but as used in this sentence, it is in the position of an adjective. It is apparently a modifier in the noun-headed word group *a science teacher*. If, however, we examine the word in contrast with a comparable adjective, both in form and function, we shall see that *science* is neither an adjective nor a true modifier.

Mr. Brown is a scientific teacher.

The word *scientific* is an adjective by form and also by function. It has the characteristic *-ic* suffix which marks adjectives. Moreover, we may use such words as *more, most, rather,* and *very* with *scientific* but not with *science.*

Mr. Brown is a very scientific teacher.

Mr. Brown is a rather scientific teacher.

We certainly cannot say

Mr. Brown is a rather science teacher.

Linguists tell us that intensifiers such as *very* and *rather* are semantically compatible with adjectives, but incompatible with nouns. Furthermore, *science teacher* and *scientific teacher* communicate quite different ideas. We shall discuss in a later chapter the grammatical principle involved here.

The semantic contrast between noun "modifiers" and adjectives is further demonstrated in the following pairs.

a college man
a collegiate man

a history text
a historic text

cost accounting
costly accounting

a child actor
a childish actor

a play writer
a playful writer

a fire squad
a firing squad

Nouns used in what appears to be the modifying function, to modify another noun, are most properly called *noun adjuncts*. The words *college, history, cost, child, play,* and *fire* as used in the above illustrations may therefore be called noun adjuncts.

Ambiguity results sometimes when a noun adjunct has a form similar to an adjective. For example,

> Miss Gonzales is a *Spanish* teacher.

We are not certain whether Miss Gonzales is a native of Spain who teaches, or a teacher of Spanish. We do not know whether *Spanish* is an adjective or a noun adjunct. The remedy is to restate the sentence more explicitly.

> Miss Gonzales is a teacher of Spanish.
>
> Miss Gonzales teaches Spanish.
>
> Miss Gonzales, our teacher, is Spanish.

Adjectives as Objective Complements

Two further ways in which adjectives are used in a sentence should be pointed out before we end the discussion.

1. The news made me *happy.*
2. I was made *happy* by the news.

In sentence 1 the adjective *happy* is a complement, not of the subject, as in the case of the predicate adjective discussed previously, but of the object *me.* Other illustrations of this usage follow.

> They called the man *stupid.*
>
> He painted the fence *white.*
>
> She swept the floor *clean.*
>
> She kept the baby *warm.*

That we cannot call the adjective a modifier of the noun it follows may be seen by observing the semantic difference between the two contrasting word orders.

> They called the man *stupid.*
>
> They called the *stupid* man.
>
> She kept the baby *warm.*
>
> She kept the *warm* baby.

In sentence 2, the adjective is used as a complement after a verb in the passive voice. The use is comparable to the noun complement after a verb in the passive voice, which we have called a retained object. Other illustrations of this usage follow.

> The man was kept *warm* by the blanket.
> The bed was made *ready* for the patient.
> The door was slammed *shut* by the child.
> The meat was boiled *tender* in the iron kettle.

Summary

Adjectives, like nouns and verbs, are identified in communication by their form, position, and function. Some adjectives have characteristic suffixes such as *-ful*, *-ish*, and *-able*. Others may be inflected for the comparative and superlative degrees by adding *-er* and *-est* as endings. All adjectives may be used with intensifiers such as *very*, *rather*, *more*, and *most*. If there is one test of an adjective, it is semantic harmony with an intensifier.

The two most common functions of the adjective are the attributive or modifying function and the predicate function. An adjective which modifies a noun usually precedes the noun and comes between the determiner and the noun. It may follow the noun, but it never precedes the determiner. In the predicate function the adjective follows the verb, which in this case is called a linking or copulative verb. The most common linking verbs are forms of *to be*, *seem*, *become*, *appear*, *look*, *sound*, *feel*, *taste*, and *smell*. Adjectives are also sometimes used as complements of direct objects and as complements after verbs in the passive voice.

Exercise A

Identify the adjectives in the following passage.

Perhaps one of the most curious revolutions in literary history is the sudden bull's-eye light cast by M. Longon on the obscure existence of François Villon. His book is not remarkable merely as a chapter of biography exhumed after four centuries. To readers of the poet it will recall, with a flavor of satire, that characteristic passage in which he bequeaths his spectacles — with humorous reservation of the case — to the hospital for blind paupers known as the Fifteen-Score. Thus equipped, let the blind paupers go and separate the good from the bad in the cemetery of the Innocents! For his own part the poet can see no distinction. Much have the dead people made of their advantages. What does it matter now that they have lain in state beds and nourished portly bodies upon cakes and cream! Here they all lie, to be trodden in the mud; the large estate and the small, sounding virtue and adroit or powerful vice, in very much the same condition; and a bishop not to be distinguished from a lamplighter with even the strongest spectacles.

Such was Villon's cynical philosophy. Four hundred years after his death, when surely all danger might be considered at an end, a pair of critical spectacles have been applied to his own remains; and though he left behind him a sufficiently ragged reputation from the first, it is only after these four hundred years that his delinquencies have been finally tracked home, and we can assign him to his proper place among the good or wicked. It is a staggering thought, and one that affords a fine figure of the imperishability of men's acts, that the stealth of the private inquiry office can be carried so far back into the dead and dusty past. We are not so soon quit of our concerns as Villon fancied. In the extreme of dissolution, when not so much as a man's name is remembered, when his dust is scattered to the four winds, and perhaps the very grave and the very graveyard where he was laid to rest have been forgotten, desecrated, and buried under populous towns — even in this extreme let an antiquary fall across a sheet of manuscript, and the name will be recalled, the old infamy will pop out into daylight like a toad out of a fissure in the rock, and the shadow of the shade of what was once a man will be heartily pilloried by his descendants. A little while ago and Villon was almost totally forgotten; then he was revived for the sake of his verses; and now he is being revived with a vengeance in the detection of his misdemeanors. How unsubstantial is this projection of a man's existence, which can lie in abeyance for centuries and then be brushed up again and set forth for the consideration of posterity by a few dips in an antiquary's inkpot![1]

Exercise B

Some of the adjectives in the following list may be compared by adding -er, and -est; some by use of the intensifiers more and most, and less and least; and some by both methods. Others may be compared by changing form. (Still others cannot be compared at all. Why?) Discuss the comparison of each adjective in the list.

[1] Robert Louis Stevenson, "François Villon."

hateful	early
good	curious
slow	black
rich	handsome
intelligent	polite
perfect	heavenly
dead	educated
careless	bad
beautiful	dejected
economical	stupid
cruel	American
friendly	wealthy

1. Write five sentences containing the simple form of five of the above adjectives.
2. Write five sentences containing the comparative form of five of the above adjectives.
3. Write five sentences containing the superlative form of five of the above adjectives.

EXERCISE C

Identify the predicate adjectives in the following sentences and indicate which verbs are linking verbs.

1. I felt bad when my brother sailed overseas.
2. My mother was very angry when the windows were broken.
3. It seems strange to return and find all your old schoolmates married.
4. The door slammed shut when the wind blew so hard.
5. The teacher looked furious when Henry dropped his books.
6. The man appeared suddenly from the large crowd and he seemed to be highly excited.
7. It sounds almost impossible to me, but I am sure that you mean well.
8. The cave smelled damp and musty, and we were afraid to go very far into it.
9. Mr. Smith got well fast when he heard the good news about his son.
10. You are being very stubborn in your attitude about studying.
11. When he tasted the milk, he found that it was sour.
12. The sky grew dark and the storm clouds raced wildly to the north.
13. It is the truth, then, that he remained loyal to the king.

14. When the man becomes penitent, he will come to confess his sins.

15. The weather is bad, and the forecast is that it will continue cold for two more days.

EXERCISE D

1. List five adjectives ending in the suffix *-ful*. Write three sentences using one of the adjectives in each in the attributive function.

2. List six adjectives ending in the suffix *-ish*. Write three sentences using two of the adjectives in each in the attributive function, but following the noun instead of preceding it.

3. List six adjectives ending in the suffix *-able*. Write three sentences using one of the adjectives in each in the predicate function. Use different verb forms.

4. List six adjectives ending in the suffix *-ive*. Write three sentences using one of the adjectives in each as a noun modifier.

5. List two adjectives ending in the suffix *-ary*. Write two sentences using one of the adjectives in each in the attributive function.

6. List six adjectives ending in the suffix *-some*. Write three sentences using one of the adjectives in each in the predicate function as objective complement.

7. List six adjectives ending in the suffix *-less*. Write six sentences using one of the adjectives in each in the predicate function. Use different linking verbs.

8. List six adjectives ending in each of the following suffixes: *-ate*, *-al*, *-ous*, *-en*, *-an*, *-y*, *-ly*, *-like*, *-ed*, *-ent*, *-ant*.

EXERCISE E

Identify the adjectives in the following passage. Explain the grammatical signals of identification in each case. Describe the function of each adjective and note the degree of comparison, if any.

Mark Jennings stood the picture up on the wide counter and he and Stephen Elwin stepped back and looked at it. It was one of Rouault's kings. A person looking at it for the first time might find it repellent, even brutal or cruel. It was full of rude blacks that might seem barbarically untidy.

But the two men knew the picture well. They looked at it in silence. The admiration they were sharing made a community between them which at their age was rare, for they had both passed forty. Jennings waited for Elwin to speak first — they were friends but Elwin was the customer. Besides, the frame had been designed by Jennings and in buying a reproduced picture the frame is of great importance, accounting for more than half the cost. Elwin had bought the picture some weeks before but he was seeing it framed for the first time.

Elwin said, "The frame is very good, Mark. It's perfect." He was a rather tall man with an attractive, competent face. He touched the frame curiously with the tip of his forefinger.

Jennings replied in a judicious tone, as if it were not his own good taste but that of a very gifted apprentice of his. "I think so," he said. And he too touched the frame, but intimately, rubbing briskly up and down one moulding with an artisan's possessive thumb, putting an unneeded last touch. He explained what considerations of color and proportion made the frame right for the picture. He spoke as if these were simple rules anyone might find in a book.

The king, blackbearded and crowned, faced in profile to the left. He had a fierce quality that had modulated, but not softened, to authority. One could feel of him — it was the reason why Elwin had bought the picture — that he had passed beyond ordinary matters of personality and was worthy of the crown he was wearing. Yet he was human and tragic. He was not unlike the sculptured kings of Chartres. In his right hand he held a spray of flowers.[2]

[2] From Lionel Trilling, "The Other Margaret," *Partisan Review*, Fall, 1945.

9

Adverbs

OF ALL THE CLASSES of English words, the adverb is the most difficult to describe. Like the adjective, the adverb is a modifier; but
whereas the adjective in either its attributive or its predicate
function refers to a noun, the adverb normally refers to a verb.
The word *adverb* literally means "to a verb." In our noun-verb
language it seems logical to make a distinction between noun
modifiers and verb modifiers. And indeed, for effective communication it is essential to recognize the difference between the
two. To avoid ambiguity, the writer must supply the structural
clues by which adverbs may be identified, and the reader must
be sensitive to these clues to avoid inappropriate responses.

Unfortunately for the grammarian, however, the words that
normally modify a verb have the habit of moving around within a
sentence and forming attachments with other words. We find
them also modifying adjectives, adverbs, nouns, and sometimes
even the whole sentence. Thus the adverb is a nomad sometimes
difficult to classify. However, the structures of language that make

classification difficult for the grammarian are often the very attributes that make it a flexible tool for the writer and speaker.

In this chapter, we shall discuss first the common characteristics of form and function by which we recognize adverbs. We shall then turn to some of the idiosyncrasies which make the adverb the very interesting and useful instrument of communication that it is.

Characteristic Adverbial Suffixes

Some adverbs are recognizable because they contrast with nouns by having the suffix -*ly*.

hour	hourly
day	daily
night	nightly
week	weekly
month	monthly
year	yearly

The nurse attended the patient *hourly*.

The boy went *daily* to see his mother.

The insects fly *nightly* about the bright street lamp.

The magazine is published *weekly*.

The reports are issued *monthly*.

He goes to the doctor *yearly* for a checkup.

Some adverbs are recognizable because they contrast with adjectives by having the suffix -*ly*.

happy	happily
serious	seriously
smart	smartly
weary	wearily
hopeful	hopefully
handsome	handsomely
frantic	frantically
laughing	laughingly
eminent	eminently
final	finally

They lived *happily* ever after.

He worked *seriously* at the problem.

> She was dressed very *smartly*.
> He walked *wearily* from the room.
> She looked *hopefully* up at the doctor.
> He was paid *handsomely* for the work.

Although the suffix *-ly* is the best-known clue to the adverb, it is not in itself enough, since many adjectives also end in the suffix *-ly*. For example, *friendly*, *manly*, *costly*, and *lovely* may be used only as adjectives in a sentence.

Other suffixes which help us to recognize the form of an adverb are *-ward*, *-time*, *-way*, *-where*, *-side*, and *-long*.

-ward	backward, forward, sideward
-time	sometime, anytime, meantime
-way	someway, anyway, sideway
-where	somewhere, everywhere, anywhere
-side	outside, inside, topside
-wise	otherwise, lengthwise, likewise
-long	headlong, sidelong

> He fell *backward* out of the ring.
> They will come *sometime* to visit us.
> You may solve the problem *anyway*.
> I hope that you will find the book *somewhere*.
> He has worked *inside* all day long.
> He arranged the blocks *lengthwise* on the floor.
> She fell *headlong* down the stairs.

Again, these suffixes are not sufficient to identify adverbs without other clues, since some adjectives and nouns also have them:

a *backward* child	in the *springtime*
an *inside* story	by the *roadside*
the *headlong* flight	on the *highway*

Inflection of Adverbs

The inflectional endings *-er* and *-est*, to indicate the comparative and superlative degrees, are used with some adverbs.

> Jim walks *faster* than his brother.
> George walks *fastest* of all.

We have been asked to drive *slow* in the congested area.

We will have to drive *slower* than ever if the traffic gets any heavier.

One has to drive *slowest* of all in the school zone.

Intensifiers such as *more, most, less, least, rather, really, very,* and *quite* are used as markers of adverbs as well as of adjectives.

He drove the car *very skillfully.*

She crossed the room *rather awkwardly.*

He walks *very fast* when he is on his way home.

She speaks *quite well* of the children.

The intensifiers *more, most, less,* and *least* are used with adverbs of more than one syllable for comparison.

Smith works *more conscientiously* than any other man in the shop.

The children listen *most attentively* when I read them a story.

Plumkin writes *less effectively* every year.

Agatha dresses *most attractively* when she is going out.

It is interesting to observe that intensifiers cannot be used with all adverbs. They occur most frequently with adverbs formed by adding the suffix *-ly* to adjectives. For example, the usage in sentences 1 and 2 below is normal, whereas that in 3 and 4 is impossible.

1. They lived *very happily* in the country.
2. She talked *very stupidly* about her great wealth.
3. The crab moved *very sideways* across the sand.
4. The newspaper comes *very weekly* to our house.

The Adverbial Prefix

Another characteristic signal of form which helps us to identify an adverb is the prefix *a-* used with certain nouns.

away	abreast
aboard	aground
abroad	apart
ahead	across

The regiment moved *ahead* across the rough terrain.

Mr. and Mrs. Smith went *abroad* for a year.

The great steamer ran *aground* in the storm.

The old car began gradually to fall *apart*.

The man moved *away* from the hot fire.

Miscellaneous Adverbs

Not all adverbs may be identified by formal signals such as characteristic suffixes, the inflectional endings *-er* and *-est*, harmony with intensifiers, or prefixes such as *a-*, as illustrated above. There is in addition a rather long list of adverbs with which the language student should become familiar, adverbs which may be learned only by use and memorization. These include the following:

there	here
now	near
yesterday	still
tomorrow	straight
today	never
then	far
often	north
late	south
already	back
soon	forth

I will plan to go *there tomorrow*.

He will *never* go *back* to the old farm.

He came *late* to school *today*.

He has *already* told me the whole story.

They walked *back* and *forth* across the stage.

Other words may be added to this miscellaneous list. For example, there are structure words which we ordinarily think of as prepositions.

out	over
in	up
beyond	after
down	throughout

I was glad when the man walked *out*.

Our troops moved *in* as the enemy retreated.

I invited him to come *down* and visit us.

We walked *over* to see their new home.

Position of Adverbs as Verb Modifiers

The primary function of adverbs is to modify verbs. An adverb is normally a modifier in a verb-headed word group. The illustrative sentences so far used in this chapter have all been written with the adverbs as verb modifiers. When the adverb is a verb modifier, its position in the sentence is not fixed.

1. Mr. Jones drove his new car *proudly* down the street.
2. Mr. Jones *proudly* drove his new car down the street.
3. *Proudly*, Mr. Jones drove his new car down the street.
4. Mr. Jones drove his new car down the street *proudly*.

If two adverbs are used as modifiers of the same verb, more combinations of word order are possible.

Mr. Jones *today* drove his new car *proudly* down the street.

Today Mr. Jones drove his new car *proudly* down the street.

Mr. Jones drove his new car *today proudly* down the street.

Mr. Jones drove his new car *proudly today* down the street.

Mr. Jones drove his new car *proudly* down the street *today*.

These five sentences are all variants of sentence 1 above, shifting the adverb *today* around, but keeping the adverb *proudly* in the same position after *car*. If the student will experiment with the number of different word orders to be obtained by variously placing *today* in sentences 2, 3, and 4, and will further consider that adverbial phrases and clauses might be substituted for the adverbs in all their various positions, he will begin to see how the shifting positions of adverbial modifiers give tremendous flexibility to the English language.

Substitution Signals for Adverbs

In the preceding sentences we have used two kinds of adverbial modifiers — an adverb (*today*) for which *then* may be substituted, and an adverb (*proudly*) for which *thus* may be substituted. In the "then" class we might have such adverbs as *yesterday, tomorrow, already, never*. In the "thus" class we might have *carefully, wearily, easily, gradually.* Most "thus" adverbs are closely related to adjectives, being in fact adjectives with the adverbial *-ly* suffix added. Still another kind of adverb may be used singly or in combination with the two other kinds: this is the adverb for which *there* can be substituted.

> Joe swept the snow *away yesterday quickly.*

This is the normal word order for these three adverbs (*there-then-thus*), though shifts may be made for emphasis or for improved sentence rhythm.

> *Yesterday* Joe swept the snow *away quickly.*
> *Yesterday* Joe *quickly* swept the snow *away.*
> Joe swept the snow *away quickly yesterday.*
> Joe swept the snow *quickly away yesterday.*

However, certain combinations of word order are never patterned in English usage. For example, we never say,

> *Away* Joe swept the snow *quickly yesterday.*
> Joe swept the snow *quickly yesterday away.*
> *Quickly* Joe swept the snow *yesterday away.*

In other words, when we use combinations of different kinds of adverbs (semantically speaking) — that is, adverbs of place, time, and manner — certain patterns of word order are conventional and certain others are not.

If one wishes to use a controlled subjective signal for identifying adverbs, he may try substituting *there, then,* and *thus* for the words in question: *there* for adverbs of place, *then* for adverbs of time, and *thus* for adverbs of manner.

Adverbs as Modifiers of Adjectives

From the formal characteristics of adverbs and their primary function as modifiers of verbs, we now turn to the novel propensity of the adverb (considered from the standpoint of form and meaning) to attach itself to adjectives, adverbs, and nouns, to become a complement, and to serve as the modifier of a whole sentence.

Adverbs often serve as modifiers of adjectives, especially if the adjective is used in the predicate function, or if it is a participle.

I hope you get better *quickly*.

The man grew angry *suddenly*.

Mr. Johnson became *strangely* silent.

The boy was *acutely* distressed with pain.

The chairs seemed *gracefully* placed in the chimney corner.

The baby becomes *necessarily* annoying when she is hungry.

The Sweets are a very *happily* married couple.

The attractive appearance of the room was enhanced by *cleverly* arranged flowers.

Many of the so-called adverbial modifiers which precede the adjective are not adverbs but structure words. They intensify meaning rather than convey it in themselves. Words like *very*, *rather*, *more*, and *most* fall distinctly into this category. They are never used in the primary function of adverbs, that is, to modify verbs. We do not say

He works *very*.

He works *rather*.

Some borderline words, such as *really*, *extremely*, *intensely*, and *mostly*, may be used both as intensifiers before adjectives and as adverbs modifying verbs. Hence they are difficult to classify when used before adjectives. The question is purely academic since communication does not depend here on grammatical classification.

They lived in a *really* attractive house.

Mrs. Brown has an *exquisitely* furnished home.

This is a *perfectly* beautiful day.

The *extremely* anxious parents waited in the hospital.

There are, however, a number of adverbs which function truly as adverbs (semantically) when they are used to modify — and precede — adjectives.

The *originally* wicked man repented and was converted.

The *locally* popular sportswriter Jim Carson received the award.

The *coldly* attractive woman braved the disapproving glances ot her associates.

A *furiously* barking dog met us at the gate.

Adverbs as Modifiers of Adverbs

Adverbs occasionally serve as modifiers of adverbs. We may observe this usage in the following sentences.

She will leave New York *early* tomorrow.

The plane will arrive here *late* tonight.

The senator plans his speeches *sometimes* hurriedly.

The great ship moved *slowly* eastward.

Population is shifting *gradually* westward.

In the first sentence *early tomorrow* is a modifier word group with *tomorrow* as the headword. The word *early* modifies *tomorrow* which is functionally an adverb. The same sort of analysis may be made of the other illustrations.

Adverbs as Modifiers of Nouns

In English, words which are adverbs by form and usually by function (modifiers of verbs) sometimes attach themselves to nouns, that is, become modifiers in a noun-headed word group. We cannot call them adjectives, for they do not have the formal characteristics of adjectives, and semantically they seem to be more adverbial than adjectival. In the following illustrations, pairs of contrasting examples show the word used first as the modifier of a verb and second as the modifier of a noun.

The man looked *backward*.

The man left without a look *backward*.

We expect her to arrive *tomorrow*.

We are looking forward to her arrival *tomorrow*.

Next year we will travel *abroad* in Europe.

We hope our trip *abroad* will be enjoyable.

The family will move *there* on Tuesday.

They expect the move *there* will be profitable.

This brings us into an area of usage in which classification of the noun modifiers may be highly indeterminate. The modifying words may be adverbial in form but adjectival in sense.

the *backward* child
in *after* years
a *forward* person
faraway places
the *above* illustration

Adverbs as Complements

Adverbs are sometimes used grammatically as complements after forms of the verb *to be*. When so used, they are adverbial both in form and in sense.

The time is *now*.
I will be *there* at ten o'clock.
The house is *here*.
The opportunity was *then*.
The meeting will be *tomorrow* at four.

In these sentences the italicized words are adverbial in form and meaning, but not in function. Functionally they complete the sentence rather than modify the verb. We could not say "The time is," or "The opportunity was."

Adverbs as Sentence Modifiers

Adverbs, finally, are sometimes used to modify the whole sentence. The following sentences illustrate this usage.

Desperately, he flung himself at his opponent.
Eagerly, he gulped the food in front of him.
Intermittently, the sound would grow in volume and then fade away.
Viciously the boy attacked his fellow classmates.
Suddenly we heard the sound of a bell.

There may be some difference of opinion whether the introductory adverb in these sentences modifies the whole sentence or the main verb. The problem seems to resolve itself into a matter of interpretation by the reader or the listener, easier in some contexts than in others. For example, in the following pair of sentences we may readily distinguish the adverb which modifies the rest of the sentence and the adverb which modifies the main verb.

> *Happily*, she did not arrive here yesterday.
> She did not arrive here *happily* yesterday.

Summary

In our noun-verb language, adverbs are modifiers. They are primarily modifiers of verbs. However, in the language as we have inherited it, we find the adverb used also as the modifier of adjectives, adverbs, nouns, and whole sentences, and even as a predicate complement. Its position in the sentence is normally just before or after the verb, but it may be shifted around almost at will. It is the one word class which is freely moved about in a sentence, and its free movement gives great flexibility to our language, particularly in the process of structural substitution. The adverb is often identifiable by certain formal characteristics. Like an adjective, it may sometimes be inflected for degree with the suffixes *-er* and *-est*. Certain characteristic suffixes such as *-ly*, *-ward*, *-way*, *-time*, and *-where*, sometimes added to adjectives, sometimes to nouns, help us to identify the adverbs thus created. The prefix *a-* is used to form certain adverbs. Intensifiers such as *very*, *rather*, *more*, and *most* may be used before certain adverbs and may serve at times to identify them. The adverb is an elusive word, difficult to define, but versatile in use.

EXERCISE A

In the following selection, identify the adverbs and describe the function of each.

Mechta (Dream), the artificial planet, was as harsh a sign of Soviet space superiority as the first Sputnik. We're sorry to say that it won't be the last such demonstration the U.S. will have to watch in 1959. It was stated categorically last week in a report by the well-informed House Committee on Astronautics and Space Exploration, that the Soviets can now send a man into space — and probably bring him back. The same House committee quotes an expert opinion that the gap between Soviet space progress and our own is now not one, but five years.

In military missilry, the take-off point for space exploration, the U.S. remains significantly behind. We do not possess a large missile we can fire in anger. The Soviets do. This puts us a long way from matching Soviet space and missile superiority — and matching is not enough.

All highly placed officials in Washington know this. So it is all the more perplexing to observe the semiparalysis of direction in our space exploration effort. This affliction is hardly disguised by the professional idiot's grin of Washington spokesmen on the latest Soviet success. ("People realize," said one about Mechta, "that in this space field, first one country will squirt ahead in one direction, then another will push ahead in another.")

The major reason for the space and missile lag is not technical, either. There is nothing wrong with U.S. working scientists, hardware, or the programs on their drawing boards. Where we have failed is in giving to the space and missile programs any fundamental unity of direction, or continuity of effort. This can be fatal in a field which, like that of nuclear energy, demands pure trail blazing in its operating methods. There are no guide rails or directions from past precedents.[1]

EXERCISE B

In each of the following sentences, fill in the blank with an adverb which you think is appropriate to the context.

1. Mrs. Prim walked _____ down the quiet lane.

2. The two families _____ went to dinner and the theater together.

3. He was in the living room _____ unfolding a paper which he had taken from his pocket.

4. His great mouth was _____ open, and he was trembling _____.

5. I raised my head and looked _____ at him.

6. The wind had sprung up _____ as if to stir up my wild thoughts.

7. The old man looked in the safe _____ expecting to find all his money.

8. The Smyths are planning to spend the winter _____ this year.

9. The guards walked _____ and _____ behind the house all night.

10. The _____ famous writer delivered the main address at the banquet.

11. Bending _____ over the casket, the old mother broke into heavy sobs.

[1] From "The Warning of Mechta," an Editorial in *Life* Magazine, January 19, 1959, p. 37. Copr. 1959 Time Inc.

12. Plumkin expects to make a fortune _____ as a giant financier.

13. The money is _____ where you hid it this morning.

14. Parker stood _____ and erect, looking _____ out over crowd of silent men.

15. Agatha cooked _____, but she always kept her house _____ clean.

16. She put the hat _____ in the closet and never wore it _____.

17. He slapped me _____ on the back and asked me _____ if my father was _____.

18. Then quite _____ the storm broke over our heads and we had to run for cover.

19. She gave him a glance _____ as he walked _____.

20. Anna looked at her child _____, _____ sleeping.

Exercise C

In the following sentences, select the form in parentheses which you feel is appropriate. If you think either form may be used, indicate this fact. Explain the usage in each case.

1. The orchestra played the (beautiful, beautifully) symphony of Tschaikovsky.

2. The orchestra played the symphony (beautiful, beautifully).

3. Mr. Batson looked (weary, wearily) at the pile of work on his desk.

4. Mr. Batson looked (weary, wearily) as he walked home from his long day's work.

5. The police have asked us to drive (slow, slowly) through the school zone.

6. You will have to speak (loud, loudly) to Mr. Finch; he does not hear very (good, well).

7. Gertrude's apple pies taste (delicious, deliciously).

8. Gertrude's apple pies are (delicious, deliciously) inviting.

9. Mother was (frantic, frantically) waving at us from the train window.

10. The student seemed very (happy, happily) after the examination.

11. The student worked very (happy, happily) at his examination.

12. The Ladies Aid Society displayed a (careful, carefully) arranged exhibit at the fair.

13. Theresa looked (happy, happily) at her new evening gown.

14. The boys went away (quick, quickly) when they heard the whistle blow.

15. When we entered the large dining hall, the music was playing (soft, softly) and (slow, slowly).

16. The lawyers knew that something (definite, definitely) had to be done.

17. This decision will not appear (satisfactory, satisfactorily) to the public.

18. If you want to come to the Senior Prom you will have to dress (formal, formally).

19. The Secretary of State considered the problem (serious, seriously).

20. Plumkin was (bare, barely) in the tub when the doorbell rang.

Exercise D

1. Write out a list of ten adverbs which are formed by adding the suffix -ly to adjectives.

2. Write five sentences using adverbs from item 1 to modify the verb in each. Use a variety of positions for the adverbs.

3. Use five of the adverbs from item 1 in separate sentences to illustrate an adverb modifying an adjective in the predicate function.

4. Write five sentences using in each an adverb to modify an adjective in the attributive function.

5. Write five sentences using an adverb to modify a participle in a participial phrase.

6. Write five sentences using an adverb to modify a gerund in a gerund phrase.

7. Write five sentences using an adverb to modify an infinitive in an infinitive phrase.

8. Write out a list of adverbs ending in -ward, -wards, -time, -times, -where, -way, -side, -wise, -long.

9. Write ten sentences using the adverbs listed in item 8.

10. List as many adverbs as you can find which begin with the prefix a-.

11. Write five sentences in which you use an adverb to modify another verb.

12. Write five sentences in which you use an adverb to modify a noun.

13. Write five sentences in which an adverb is used as a complement.

14. Write five sentences in which an adverb is used to modify the whole sentence.

15. Write a sentence in which two adverbs modify the same verb. Then write as many variant sentences as you can by shifting the positions of the adverbs.

16. Write a sentence in which three adverbs are used to modify a verb — adverbs for which *there*, *then*, and *thus* could be substituted.

17. Write a series of sentence variants on item 16 by shifting the relative positions of the adverbs used.

10

Structure Words

As we have seen, the four important word classes in our language are nouns, verbs, adjectives, and adverbs. Nouns and verbs are primary, fulfilling the basic function of communication. Adjectives and adverbs are secondary, serving as modifiers and making our communication more explicit. It has been estimated that more than ninety-three per cent of the words used in the spoken language are nouns, verbs, adjectives, and adverbs.[1] The new words being ever added to the language are invariably nouns, verbs, adjectives, and adverbs.

There is, besides, a fifth general class of words, which includes prepositions, conjunctions, pronouns, interjections, and the miscellaneous words that grammarians have always found difficult to classify. Modern linguists have referred to this fifth class of words as function words or structure words. In this text, we shall refer to them as structure words.

[1] Charles C. Fries, *The Structure of English* (New York: Harcourt, Brace, 1952).

The linguists have distinguished between the structure words and the four classes of words thus far discussed (the nouns, verbs, adjectives, and adverbs) in terms of two kinds of linguistic meaning: structural and lexical. Structural meaning attaches to all words in communication by virtue of their relationships and positions. Lexical meaning is what the term "meaning" conveys to most of us: dictionary meaning, the kind of meaning we think of as inherent in a word, in and of itself, independent of sentence context. Thus nouns, verbs, adjectives, and adverbs are said to have both lexical and structural meaning, whereas structure words are relatively weak or lacking in lexical meaning, and derive their meaning almost wholly from their relations to the major actors on the language stage. Whether or not this distinction between lexical and structural meaning is an artificial one, as some critics have argued, we may agree for practical purposes that words like *boy*, *run*, *beautiful*, and *heavily* have meaning in a different way from words like *the*, *and*, *however*, *if*, *which*, and *for*.

In this sense, then, we may say that the structure words are more significant for what they do than for what they "mean." For they perform a number of important grammatical functions. They connect word groups, both subject-predicate word groups and modifier word groups. They are important elements in subordination and co-ordination. They serve as agents in the process of substitution that makes our communication more concise. They help to transmit shades of attitude and feeling in verb phrases. In this chapter we shall describe these structure words and show how they are used.

Connectives

Connectives make up the first large group of structure words. This group includes co-ordinate conjunctions, conjunctive adverbs, subordinate conjunctions, and prepositions.

The co-ordinate conjunctions were discussed in Chapter 4, but are listed again here. It is important to memorize them.

and	yet
but	so
or	neither . . . nor
nor	either . . . or
for	

In Chapter 4 we discussed the use of these words in the grammatical device of co-ordination, the adding on of subject-predicate word groups (independent clauses). Examples of compound sentences were given in which the co-ordinate conjunctions were used. The reader should now refer back to these (pages 43–44).

With the exception of *for*, *yet*, and *so*, the conjunctions listed above may be used to create other compounds — nouns, verbs, adjectives, adverbs, phrases, and other structure words. These compounds, of course, may have a great variety of functions within the sentence. We illustrate here a few of the possible compound structures which may be created by use of these conjunctions.

(a) Compound noun

   Neither medicine *nor* care will help him now.

(b) Compound verb

   Jenkins worked hard *and* saved his money for twenty years.

(c) Compound adjective

   The poor *or* underprivileged citizens will be helped by the Welfare Board.

(d) Compound adverb

   Smith sat quietly *and* patiently waiting for his wife.

(e) Compound participle

   Rushing *and* passing, the team quickly pushed its way to a touchdown.

(f) Compound gerund

   He likes to talk about hunting *and* fishing.

(g) Compound infinitive

   He wants to go to college *and* study engineering.

(h) Compound prepositional phrase

   You will find the papers *either* in the safe *or* on my desk.

(i) Compound structure words

   I recall your telling me the story, but I can't remember where *or* when.

Another class of connectives is the conjunctive adverbs, whose use in the formation of compound sentences we discussed in Chapter 4. The reader should refer back to the illustrations given on page 45. A list of conjunctive adverbs is given again here.

however	accordingly
therefore	hence
moreover	also
nevertheless	then
furthermore	likewise
otherwise	thus
consequently	besides

Conjunctive adverbs are important structure words since they too perform the function of co-ordination. They are borderline words, however, since they may also perform the function of ordinary adverbs.

Subordinate conjunctions are the connectives that perform the important function of subordination — the inclusion within a sentence of a subject-predicate word group. We have seen how this is effected in Chapter 4 (refer to pages 47–51 and note again the many illustrations of noun clauses, adjective clauses, and adverbial clauses). A list of subordinate conjunctions is given again here.

while	since	after
though	because	unless
although	as	until
if	before	whether
which	when	whenever
that	where	however
who	how	wherever
whose	why	whichever
whom	what	whatever

Note that this class of connectives includes words used to signal questions, *why*, *how*, *where*, *when*, *who*, *which*, etc. When so used, they do not have a subordinating function.

When do you plan to go to New York?

Why do spiders spin a web?

Who will go to the library for me?

How much income tax will we pay this year?

The fourth and last class of connectives is the prepositions. In Chapter 5, in the discussion of modifier word groups, illustrative sentences were given in which prepositional phrases were used (refer to pages 59–60). A list of prepositions is given below.

for	through	down
to	on	off
in	at	of
out	upon	across
by	from	beyond
up	with	beneath
over	under	against
above	among	about
during	inside	near

Pronouns

The second main group of structure words is the pronouns. The word *pronoun* may mean many things in grammar because literally it means "for a noun." In this text, we shall confine the meaning of the word to the class which has been traditionally called personal pronouns, for there are many kinds of words which may be substituted "for a noun," and to include them all in one category would entail complicated and unnecessary subclassifications. We shall consider the problem of substitution in Chapter 14.

Although personal pronouns are substitute words, they have considerable grammatical importance since they are inflected for person, number, gender, and case. They are classified as structure words: they do not belong to the primary and secondary word classes, and their meaning is primarily derivative and structural rather than lexical.

The term *person* in reference to pronouns relates to the person speaking, *first person;* the person spoken to, *second person;* or the person spoken of, *third person.*

FIRST PERSON	I, me, my, mine	we, us, our, ours
SECOND PERSON	you, yours	you, yours
THIRD PERSON	he, him, his	they, them, their, theirs
	she, her, hers	
	it, its	

The term *number* in reference to pronouns relates to quantity. *Singular* means one and *plural* means more than one.

SINGULAR	PLURAL
I, me, my, mine	we, us, our, ours
you, yours	you, yours
he, him, his	they, them, their, theirs
she, her, hers	
it, its	

The term *gender* in reference to pronouns relates to sex, *feminine, masculine, neuter*. Only the third person singular pronoun is inflected for gender.

MASCULINE	he, him, his
FEMININE	she, her, hers
NEUTER	it, its

The term *case* in reference to pronouns relates to syntax, or function in the sentence. *Nominative case* refers to the subject function, *objective case* to the object function, *possessive case* to the possessive or genitive function.

NOMINATIVE	I, you (*sing.*), he, she, it, we, you (*plu.*), they
POSSESSIVE	my, mine; your, yours (*sing. & plu.*); his, her, hers, its; our, ours; their, theirs
OBJECTIVE	me, you (*sing. & plu.*), him, her, it, us, them

The student will quickly see that the inflection of pronouns is complicated by considerable overlapping. Pronouns do not have separate and distinct inflected forms for each grammatical aspect. In the following sentences, the pronouns will be described in terms of inflections for person, number, gender, and case.

> *We* have just returned from New York. (First person, plural number, nominative case)
>
> The judge is now considering *his* case. (Third person, singular number, masculine gender, possessive case)
>
> The agent gave *us* the tickets. (First person, plural number, objective case)
>
> *You* have not told me about your trip. (Second person)

I am certain that the property will be turned over to *her*. (Third person, singular number, feminine gender, objective case)

I do not wish to trouble *them*. (Third person, plural number, objective case)

We placed the picture where *it* would show to the best advantage. (Third person, singular number, neuter gender)

He will give it to *your* teacher. (Second person, possessive case)

Determiners

The third main group of structure words is made up of what we have called determiners. These words are noun markers and precede a noun or an adjective modifying a noun. (The determiner would precede all single word modifiers before a noun.)

The money is in the bank.
This money is in the bank.
That money is in the bank.
More money is in the bank.
No money is in the bank.

A boy is in the classroom.
Some boys are in the classroom.
Few boys are in the classroom.
Two boys are in the classroom.
Three boys are in the classroom.
Those boys are in the classroom.

Most young men like music.
Many young men like music.
All young men like music.
These young men like music.
Both young men like music.

All the italicized words in the above sentences may be called determiners. Other words which may be substituted for these determiners would belong to the same class. In addition to the determiners in these sentences we could list the following:

each	every
either	another
an	neither
other	ten
any	whatever

In some textbooks of grammar certain determiners when used alone without a noun are called pronouns. For example, in the following sentence the word *this* does not precede a noun, but is used independently.

> *This* is my brother.

In this text, however, we are limiting the term *pronoun* to the personal pronouns. The independent use of words like *this*, *that*, *these*, *those*, etc., will be discussed in Chapter 14.

Auxiliary or Helping Verbs

The fourth main group of structure words consists of the words which we have traditionally called auxiliary or helping verbs. The following list includes most of these words.

shall	might	am
will	must	is
should	has	are
would	had	was
can	have	were
could	do	been
may	did	being
having	to be	ought to
used to	got	get
getting	going to	keep
kept		

As we have seen in Chapter 7, these auxiliary verbs are used in a great variety of ways with verbs to express many shades of time, attitude, intent, aspect, and condition.

> I *studied* English this term.
> I *have studied* English this term.
> I *had studied* English this term.
> I *had to study* English this term.

I *ought to have studied* English this term.

I *should have studied* English this term.

I *might have studied* English this term.

I *have been studying* English this term.

I *did study* English this term.

I *was going to study* English this term.

I *kept studying* English this term.

I *should have been studying* English this term.

I *might have been studying* English this term.

I *must have studied* English this term.

I *must have been studying* English this term.

I *could have been studying* English this term.

I *ought to have been studying* English this term.

Some of the words which we have called auxiliary verbs are used independently as finite verbs and inflected as verbs. This list includes forms of *to be, have, get, do,* and *keep.* When so used, they are verbs in their own right.

I hope you *get* well quickly.

I *am* happy to be here.

George *has* ten dollars.

They *do* very skillful work.

He *keeps* his car in the garage.

Auxiliary verbs in their "helping" function are structure words having meaning only in the context of the verb phrase of which they are part. Grammatically, they resemble modifiers; in fact, they have been called modifiers of the main verb by some grammarians.

Particles

The last group of structure words is made up of a large number of miscellaneous words, useful in communication but indeterminate in nature. We shall call them particles, a term long used by grammarians, though not always with the same meaning. In this classification, particles will include what have been traditionally called interjections and a large group of unclassifiables.

oh	very	rather
indeed	too	more
not	most	less
least	really	fairly
quite	not	almost
anybody	somebody	everybody
nobody	nothing	everything
anything	yes	no
please	hello	good-by

The student will recognize the words which in Chapters 8 and 9 were called intensifiers, a term that describes their function in relation to adjectives and adverbs. Words such as *very, rather, more, most, less, least, fairly,* and so on, when used as modifiers of adjectives and adverbs, reinforce or strengthen (or perhaps weaken) the force of the modifier.

Certain structure words, *more, most, any, some,* and others, may be classified as determiners when used before nouns and yet may be listed with the particles as intensifiers. They have a different structural value as determiners from what they have as intensifiers.

Words such as *nobody, anybody, somebody,* and the like are structure words used as substitutes for nouns in a functional sense. We will discuss them more fully in Chapter 14.

Importance of Structure Words

To appreciate the grammatical value of structure words, let us examine a sentence taken from an editorial in a large city newspaper.

> *The* City *of* Phoenix took *some* big jumps *in* statistics *in* 1958, *which* was *a* record year *of* growth, *but two* figures reassuringly *either* stayed put *or did not* increase *as might have been* expected.

DETERMINERS	CONNECTIVES	
The	of	of
some	in	but
a	in	either . . . or
two	which	as

AUXILIARY VERBS	PARTICLES
did	not
might have been	

The determiners point to the nouns and give shades of meaning in context. The connectives give coherence to the sentence. The connectives which we call prepositions enable the writer to include the modifier word groups (phrases) within the framework of the sentence. They too express shades of meaning. The connective *which* enables the writer to include the subordinate clause (*which . . . growth*) which relates to *1958*. The connective *as* permits inclusion of the elliptical (it has no subject) clause *as . . . expected* to modify the verb *increase*. The connective *but* adds on to the first main statement the independent clause *two . . . expected;* it also supplies a tone of contrast. The connective *either . . . or* permits use of the compound verb forms and shows alternative possibilities. The auxiliary verbs *did* and *might have been* add tone and meaning to the main verbs. The particle *not* has the pure force of a negative.

Summary

Nouns, verbs, adjectives, and adverbs are the four important word classes in English. Other words in our language, however, help to supply the framework of communication. They do not have meaning in the same way that nouns, verbs, adjectives, and adverbs do, but they contribute to coherence and the logical relation of ideas. They help indicate or identify the more meaningful words; provide substitute structures to make our statements more concise; express delicate shades of mood, time, attitude, and condition; communicate negation and emotion.

This fifth class of words, the structure words, may be divided into five groups: connectives, pronouns, determiners, auxiliary verbs, and particles.

Connectives include conjunctions, conjunctive adverbs, subordinate conjunctions, and prepositions. Their chief function is to add onto or include within a sentence subject-predicate word groups or modifier word groups. The conjunctions are also used to form compounds within the sentence.

Pronouns — the term here is limited to personal pronouns — are words substituted for nouns which have already been used within the context of the communication. Pronouns are inflected for person, number, gender, and case.

Determiners, words like *a*, *an*, *the*, *this*, *that*, *some*, are pointers, indicators, markers of nouns. They are useful as delicate signals to the listener or reader that the primary communication word, the noun, is coming up. They also supply shades of meaning in context.

Auxiliary verbs are used in great number and in a great variety of ways before the main verb, which they not only identify but qualify with subtle shades of meaning.

Particles are a miscellaneous group of words which fill a number of different functions. They communicate emotional tone, function as intensifiers before adjectives and adverbs, and supply negation. They serve at times as noun words, as substitute forms in generalizations. They communicate conventional greetings and salutations. Particles, like most structure words, are hardly meaningful in themselves but are useful in the larger context of communication.

EXERCISE A

Identify the structure words in the following paragraphs and discuss their function.

1. They pushed us into a large white room and my eyes began to blink because the light hurt them. Then I saw a table and four fellows seated at the table, civilians, looking at some papers. The other prisoners were herded together at one end and we were obliged to cross the entire room to join them. There were several I knew, and others who must have been foreigners. The two in front of me were blond with round heads. They looked alike. I imagine they were French. The smaller one kept pulling at his trousers, out of nervousness.

This lasted about three hours. I was dog-tired and my head was empty. But the room was well-heated, which struck me as rather agreeable; we had not stopped shivering for twenty-four hours. The guards led the prisoners in one after the other in front of the table. Then the four fellows asked them their names and what they did. Most of the time that was all — or perhaps from time to time they would ask such questions as: "Did you help sabotage the munitions?" or, "Where were you on the morning of the ninth and what were you doing?" They didn't even listen to the replies, or at least they didn't seem to. They just remained silent for a moment and looked straight ahead, then they began to write.[2]

[2] Jean-Paul Sartre, "The Wall."

2. The big car rolled smoothly into the night. The sharp bright smudge of the headlights slid under the darkness with mathematical exactitude. Dressed in his hunting clothes, the boy sat beside his uncle and watched the road. He sat rather stiffly. His new boots, greased by his mother, prodded the boxes of shells piled carelessly onto the floor of the car. He was not comfortable. The shells gave him no easy rest for his feet, his clothes were strange in their bulk, and he could not make up his mind how to act with his Uncle Bomar. This was to him at the moment the most serious matter in the world. He tied himself into knots thinking about it. He rather felt that the childish deference to an elder was out of place now that they were going hunting together, and not merely hunting but to the Lake for ducks. The invitation was plainly Bomar's way of accepting him as a man. Bomar did not take boys duck shooting. Quail or dove hunting, but never duck. He had begged too often not to know. The boy felt that at last he was ready for a man's pleasures and responsibilities. This thought made him all the more anxious to behave as he should. This and the way his mother had seen them off.[3]

Exercise B

Identify all the connectives in the following sentences, and explain their functions.

1. The man and his wife were injured in the collision.
2. It was the evening of the third day, but still no visitor had arrived.
3. He was obliged to borrow money or to go bankrupt.
4. Plumkin climbed the hill and saw what was on the other side.
5. There is an old castle beyond the village which belonged to the Earl of Westchester.
6. The men will either go back to work or lose their jobs.
7. He spoke of his mother and of the many times that he had made her sad.
8. I do not know where he has gone or what he is doing.
9. Smith graduated from college last June; however, he has been unable to find a job.
10. The road was slippery because it had just been snowing.
11. He told us the true and complete story of his life.
12. He rose to address the crowd and received a tremendous ovation.

[3] From Andrew Lytle, "The Mahogany Frame," in *A Novel, A Novella, and Four Stories*, © 1958 by Andrew Lytle; reprinted by permission of Ivan Obolensky, Inc.

13. When I awoke the next morning, I found the house deserted and cold.

14. He was old and wore glasses, and his hair as it fell across his forehead was thin and white.

15. The man nodded knowingly, although in his heart he was confused.

EXERCISE C

In the following passage, supply the inflected form of the pronoun which best suits the context. Discuss the person, number, gender, and case of the pronouns used.

Bob and his brother Jim live in the country. _____ father owns a large ranch which _____ bought many years ago. Bob and _____ brother raise cattle. _____ have forty head of good stock which they have raised by _____. Next year Bob is planning to go to college where _____ hopes to study agriculture. He believes that this kind of education will help _____ to become a successful rancher. He made up his mind last month when his father asked him, "What are _____ plans for the future, Bob?" Bob thought for awhile and said to his father, "_____ hope to be able to spend four years in college, because I am sure that it will help _____ to learn a great deal about raising cattle."

Bob's sister is younger than _____ or Jim. _____ is a sophomore in high school. _____ name is Mary Jane. Last year her mother took _____ to Chicago. _____ spent two weeks in the city enjoying all _____ stores and fine theaters. Their cousins invited _____ to go for a sail on Lake Michigan which _____ all enjoyed very much. When Mary Jane and her mother returned home, _____ had much to talk about.

"The vacation was wonderful," said Mary Jane, "but _____ are both glad to be home." And then she thought for a moment. "We hope that _____ are just as glad to see _____ back home again."

EXERCISE D

In the following sentences, supply the appropriate inflected form of the required pronoun.

1. It is nearly time for (he, him) to be leaving for the trip.

2. I could easily see that he did not care for (you, your) playing tonight.

3. This matter is entirely between you and (I, me).

4. Mr. Brown is one of those busy men who are always willing to do (his, their) part.

5. For a moment I thought you were (she, her).

6. The group treated (its, their) new president with great respect.

7. Everyone in the audience remained in (his, their) seat while the classes marched out of the hall.

8. I do not like (you, your) running around with that crowd.

9. They decided to go to Europe with my husband and (I, me).

10. The committee invited them as well as (we, us) to the reception.

11. Twenty-five of (we, us) regulars were chosen for the special assignment.

12. It was not easy for (they, them) and (we, us) to make this decision.

13. Somebody in the organization must have broken (his, their) promise.

14. Every citizen has a sacred duty to defend (his, their) country.

15. The captain chose Bill as well as (I, me).

Exercise E

1. Substitute as many determiners for *the* in the following sentence as you can think of:

    The painting is beautiful.

2. Substitute as many determiners for *the* in the following sentence as you can think of:

    The paintings are beautiful.

3. Substitute other determiners for *a* in the following sentence:

    The rains washed soil away from a house.

4. Substitute other determiners for *these* in the following sentence:

    How much did you pay for these books?

5. Substitute other auxiliary verbs for *may* in the following sentence:

    Charles may enter college next fall.

6. Substitute other auxiliary verbs for *have:*

    Mr. Smith and his wife have gone to the country.

7. Substitute other auxiliary verbs for *kept:*

    Mary kept looking out of the window for her girl friend.

8. Substitute other auxiliary verbs for *was:*

    Mrs. Brown was elected chairman of the Woman's Club.

9. Substitute other auxiliary verbs for *should have been:*

    George should have been promoted last year.

10. Substitute other auxiliary verbs for *has been:*

    James has been nominated to give the speech of welcome.

11. Substitute other intensifiers for *very:*
   The flowers made Mother very happy.
12. Substitute other intensifiers for *rather:*
   A rather dignified young man entered the room.
13. Substitute other intensifiers for *real:*
   The children were asked to be real quiet during the evening.
14. Substitute other intensifiers for *more:*
   Sarah writes her reports more effectively this year.

Form and Function—
Functional Shift

IN THE subject-predicate structure of English, the key word of the subject is the noun, or a word or word group substituted for a noun. The key word in the predicate is the verb, which is sometimes followed by a complement — usually a noun or an adjective, or substitute forms for these words. Modifiers are built up about the nouns and the verbs and sometimes about the modifiers themselves. By means of structure words we add subject-predicate word groups to the main sentence, include subject-predicate word groups, and attach modifier word groups.

There are, therefore, three *main* functions in the language — subject, predicate, and modifier. Within the subject there will be a noun (or noun substitute) and its modifiers; within the predicate there will be a verb, which may have modifiers, and possibly one or more complements, which also may have modifiers. We have been accustomed to call the noun modifiers adjectives and the verb modifiers adverbs.

155

Word Order as a Signal of Function

Function within a sentence is determined by the relative positions of the words, that is, by word order. We have learned that the order of the main elements is fixed — subject, verb, complement. We respond habitually to this fixed word order.

> John ate the fish.
>
> The fish ate John.

Our response to the first statement might be a bored "So what?" To the second statement we might reply with an amazed "Indeed!"

Modifiers attach themselves usually to some headword. This attachment is signaled by their position.

> The *kind old* lady
>
> The man *in the gray-flannel* suit
>
> The boy *who lives across the street*
>
> The work *to be done*
>
> The street *being paved this month*

In each of the above illustrations, the separate word or the word group modifies the noun which it precedes or follows. We respond to the word order to which we have become habituated. We are sensitive, that is, to position.

> The man walked *rapidly*.
>
> The man walked *down the street*.
>
> The man walked *wherever the path led him*.
>
> The man walked *to get the exercise*.

In these sentences each of the modifying words or word groups relates to the verb. We know this because of the position of the modifier. Indeed, we respond to adverbial modifiers even when they are shifted to a number of different positions, provided they remain within the conventional patterns of English usage.

Word order, then, is the dominant structural signal of meaning. Word order reveals syntax or function, and this determines meaning and hence response.

Other Structural Signals of Function

The other structural signals which provide clues to function and therefore to meaning are structure words and inflectional changes. These signals reinforce word order in its revelation of function.

> The cook will fish.
> The fish will cook.

Structure words as well as position provide the clues in the above sentences. In the first, the determiner *the* identifies *cook* as a noun, and the auxiliary verb *will* identifies *fish* as a verb. In the second sentence, the determiner *the* identifies *fish* as a noun, and the auxiliary *will* identifies *cook* as a verb.

> The boy is coming home.
> The boys are coming home.

Here we find three formal clues to meaning. First, the change of *boy* to *boys* (inflection for plural meaning) is characteristic of nouns and helps to identify them. We are habituated to this change — *girl, girls; book, books; steak, steaks; pen, pens.* Second, the change of *is* to *are* (inflection for plural meaning) is characteristic of this particular verb, and we have responded to it and used it since early childhood. The inflection helps us to identify the verb. The third signal is agreement. When the subject assumes the plural form *boys*, the verb assumes the plural form *are*. The changes occur at the same time and indicate subject-predicate relationship. All these formal signals reinforce the signal of word order to help the listener or reader identify the function groups of the sentence and therefore to respond appropriately (to interpret meaning).

> The cook manned the boat.
> The man cooked the fish.

In these two sentences, the verb is identified by inflectional endings as well as position. The *-ed* suffix gives the reader the verb signal. In the first sentence, the determiner *the* identifies *cook* as a noun and therefore the subject in this position. In the second sentence, it so identifies *man*.

We have pointed out that modifiers of nouns are identified by their position in relation to the noun, and that modifiers of verbs are usually identified by means of their position. But they may also be identified by certain characteristics of form. As discussed in Chapters 8 and 9, adjectives and adverbs are sometimes inflected, and these inflectional changes are often clues to their identity. Moreover, many adjectives and adverbs have characteristic endings, suffixes, which serve also as means of identification.

> the *poor* people of Paris
> the *poorest* people of Paris
> the *beautiful* sunset
> the *most beautiful* sunset
> a *religious* meeting
> an *attentive* student
> an *interesting* story
> a *wealthy* man

In all except the first of the illustrations above, form reinforces position in identifying function. The inflectional change or the characteristic suffix signals the adjective, the modifier of the noun.

> Mary looked *long* at the candy.
> Mary looked *longer* at the candy.
> Bill drove *rapidly* down the street.
> Bill drove *more rapidly* on the highway.
> The birds flew *away*.
> The men climbed *upward*.

In the adverbial modifiers italicized above, the function is determined mainly by the position of the modifier in relation to the verb. However, the inflected ending, the intensifier *more*, and the characteristic prefix and suffixes all help to strengthen this identification. In other words, the formal characteristics of the modifier are grammatical devices to make its function clear, but the function is determined largely by word order.

The importance of position, or word order, in determining function and therefore meaning may be seen readily in situations where form and function apparently conflict.

> Only the *wealthy* can stay at this hotel.

Here *wealthy* has the formal characteristics of an adjective. It ends in -*y* and it is inflected like an adjective and not like a noun.

However, in this sentence it is not a modifier and therefore does not have the function of an adjective. By its position in the sentence we recognize it as having a noun function, that is, it is used as the subject. Our response to it is the same as if it were a noun in form. Its function in the sentence is determined by the word order and not by the form of the word.

The *fraternity* men celebrated *hell* week.

In the above sentence, the italicized words are modifiers, as we know from their positions before the nouns they modify. However, *fraternity* has the formal characteristic of a noun, the *-ity* suffix. Also it is inflected like a noun and not like an adjective. We know, too, that the adjective conveying the idea of fraternity is *fraternal*. Again, the word *hell* is not inflected like an adjective, nor does it have the appropriate adjective suffix *-ish* (*hellish*). By form the words are nouns, by position they are modifiers. Functionally they are modifiers and we so interpret the sentence.

Relation of Form to Function

The student of grammar should understand the relation of form and function in our language. Function in the sentence relates principally to subject, verb, complement, modifier, and connective. Meaning, in terms of appropriate response, is determined by function, which is signaled primarily by word order and reinforced by structure words and formal characteristics of words. In a highly inflected language such as Latin, form and function are in almost perfect agreement. In English, which has very little inflection, form and function as determined by word order do not always agree. In this event, structure words may reinforce word order in signaling function.

Functional Shift

Because English is mostly a non-inflected language, it is possible to use the same word in different functions. This use of a word to fulfill various functions within a sentence is called functional shift. The same word may be inflected in different ways according to its function.

In the following pairs of sentences, a word is used first as a noun and second as a modifier of a noun.

> The criminal was sent to *prison*.
> The *prison* walls were high and dark.

> Plumkin hates all *women*.
> Plumkin is a *woman* hater.

> Mr. Smith owns many *cattle*.
> Mr. Smith owns a *cattle* ranch.

> The *apples* were red and ripe.
> The *apple* tree was all in bloom.

In the following sentences, a word is used first as an adjective and second as a noun.

> He told me the *bad* news.
> He always remembers the *bad* about people.

> The *American* people are happy and prosperous.
> The *Americans* are happy and prosperous.

> This man has many *selfish* habits.
> We will have to class him among the *selfish*.

> The *savage* dog was tied with a heavy chain.
> The *savages* attacked the settlers.

> The *insane* man was sent to a hospital.
> He was sent to a hospital for the *insane*.

In the following pairs of sentences, a word is used first as a noun and second as a verb.

> His *elbow* was aching from the blow.
> He *elbowed* his way through the crowd.

> Water poured rapidly through the *sluice*.
> The great crowd *sluiced* its way through the gates.

> Cyrano was sensitive about his great *nose*.
> The detective *nosed* his way about the house.

The *man* joined the crew of the merchant ship.
The crew *manned* the ship and sailed out of the harbor.

The woman covered her floors with *carpet*.
She *carpeted* her floors from wall to wall.

In the following pairs of sentences, a word is used first as a structure word and second as a noun.

Nobody is as foolish as that.
Mary married a *nobody*.

Everything in the room was mixed up.
She is his *everything*.

The man ran *out* the door.
Jim managed to get the third *out* to retire the side.

The children were running *up* and *down* the stairs.
Life is filled with *ups* and *downs*.

Yes, I will be glad to attend the meeting.
I hope you can give me a *yes* for an answer.

In the following pairs of sentences, a word is used first as an adverb and second as a modifier of a noun.

The road turns *north* two miles from here.
The road *north* leads to Smithtown.

John did not look *backward* when he left.
A look *backward* will let you know who is following.

The army moved *forward* two miles.
The advance *forward* was slow.

The group will meet *tonight* in the lecture room.
The meeting *tonight* will be in the lecture room.

Alfred is planning to go *abroad* next summer.
A trip *abroad* will do him good.

In the following pairs of sentences, a word is used first as a verb and second as a noun.

The students will *dance* in the gymnasium.
The *dance* will be held in the gymnasium.

I hope to *break* the good news tomorrow.
A coffee *break* is excellent relaxation.

John can *run* a mile in five minutes.
Our team made a *run* in the first inning.

The captain *shouted* a warning to us.
We heard the *shout*, but it was too late.

The two men will *fight* tomorrow night.
We expect the *fight* to be a good one.

In the following pairs of sentences, a word is used first as a verb and second as an adjective.

Mother hung the clothes on the line to *dry*.
The *dry* clothes were folded and put away.

Agnes *wet* her feet coming home from school.
Agnes had *wet* feet when she came home from school.

John will *clean* his hands before dinner.
John will have *clean* hands before eating.

She will *thin* the cream with a little milk.
This cream is too *thin* to whip.

He *busied* himself writing letters to his friends.
He was a *busy* man today.

In the illustrations above, we have seen a word used in two different functions: adjective-noun, noun-verb, adjective-verb, etc. In some instances the word is inflected according to its function in the sentence. The following illustrations show how the same word may be used in three different functions.

A word is used as a verb, a noun, and a modifier of a noun.

Mr. Jones *fished* all day long.
Mrs. Jones fried the *fish* in butter.
The *fish* market has been closed.

A word is used as an adjective, an adverb, and a noun.

He fell into a *dead* sleep.
The car stopped *dead* in the middle of the road.
His speech honored the nation's *dead*.

A word is used as an adverb, a verb, and a noun.

> The car turned *right* at the end of the drive.
> The crew *righted* the engine which had been derailed.
> He followed traffic and kept to the *right*.

A word is used as an adverb, an adjective, and a verb.

> The hungry child looked *long* at the steaming food.
> The south road is *longer* than the north road.
> He *longed* for his mother's cooking.

In the following sentences, a word is used in four different functions: noun, verb, adjective, and adverb.

> Our country *home* is in the mountains.
> The pigeons *homed* swiftly across the plain.
> He is very fond of *home* cooking.
> The old man came *home* to rest.

A few words in our language may be used in more than four different functions. In the following sentences, a word is used as a structure word (a connective), an adverb, an adjective, a noun, and a verb.

> Jerry ran *down* the street.
> Jerry jumped *down* and ran away.
> Jim appears discouraged and *down*.
> Life is filled with ups and *downs*.
> The fighter *downed* his opponent in four rounds.

That functional shift gives flexibility to our language we may easily see by examining each function within the sentence and observing the many word forms which may be used.

1. Subject of a sentence

> The *people* love their country.
> The *young* love their country.
> *They* love their country.
> The *dance* was enjoyed by everybody.
> *Now* gives us the opportunity.
> *Everyone* is enjoying himself.
> *Traveling* is an education in itself.

The subject of a sentence is a function normally filled by a noun, but it may be filled by a word substituted for a noun. (We have seen in Chapter 4 that word groups may also be substituted for a noun subject.) In the above sentences, words which are usually classified by form as nouns, adjectives, pronouns, adverbs, and verbs are used in the subject function.

2. The predicate — the verb

> Mr. Smith *educated* his family very thoroughly.
>
> The fire will *smoke* for days.
>
> They *calendared* the event in July.
>
> The wet coat will *dry* in the sun.
>
> The ship will *near* the iceberg in another hour.
>
> They have *upped* the price of kerosene.

The main word in the predicate is the verb. Any word which may be used as a verb can be inflected like a verb. In the above sentences, words which are usually classified by form as verbs, nouns, adjectives, adverbs, and connectives are used in the verb function.

3. The predicate — the complement

> The hint escaped my *attention*.
>
> She gave me a nasty *dig*.
>
> We promised *him* a party.
>
> The ministry is a *calling* which attracts unselfish men.
>
> The state gives the *aged* a pension.
>
> Life rewards the *ambitious* with success.
>
> He is coming, but I do not know *when*.

The complement is a function normally filled by a noun or by an adjective after a linking verb. In the above sentences, words which are usually classified by form as nouns, pronouns, verbs, adjectives, and connectives are used in the complement function.

4. Modifier of a noun

> Mr. Jones accepted the *attractive* offer.
>
> This is strictly a *business* deal.
>
> *Their* papers were written well.

A *smiling* man entered the room.

I am planning a trip *abroad*.

The fire caused a *near* panic.

We think of the modifier of a noun as an adjectival function. In the above sentences, words which are usually classified by form as adjectives, nouns, pronouns, verbs, adverbs, and connectives are used in the adjectival function.

5. Modifier of a verb.

The horses ran *swiftly* across the pasture.

The boys looked *long* at the newcomer.

He looked *up* as we came *in*.

The children came *running*.

The store will open *Sunday*.

We think of the modifier of a verb as an adverbial function. However, in the above sentences, words which are usually classified by form as adverbs, adjectives, connectives, verbs, and nouns are used in the adverbial function.

Other functions within the sentence include appositives, the object of a preposition, and connectives. Other form classes may be substituted for an appositive, which is normally a noun, and for an object of a preposition, which is normally a noun. What has been said in relation to complements is applicable to both these functions. For connectives, which are structure words, no substitution is possible. The list of connectives (pages 140–143) is limited and would well be memorized, since connectives have no formal characteristics.

Summary

Words are classifiable by form and by function. In many instances the formal characteristics of a word reinforce its function within the sentence. On the other hand, form and function sometimes conflict. From the standpoint of structure, the function of the word within the sentence — its position in the sentence with relation to other words — is the dominant element in communication. We respond to a word as a noun because it is the subject of a sentence or a complement or the object of a preposition or an appositive, not necessarily because it looks like a noun or usually functions as a noun. We respond to a verb because it is used as a verb, not necessarily because it looks like a verb, for a word may normally be used as a noun or an adjective or an adverb and still serve as a verb in a sentence.

Since English is a relatively uninflected language, that is, since most words are not changed in form according to their syntax, we find that words have variety of function within the sentence. Thus the same word may be used as a noun, as a verb, and as a modifier. This principle of changing function is called functional shift. It permits a flexibility of communication that is not possible in languages in which inflection is a necessary component of change of function.

Functional shift makes classification difficult and has thereby caused no end of controversy, confusion, and differences of opinion among students of grammar. For a word in English has no absolute classification as noun or verb or adjective or adverb. Its form does not determine its class or use, though may help to identify its function. The listener or reader responds to the word in the context of the sentence and does this adequately and appropriately when he recognizes its function. Classification of words, then, rests finally on use, on function within the pattern of the sentence.

Exercise A

Identify the function of each italicized word in the following passage. How does the form of the word help you to determine its function within the sentence? If the form of the word does not reinforce the identification of function, by what means are you able to determine the function? Do you find any words in which form and function conflict?

The *possessions* of Christopher Alexander Pellett were these: his name, which he was always *careful* to retain intact; a suit of ducks, no *longer* intact, in which he *lived* and *slept;* a *continuous* thirst for liquor, and a set of red whiskers. Also *he* had a friend. Now, no man can gain friendship, even among the gentle islands of Polynesia, except by virtue of some *quality* attaching to *him.* Strength, humor, villainy: he must show some trait by which the friend can *catch* and *hold.* How then, explain the *loving devotion* lavished upon Christopher Alexander Pellett by Keraki, the *company* boat *boy? This* was the mystery at Fufuti.

There was no harm in Pellett. He *never* quarreled. He never raised his fist. *Apparently* he had never learned that a white *man's* foot, though it wobble ever so much, is given him wherewith to kick natives out of the road. He never even *cursed* anyone except himself and the Chinese half-caste who sold him *brandy:* which was certainly *allowable* because the brandy was very *bad.*

On the other hand, there was no perceptible *good* in him. He had long lost the *will* to toil, and latterly the skill to beg. He did not *smile,* nor dance, nor exhibit any of the *amiable* eccentricities that sometimes recommend the *drunken* to a certain *toleration.* In any other part of the world he must have *passed* without a struggle. But some chance had *drifted him* to the beaches where life is as *easy* as a song and his particular fate had given *him* a friend. And so he persisted. That was all. He persisted, a sodden *lump* of flesh preserved in alcohol. . . .[1]

EXERCISE B

1. Use the word *game* in three separate sentences: (*a*) as a noun, (*b*) as a verb, (*c*) as an adjective.
2. Use the word *group* in three separate sentences: (*a*) as a noun, (*b*) as the modifier of a noun, (*c*) as a verb.
3. Use the word *equal* in three separate sentences: (*a*) as an adjective, (*b*) as a verb, (*c*) as a noun.
4. Use the word *milk* in three separate sentences: (*a*) as a noun, (*b*) as a noun modifier, (*c*) as a verb.
5. Use the word *past* in four separate sentences: (*a*) as an adjective, (*b*) as a noun, (*c*) as an adverb, (*d*) as a connective.
6. Use the word *lost* in three separate sentences: (*a*) as an adjective, (*b*) as a noun, (*c*) as a verb.
7. Use the word *round* in five separate sentences: (*a*) as an adjective, (*b*) as a noun, (*c*) as a connective, (*d*) as a verb, (*e*) as an adverb.
8. Use the word *alone* in two separate sentences: (*a*) as an adverb, (*b*) as an adjective.
9. Use the word *back* in four separate sentences: (*a*) as a noun, (*b*) as a verb, (*c*) as an adjective, (*d*) as an adverb.
10. Use the word *short* in four separate sentences: (*a*) as an adjective, (*b*) as an adverb, (*c*) as a noun, (*d*) as a verb.

[1] John Russell, "The Price of the Head."

11. Use the word *free* in four separate sentences: (*a*) as an adjective, (*b*) as an adverb, (*c*) as a verb, (*d*) as a noun.

12. Use the word *laughing* in four separate sentences: (*a*) as an adjective, (*b*) as a noun, (*c*) as a verb, (*d*) as an adverb.

EXERCISE C

Fill in the blanks according to directions. Write separate sentences for each substitution.

1. The _____ at Kelsey's Ranch is very enjoyable.
   (*a*) a noun
   (*b*) a verb form

2. She is the _____ speller in the whole school.
   (*a*) an adjective
   (*b*) a noun adjunct

3. I gave _____ to Mr. Cooper.
   (*a*) a structure word
   (*b*) a noun

4. Mr. Calhoun will _____ the horse for the race.
   (*a*) a verb
   (*b*) a word with a noun suffix
   (*c*) a word that may be inflected as an adjective

5. We gave Fred the _____.
   (*a*) a noun
   (*b*) an adjective
   (*c*) a word that may be inflected as a verb.

6. _____ is a thrilling experience.
   (*a*) a verb form
   (*b*) a word with a noun suffix

7. The new building will be painted _____.
   (*a*) an adverb
   (*b*) an adjective
   (*c*) a noun

8. Mary is always reading _____ stories.
   (*a*) a noun adjunct
   (*b*) a verb form
   (*c*) a structure word
   (*d*) a possessive noun
   (*e*) an adjective with a characteristic suffix

9. The man looked _____ as we walked in.
   (*a*) an adverb
   (*b*) an adjective
   (*c*) a word sometimes used as a connective

10. The government gives the _____ a pension.
   (*a*) a noun inflected for plural number
   (*b*) a word with an adjective suffix
   (*c*) a verb form

12

Verbals

VERBALS ARE the bad boys of grammar. From the standpoint of form they are verbs: infinitives, present participles, and past participles. From the standpoint of meaning they are verbs. They may have subjects, complements, and adverbial modifiers just as verbs do. But from the standpoint of function they serve as subject, complement, or modifier. They are the delight of the expert writer, but the sorrow of the student of grammar who is often confused by their versatility.

In the study of functional shift, we have seen that many words may be used in a variety of functions. The same word, for example, may be used as an adjectival modifier or as a verb.

> The dishes are *dry*.
>
> Mary will *dry* the dishes.

In the first sentence, *dry* is a predicate adjective; in the second, a verb. In this illustration it may be observed that when *dry* is an adjective it will be inflected like an adjective; when *dry* is a verb it will be inflected like a verb.

> The dishes are *driest* when rinsed with hot water.
>
> Mary has *dried* the dishes.

Verbals are verb forms whose function has shifted. But unlike other more compliant words, they still wish to retain some of their original privileges, and they do. Even though they may be subjects, or complements, or modifiers, they may still have subjects, complements and adverbial modifiers themselves. Besides, they are always inflected as verbs. In other words, verbals, unlike other words whose function has shifted, have a double function. They have the adopted function (subject, complement, or modifier) and also some of the verb function.

The Infinitive

In terms of form, there are three kinds of verbals: the infinitive (the plain form of the verb preceded by *to*), the *-ing* form (corresponding to the present participle of the verb), and the form corresponding to the past participle of the verb (usually the *-ed* or *-en* form and so characterized in this chapter). Examples of the infinitive are given below.

to see	to be seen
to drive	to be driven
to make	to be made
to grow	to be grown

The forms in the right-hand column, variants of the simple infinitive form, are sometimes called the passive of the infinitive.

> I want *to see* his new car.
>
> He wishes *to be seen* in his new car.

The infinitive may be used in a variety of functions in the sentence. Let us look at it first as the subject of a sentence.

> *To sing* is a great delight.
>
> *To go* would be a pleasure.
>
> *To listen* is not always pleasant.
>
> *To look* would make me ill.
>
> *To be praised* would embarrass me.

In each of the above sentences, the infinitive has a noun function in that it is the subject. However, the infinitive may have adverbial modifiers and also in many cases may take a complement.

> *To sing happily* is a great delight.
> *To sing in the morning* is a great delight.
> *To sing when the sun shines* is a great delight.
> *To sing ballads* is a great delight.

In these sentences, the subject is no longer the infinitive alone, but is the word group composed of the infinitive and its modifiers, or of the infinitive and its complement with modifiers, if any. We call such a word group an infinitive phrase. One may substitute a long infinitive phrase for a noun as the subject of a sentence.

> A *song* is a great delight.
> *To sing ballads happily in the morning when the sun shines* is a great delight.

An infinitive may be used as a complement.

> The lady wishes *to sing*.
> The child wants *to play*.
> Men desire *to succeed*.
> The team hopes *to win*.
> Smith is asking *to be elected*.

Each of the infinitives in the above sentences is used as a complement, a direct object. However, each may have adverbial modifiers and possibly a complement of its own.

> The team hopes *to win easily*.
> The team hopes *to win in the tournament*.
> The team hopes *to win when it meets Smithtown*.
> The team hopes *to win the basketball game*.

In these sentences, the direct object is now the infinitive phrase, which is italicized. Illustrated below is an infinitive phrase substituted for a noun as the direct object of a verb. In other words, the infinitive phrase performs the noun function.

> The team wants a *victory*.
> The team wants *to win in the tournament when it meets Smithtown*.

An infinitive may be used as the modifier of a verb.

> He has come *to sing.*
> He has gone *to explore.*
> He always plays *to win.*
> He is struggling *to succeed.*
> The sick woman is fighting *to live.*

Each of the infinitives above performs the function of an adverbial modifier, yet each retains some of its verbal function in its ability to take adverbial modifiers or even a complement.

> He has gone *to explore the North.*
> He has gone *to explore where there is no human life.*
> He is going *to explore soon.*
> He is going *to explore Patagonia.*

These sentences illustrate the use of an infinitive phrase as the modifier of a verb. The phrase consists of the verbal (the infinitive) with its complement and modifiers. The following example shows the infinitive phrase again used as a substitute word group, this time in place of a single adverbial modifier.

> Mary Brown worked *eagerly.*
> Mary Brown worked *to become ultimately an expert typist.*

An infinitive may be used as the modifier of a predicate adjective.

> Jim is eager *to go.*
> George is anxious *to work.*
> Mary is ready *to sing.*
> The party seems willing *to compromise.*
> Mr. Johnson appeared too worried *to eat.*

In each of the above sentences the infinitive modifies the predicate adjective, functioning as if it were an adverb. In this function, as in others, it still keeps its verbal characteristics. It may have adverbial modifiers and it may sometimes take a complement.

> The party seems willing *to compromise finally.*
> The party seems willing *to compromise at last.*
> The party seems willing *to compromise when the agreement is drawn up.*
> The party seems willing *to compromise the whole difficulty.*

In each example here, the infinitive phrase consists of the infinitive with its modifiers or complement. Since it modifies the predicate adjective, it is a modifier word group.

An infinitive may be used after a linking verb as a subjective complement.

> To see is *to believe.*
>
> Henry appears *to be improving.*
>
> Mother seems *to know.*
>
> John was *to go*, but he became ill.
>
> The hot weather seems *to be going.*

The infinitive in each of the above sentences is a complement after a linking verb, a predicate complement or a subjective complement. It may have adverbial modifiers or possibly a complement of its own.

> Mother seems *to know already.*
>
> Mother seems *to know about Jack's accident.*
>
> Mother seems *to know since she has already told Father.*
>
> Mother seems *to know the whole story.*

The italicized word groups in the above sentences are infinitive phrases, each being the complement of a linking verb. Actually the infinitive phrase so used is a substitute word group, as may be demonstrated by the following:

> Donald seems *studious.*
>
> Donald seems *to know the facts about economics.*

The infinitive is unique in its function as the verb part of an infinitive phrase which has a subject.

> I want *him to know the whole story.*

The italicized word group is an infinitive-phrase object of the verb *want.* Actually the phrase is a subject-predicate word group, but the verb is not a finite verb (as it is in a sentence or a clause). The verb function is taken by the infinitive. So here we have an infinitive usurping still another function of the verb, taking a subject and actually performing as the verb in a subject-predicate word group. When the subject of the infinitive is a pronoun, it is in the objective form. Other examples of this structure follow.

Finnegan asked *me to show him the property.*

I told *the boys to move quietly from the building.*

The Smiths invited *us to come to their house for Christmas.*

The captain ordered *the regiment to advance when the barrage moved forward.*

The officer has the responsibility to order *his men to advance when it is necessary.*

In the last sentence, the infinitive phrase is object of another infinitive, *to order.* In some constructions the infinitive phrase having a subject may be object of the preposition *for.*

I think it is very foolish for *you to go on this long trip.*

For *him to complete the job* would take three months.

I made an appointment for *Mary to see the dentist.*

Sometimes in the subject construction the *to* of the infinitive is omitted.

Helen saw *Plumkin eat her ice cream cone.*

Sister made *the baby cry.*

He let *me rent his house for two months.*

Freddy watched *his daddy wash the car.*

The Gerund

The second type of verbal, the *-ing* form, is called a gerund when used in any of the functions of a noun — subject, complement, appositive, object of a preposition. (When it is used as an adjective, it is called a participle.)

The gerund may be used as the subject of a sentence.

Traveling is always a great pleasure.

Stealing is dishonest.

Walking is a very healthful exercise.

Putting is a difficult skill.

Rowing strengthens the arm muscles.

Each of the verbals in the above sentences functions as the subject and is called a gerund since the subject function is a noun function. The gerund still retains some of its verbal characteristics. It may have adverbial modifiers, or it may take a complement.

Rowing rapidly strengthens the arm muscles.

Rowing in rough water strengthens the arm muscles.

Rowing when the water is rough strengthens the arm muscles.

Rowing a heavy barge strengthens the arm muscles.

In each of the above sentences the gerund with its modifiers or complement is called a gerund phrase. It is a word group which can substitute for a noun as the subject of a sentence:

Golf is a very healthful exercise.

Playing golf in the fresh air when the sun is shining is a very healthful exercise.

The gerund may be used as a complement, as the direct object of a verb.

Mabel dislikes *writing.*

The dress needs *mending.*

The job requires *traveling.*

Jimmy loves *swimming.*

Kathy adores *dancing.*

In the above sentences, the verbal is the direct object of the verb and is called a gerund since it functions like a noun. Again, each gerund retains some of the characteristics of a verb: it may have adverbial modifiers or may take an object.

Mary dislikes *writing rapidly.*

Mary dislikes *writing to her boy friends.*

Mary dislikes *writing when the weather is hot.*

Mary dislikes *writing grocery lists.*

These sentences illustrate the gerund with its modifiers or complement, the gerund phrase, used as the direct object of the verb. It may be thought of as a substitute word group for a noun in this function:

Jim likes a *swim.*

Jim likes *swimming in the cool ocean when the weather is hot in the summertime.*

The gerund may be used as the complement after a linking verb.

Freddy's chief fault was *bragging*.

My favorite pastime is *bowling*.

Mary's best subject is *reading*.

Her only interest is *dancing*.

Helen's duty was *baby-sitting*.

In each of the above sentences, the verbal is used as a noun in the predicate complement function. It may have adverbial modifiers and sometimes a complement.

Her only interest is *dancing continually*.

Her only interest is *dancing in contests*.

Her only interest is *dancing where she can display her great ability*.

Her only interest is *dancing the tango*.

Each of the above italicized word groups is a gerund phrase used as the predicate complement of a form of the verb *to be*.

The gerund may be used as the object of a preposition, as illustrated in the following sentences.

Harold is tired of *playing*.

Joe Smith was arrested for *speeding*.

There is always time for *reading*.

This news came too late for *printing*.

The latest in *styling* is a high neck with a low waistline.

Since a verbal so used fulfills a noun function, it is a gerund. It retains some of the verb functions, and may have adverbial modifiers and possibly a complement.

Harold is tired of *playing so strenuously*.

Harold is tired of *playing in the park*.

Harold is tired of *playing when lunchtime comes*.

Harold is tired of *playing games*.

Each of the italicized word groups in the above sentences is a gerund phrase used as the object of a preposition. It may be thought of as a word group substituting for a noun:

There is plenty of time for *recreation*.

There is plenty of time for *playing baseball when the warm weather comes*.

The gerund may be used as an appositive.

> His offense, *stealing*, was punishable with imprisonment.
> Her ambition, *acting*, was never realized.
> That was his worst habit, *drinking*.
> Mother gave Father a job, *dishwashing*.

Each of the verbals above is in apposition with a noun. Since this is a noun function, the verbal is a gerund. It may have adverbial modifiers or even take a complement:

> His offense, *stealing from department stores*, was punishable with imprisonment.
> His offense, *stealing automobiles*, was punishable with imprisonment.

The gerund may have a verb function in a word group by having a subject. The word group will be a verbal phrase.

> We saw *him coming down the road.*
> Father caught *Jimmy smoking a big cigar.*
> Mother doesn't want *Agnes working in the delicatessen store.*
> The teacher doesn't want *anybody coming in after the bell rings.*
> The fighter sent *him spinning through the ropes.*

In each of the above sentences, the noun (or noun substitute) and the verbal in the italicized word group have a subject-predicate relationship. In this way the verbal, although not a finite verb (being an *-ing* form without an auxiliary verb), takes on a true verb function. The word group functions like a noun in each sentence and therefore may be called a gerund phrase.

The Participle

When the *-ing* form of a verb is used as the modifier of a noun in the adjective function, it is called a participle. It may occupy a position before the noun it modifies, or it may immediately follow the noun.

> The *barking* dog keeps me awake at night.
> The *blinking* owl peers into the darkness.
> *Blinking*, the owl peers into the darkness.
> *Listening*, we heard the soft patter of steps.

> The old man, *sleeping*, did not hear his son enter the room.
>
> Shepherds, *watching*, saw the bright star in the heavens.

Each of the italicized words in the above sentences is a verbal which modifies a noun or a noun substitute. As such it performs the function of an adjective and is called a participle, in contrast to the verbal used in a noun function, which, as we have seen, is called a gerund.

A verbal used to modify a noun (a participle) may have adverbial modifiers or possibly a complement. Participles, like gerunds, retain their verb prerogatives. Participles with adverbial modifiers usually either introduce the sentence or follow the noun they modify, though they may come at the end of the sentence.

> The dog, *barking noisily*, keeps me awake.
>
> The dog, *barking at the neighbors*, keeps me awake.
>
> The dog, *barking when it gets cold at night*, keeps me awake.
>
> The dog, *chewing a hard bone*, keeps me awake.
>
> *Humming a beautiful melody which expresses the joy in her heart*, Pippa walks through the town.
>
> Pippa walks through the town *humming a beautiful melody which expresses the joy in her heart*.
>
> Pippa, *humming a beautiful melody which expresses the joy in her heart*, walks through the town.

Each of the italicized word groups above is a participial phrase. A participial phrase is made up of a participle with modifiers and complement, if there is a complement. The participial phrase in each of the above sentences modifies a noun or a noun substitute. The last three sentences illustrate the three positions which the participial phrase may have within the sentence.

The participle, and hence the participial phrase, may modify a noun in any of its functions.

> I like tomatoes *growing on the vine*.
>
> He told us about men *fighting for their lives*.
>
> Mr. Brown is a man *working hard to become successful*.
>
> The manager, a man *completing his twenty-fifth year with the company*, will be given a testimonial dinner on Friday night.

A participle may be used as a predicate adjective after a linking verb.

Her costume was *striking*.

His attentions became *annoying*.

Sally's manners are *becoming*.

Clara always manages to be very *entertaining*.

Something in your plan seems *lacking*.

Each of these verbals is a participle used as a predicate after a linking verb. Here, this is an adjectival function. (It may also be a noun function, as we have seen.)

The participle used in the predicate function as above may have adverbial modifiers, but may not take a complement.

His attentions became *very annoying*.

His attentions became *annoying to me*.

His attentions became *annoying whenever he came to dinner*.

The question now arises: What is the difference between a verb phrase having as its main verb an -*ing* form of the verb with some form of *to be* as an auxiliary, and a participle used as a complement after some form of the verb *to be?*

Her costume is *striking*.

The bell is *striking*.

Usually, as in the above sentences, the context of meaning supplies the clue to the contrast between verbal and verb. In the first sentence, *striking* is a participle, a verbal. In the second, *striking* is part of the verb phrase. An objective test of the adjective or participle is to insert *very* before the verb form.

Her costume is *very striking*.

In this sentence the word *very* is compatible with *striking*. But if *very* were inserted in the second sentence we would obtain an incongruous effect:

The bell is *very striking*.

Sometimes a structure word or a complement supplies the signal for the determination of verb or verbal.

Mrs. Smith was *very entertaining* last night.

Mrs. Smith was *entertaining her friends* last night.

In the first sentence we know that *entertaining* is used in the adjective function because of the modifier *very*. Therefore it is a *verbal*, a participle. In the second sentence, the complement *friends* is the signal that *was entertaining* is a verb phrase and that *entertaining* is part of the verb and not a verbal.

A participle may be used as an objective complement.

> Mary found the book *interesting*.
> The crowd considered the game *exciting*.
> The critics believed the play *convincing*.
> The girls thought Plumkin *boring*.

The contrast between this function and the modifying function of the participle may be seen by studying the two sentences which follow.

> Mary found the book *interesting*.
> Mary found the *interesting* book.

When the participle is in the function of an objective complement, it may have adverbial modifiers, but cannot itself take a complement.

> Mary found the book *interesting in the last chapter*.
> Mary found the book *interesting where she least expected*.
> Mary found the book *extremely interesting*.

Each of the word groups italicized in the above sentences is a participial phrase used as an objective complement.

One of the rare adverbial uses of the *-ing* form of the verb may be illustrated in the following sentences.

> The woman left *crying bitterly*.
> The girls ran *laughing at their funny costumes*.
> The boys came *running to their mother*.

These verbal phrases have an adverbial function both structurally and semantically. For example, we may substitute the verbal phrase for the adverb *thus:*

> The boys came *thus*.
> The boys came *running to their mother*.

Furthermore, the position of the verbal phrase following the verb gives it a strong adverbial relationship, and if the verbal phrase is shifted to a position before or after the noun subject, the original meaning is distorted.

Finally, the *-ing* form of a verb may be used as the modifier of an adjective.

> The *dripping* wet leaves brushed against his face.
>
> The weather tonight is *freezing* cold.
>
> The water is *boiling* hot.
>
> Father looks *fighting* mad over there.

The third kind of verbal, from the standpoint of form, is the *-ed* or *-en* form (or the form corresponding to the past participle of a verb). Since this form is always used in an adjectival function as a verbal, it is considered a participle when so used.

> The *frightened* deer ran into the clearing.
>
> The *boiled* lobster was delicious.
>
> The *frozen* strawberries were served for dessert.
>
> The *melted* snow helped to flood the river.

The noun modifiers italicized in the above sentences are verbals with an adjectival function and are therefore participles. They may have adverbial modifiers, but may not take a complement.

> The snow, *melted by the rains*, helped to flood the river.
>
> The snow, *melted gradually when the sun came out*, soaked into the ground.

Each of the participial phrases italicized above modifies the noun it follows. The participial phrase may, however, precede the noun it modifies.

> *Driven by the wind*, the dust spread over the city.
>
> *Excited by the fierce dogs*, the horses ran wildly across the field.

The *-ed* or *-en* participle may be used with the auxiliaries *having*, *being*, or *having been*.

> The jury, *having convicted* the prisoner, was discharged.
>
> The prisoner, *having been convicted* by the jury, was sent to the penitentiary.
>
> The horses *being driven* into the corral will be sold tomorrow.

In the first of these sentences, the participle is an active verb form, whereas in the second and third sentences it is a passive verb form. In all the sentences, the participial phrase is a word group modifying the noun it follows.

The *-ed* or *-en* participle may be used as a predicate adjective.

> Dorothy is *tired.*
> Jim looks *annoyed.*
> Mother seems *worried.*
> Father appears *excited.*
> I believe you are *mistaken.*

The italicized verbals in the above sentences fulfill an adjectival function, the predicate function, and therefore are participles. They may take adverbial modifiers but not complements.

> Father appears *very excited.*
> Father appears *excited tonight.*
> Father appears *excited at the good news.*
> Father appears *excited whenever he reads a detective story.*

These italicized word groups are participial phrases used in the predicate complement function.

The *-ed* or *-en* participle may be used in the objective complement function.

> We found Timkins *shaken by the news.*
> I was happy to see her *relieved of much of the work.*
> They did their best to get me *fired from the job.*
> We want the job *completed by January.*

The italicized word groups above are participial phrases used in the objective complement function. The contrast between a participial modifier and a participle used as an objective complement may be seen in the following pairs of sentences.

> He had my coat *mended.*
> He had my *mended* coat.
>
> My father had the car *inspected.*
> My father had the *inspected* car.

Summary

Verbals are verb forms whose function has shifted. Unlike other word classes whose functions may shift, verbals not only adopt the new function but retain some of the old. A verbal may be used like a noun in the subject function, but still behave like a verb in taking adverbial modifiers or even a complement.

There are three kinds of verbals from the standpoint of form: the infinitive form, which is the plain form of the verb preceded by the preposition to; the *-ing* form of the verb, which by dictionary designation is the present participle; and the *-ed* or *-en* form of the verb, which by dictionary designation is the past participle.

Functionally, an infinitive may have a variety of uses. Serving as a noun, it may be the subject of a sentence, the direct object of a verb, or an appositive. It may serve as a modifier of a verb, of a noun, or of an adjective. It may follow a linking verb as a predicate complement. An infinitive may even be a non-finite verb in a subject-predicate word group used as an infinitive phrase. The classification of the verbal which we call an *infinitive* is based on its form and not on its function.

The *-ing* verbal also has a number of functions in a sentence. It may be used like a noun as the subject of a sentence, as the object of a verb, as a predicate complement, as the object of a preposition, or as an appositive. In all of the noun functions, the *-ing* verbal is called a gerund. This classification is based on function.

When the *-ing* verbal is used as an adjective it is called a participle. This too is a functional classification. The participle may modify a noun in any of its functions. It may serve as a predicate adjective after a linking verb, or even as an objective complement.

The *-ing* verbal may sometimes function as an adverb, either as a modifier following a verb or as the modifier of an adjective.

In the *-ed* or *-en* forms, the verbal is used adjectivally, as the modifier of a noun, as a predicate adjective, or as an objective complement. The *-ed* and *-en* verbals are therefore classified as participles.

Since a verbal may have adverbial modifiers or even take a subject or a complement at times, it may serve to build up a word group, which takes on the original function of the verbal, as subject, complement, or modifier. The word group is called an infinitive phrase, a gerund phrase, or a participial phrase according to its form and function. If formed with an infinitive, it is called an infinitive phrase, no matter what its function may be. If formed with an -*ing* verbal, it will be a gerund phrase if used as a noun, a participial phrase if used as an adjective. If the word group is formed with an -*ed* or -*en* verbal, it will function only adjectivally and will therefore be a participial phrase.

Exercise A

1. Identify the function of each infinitive.
   (a) Donny doesn't want to come.
   (b) To speak is often difficult.
   (c) It is difficult to write.
   (d) She has the will to live.
   (e) We are ready to go.
   (f) They asked him to leave.
   (g) The man to watch is Johnson.
   (h) It is too late to read.
   (i) You have no right to order him to go.
   (j) You are driving too fast to look.

2. Identify the function of each -*ing* verbal.
   (a) Singing is good recreation.
   (b) His hobby is reading.
   (c) She talked of leaving.
   (d) This composition needs revising.
   (e) She doesn't want anybody looking.
   (f) The water is freezing cold.
   (g) Walking is healthful exercise.
   (h) His great art, composing, will bring him fame.
   (i) Father saw him coming down the road.
   (j) Johnny has gone swimming.
   (k) The burning forest lighted up the sky.
   (l) The meal was satisfying.
   (m) The people, entering, could not see in the dark.
   (n) He believed his position rewarding.
   (o) The play was thought exciting.

3. Identify the function of each *-ed* or *-en* verbal.
   (*a*) The beaten fighter fell to the canvas.
   (*b*) The people were shocked at the brutality.
   (*c*) The old man, saddened and dejected, gave in to his grief.
   (*d*) He found his father discouraged.
   (*e*) Her nerves seemed shaken.
   (*f*) We saw the man injured.
   (*g*) Encouraged and satisfied, the man began the difficult task.

Exercise B

Identify and describe the function of each of the verbals and verbal phrases.

1. The actors are ready to go on stage.
2. We have seen her dancing at the Palace.
3. Acting on the advice of the lawyer, Mr. Brown withdrew his suit.
4. Our house needs painting and many repairs.
5. He granted her desire to look once more at the valuable stone.
6. Charlie seemed hurt when I told him he was fired.
7. To see this property yourself will help to convince you.
8. Without looking back at his guards, the prisoner ran to escape through the open gate.
9. It is just wonderful to have you here.
10. The captain was told to have his men ready at dawn.
11. The general ordered the regiment to advance to the river.
12. Fatigued and disgusted, Plumkin climbed down from the flagpole.
13. The boys, swimming across the lake, had to fight a strong headwind.
14. We went there after the theater to eat lobsters and drink Martinis.
15. The financial difficulty is depressing to Simpson.
16. Thompson went fishing in Lake George.
17. We found the woman stunned by the collision.
18. They caught the boy stealing money from the cash drawer.
19. I do not approve of young people going to places like this.
20. There is a time to laugh and there is a time to cry.
21. The order was to demolish the bridge as soon as we could.
22. I wrote down my occupation, farming.

23. Mrs. Washburn wanted to be seen in her new car.

24. Jimmy seems to be improving in his composition work.

25. He walked around the floors feeling lost and out of place.

26. Sally dislikes walking to school every morning.

27. Jim's main interest was wrestling.

28. The old folks are contented in their new home.

29. George's clothes were dripping wet when he stopped in to tell us the good news.

30. There will be no fooling about this matter; I intend to win the case.

Exercise C

1. Write a sentence with an infinitive phrase used as the object of a verb.

2. Write a sentence with a gerund phrase used as the subject of a sentence.

3. Write a sentence with a gerund phrase used as the object of a preposition.

4. Write two sentences with participial phrases modifying the subject. Use an *-ing* verbal in one sentence and an *-ed* verbal in the other.

5. Write two sentences using infinitive phrases as modifiers of an adjective.

6. Write a sentence with a gerund phrase used as the object of a verb.

7. Write a sentence with a gerund phrase used as the predicate complement of a linking verb.

8. Write a sentence with an infinitive phrase having a subject.

9. Write a sentence with an infinitive phrase used as an appositive.

10. Write a sentence with a participial phrase used as an objective complement.

11. Write a sentence with an infinitive phrase used as the subject of the sentence.

12. Write a sentence with a participial phrase modifying the direct object.

13. Write a sentence with an infinitive phrase modifying the verb.

14. Write a sentence with a verbal phrase in which an *-ing* form takes a subject.

15. Write a sentence with a gerund phrase used as an appositive.

16. Write a sentence with a participial phrase used as a predicate complement.

Exercise D

1. In the following sentence, change one of the subject-predicate word groups to a verbal phrase:

    The men heard the whistle blow and they went to work.

2. In the following sentence, change the subordinate clause to an infinitive phrase:

    The chief decided that he would blow up the dam.

3. Rewrite the following sentence, changing the subordinate clause to a gerund phrase object of a preposition:

    Cassidy thought that he would go to Europe to visit Paris.

4. Reconstruct the following sentence, using two gerunds.

    I believe what I can see.

5. Rewrite the following sentence so that it will have an infinitive phrase modifying the verb:

    Mr. Johnson went to New York so that he would have the opportunity of visiting his Aunt Mamie.

6. Change the following sentence so that it will be written with a participial phrase used as a predicate complement:

    George annoyed me with his hostile attitude.

7. Rewrite the following sentence, using an infinitive with a subject and making the whole construction the object of the verb:

    Mr. Jones asked me if I might go with him to Boston.

8. Revise the following sentence so that it will have a gerund phrase as the direct object of the verb:

    The children enjoyed it when they could play in the garden.

9. Change the subordinate clause in the following sentence to a participial phrase:

    We watched the old man as he walked down the road.

10. Rewrite the following sentence with an infinitive phrase used as an appositive:

    When one has lots of money, he may enjoy himself.

11. Revise the following sentence, using an infinitive phrase to modify a predicate adjective:

    Brown and Smith are always anxious that their customers will be satisfied.

12. Rewrite the following sentence, using a participial phrase and an
    infinitive phrase:

> When the students heard about the results of the election,
> they decided that they would celebrate the great event.

EXERCISE E

*In the following selection, the author has used no verbals.
Revise the passage using verbals wherever you think it is possible without damaging the meaning. Discuss the effect which
your revision has on the original style and its impact on the
reader.*

Imagine, if you can, a small room, hexagonal in shape, like the cell of
a bee. It is lighted neither by window nor by lamp, yet it is filled with a
soft radiance. There are no apertures for ventilation, yet the air is fresh.
There are no musical instruments, and yet, at the moment that my
meditation opens, this room is throbbing with melodious sounds. An
arm-chair is in the center, by its side a reading-desk — that is all the
furniture. And in the arm-chair there sits a swaddled lump of flesh — a
woman, about five feet high, with a face as white as a fungus. It is to her
that the little room belongs.

An electric bell rang.

The woman touched a switch and the music was silent.

"I suppose I must see who it is," she thought, and set her chair in
motion. The chair, like the music, was worked by machinery, and it
rolled her to the other side of the room, where the bell still rang im-
portunately.

"Who is it?" she called. Her voice was irritable, for she had been inter-
rupted often since the music began. She knew several thousand people;
in certain directions human intercourse had advanced enormously.[1]

---

[1] E. M. Forster, "The Machine Stops"; from *The Eternal Moment and Other
Stories* by E. M. Forster, copyright, 1928, by Harcourt, Brace and Company,
Inc.; renewed, 1956, by E. M. Forster. Reprinted by permission of the
publishers.

Agreement

13

IN THIS TEXT, the word *agreement* will refer to the bound relationship of subject and verb in terms of number. In general, the singular and plural forms of the subject take or select different forms of the verb. We think of this selection or correspondence as concord or agreement.

The *bus leaves* at ten o'clock.
The *buses leave* at ten o'clock.

The *man is building* the house.
The *men are building* the house.

He was in the library.
They were in the library.

This belongs in the hall closet.
These belong in the hall closet.

Limitations of Agreement in English

If English were a highly inflected language like German or Latin, we could quickly describe the distinctions in verb forms for the three persons and the two numbers in all of the tenses. However, in our language we do not find a complete correspondence of form and function.

The *man finished* the house last week.

The *men finished* the house last week.

The *man will finish* the house next week.

The *men will finish* the house next week.

In the above pairs of sentences we may observe that the singular and plural forms of the subject do not select different forms of the verb. The first pair illustrates a singular and a plural subject used with a verb in the past tense. The second pair illustrates a singular and a plural subject used with a verb in future tense formed with the auxiliary *will*. We may say that there is no concord, no agreement between subject and verb.

The *man has finished* the house.

The *men have finished* the house.

The *man had finished* the house by last Monday.

The *men had finished* the house by last Monday.

The *man will have finished* the house by next week.

The *men will have finished* the house by next week.

Here we find agreement between subject and verb in the first pair of sentences. The tense of the verb in each is called the present perfect tense. In the second pair of sentences there is no agreement of subject and verb. The tense of the verb in each is called the past perfect tense. In the third pair of sentences there is no agreement of subject and verb. The tense of the verb in this pair is called the future perfect tense.

Let us examine concord or lack of concord in sentences which have verb auxiliary forms.

The *boy would like* to go.

The *boys would like* to go.

The *boy is going* with his father.

The *boys are going* with their fathers.

The *boy ought to go* to school.

The *boys ought to go* to school.

The *house does need* painting.
The *houses do need* painting.

The *girl was chosen* to lead the group.
The *girls were chosen* to lead the group.

The *child has been sleeping* all day.
The *children have been sleeping* all day.

Mother did go to church this morning.
Mother and Father did go to church this morning.

The *boy had been playing* ball all morning.
The *boys had been playing* ball all morning.

The *man may finish* the job this morning.
The *men may finish* the job this morning.

We may observe that certain forms of auxiliary verbs change in agreement with the subject. These are forms of *to be*, *have*, *do*, or any verb which may in itself be inflected. With auxiliary verbs such as *may*, *will*, *can*, *would*, *might*, etc., there is no agreement between subject and verb in relation to number. Agreement or concord between subject and verb for forms of *to be*, *have*, *do*, etc., is found only in the present form of the verb, except that in the case of the verb *to be* agreement occurs also in the past form. In general, agreement or concord between subject and verb exists in the present tense. The verb *to be*, of course, is the exception.

If the subject of a sentence is a pronoun instead of a noun, we may observe additional irregularities and complications in the matter of agreement.

I like sweet potatoes.
We like sweet potatoes.

You go to the library.   (sing.)
You go to the library.   (plu.)

He sings in the choir.
They sing in the choir.

In these sentences we may observe that agreement between subject and verb (in the present tense) occurs only when the third person of the pronoun is used. Otherwise there is no contrast between the singular and plural forms of the verbs.

Let us examine the past forms.

> *I liked* sweet potatoes.
> *We liked* sweet potatoes.
>
> *You went* to the library.   (sing.)
> *You went* to the library.   (plu.)
>
> *He sang* in the choir.
> *They sang* in the choir.

We may see from the above sentences that concord for number between subject and verb does not occur in the past tense when the subject is a pronoun. The verb *to be* is an exception: not only do we find agreement in the past forms, but also in the present form for the first person (as well as for the third person).

> *I am* happy in the new house.
> *We are* happy in the new house.
>
> *I was* present at the inauguration.
> *We were* present at the inauguration.
>
> *He was* in the living room.
> *They were* in the living room.

When the subject is a pronoun, there is agreement between subject and verb when the pronoun is in the third person and the verb is in the present tense. The exception is the verb *to be*. When forms of this verb are used, there is agreement for the first person present and also for the first and third person past tense, besides the normal agreement for the third person present. This may sound complicated, but we are so habituated to the use that we seldom, if ever, vary from it. It is only the verbal description which seems complicated. But such is our language when we set out to describe it.

Trouble Spots for the Writer

For the student of composition, the principle of agreement is complicated by various factors. The first is the one we have just discussed, namely, that agreement is not general and that even where agreement is found there are irregularities. Other complications stem from the fact that complex sentence structure or the nature or form of the subject may obscure the number of the subject, which determines the inflected form of the verb to which it is bound. In the discussion to follow, we shall point out some of the trouble spots for the writer and indicate, with illustrations, the conventional usage which constitutes standard written English.

At times a phrase or a clause intervenes between subject and verb. If this word group has a plural noun, the number of the noun in the word group may obscure the number of the subject and cause the student to respond to the wrong signal.

> *One* of the graduates *was appointed* to the committee.
>
> *Henry,* as well as his three sisters, *is going* to attend college.
>
> *Parsons,* together with his four friends, *is playing* poker.
>
> *Studying literature,* in addition to extracurricular activities, *is* part of the pleasure of college life.

In each of the above sentences, the subject is singular and the intervening word group contains a plural noun. The verb form is the singular in each sentence to agree with the subject.

When a sentence is inverted, with the verb coming before the subject, the student may misinterpret the word order and fail to fulfill the principle of agreement. All of the following sentences are inverted for one reason or another, and in each the subject agrees in number with the verb.

> There *are* three *boys* in the party.
>
> There *come* the *children.*
>
> Here *are* the *books* I promised you.
>
> Here *is* the *grapefruit* I picked.   (one)
>
> Here *are* the *grapefruit* I picked.   (more than one)
>
> Where *are* my *father* and *mother?*
>
> *Is* any *one* of the students *going* to the party?
>
> Throughout the lecture *are shown* interesting *views* of New England.

Compound subjects often give the writer trouble because no set rules can be established. When the compound subject is joined with *and,* the verb is usually in the plural form.

> *Mr. White and Miss Brown are coming* to the party.
>
> *Tennis and golf provide* good exercise.
>
> *Fishing and hunting are* excellent sports.

Sometimes, however, the sense of a compound subject with the connective *and* is singular, and the writer may use a singular verb.

> *Bacon and eggs* is a favorite American breakfast.
>
> *A trip to Bermuda and a thousand dollars was* the first prize in the beauty contest.
>
> The *satisfaction* and *enjoyment* of the work *was* ample reward for the effort.

We find this lack of agreement sometimes in an inverted sentence, especially one beginning with *there.*

> There *is wit and humor and satire and a touch* of irony throughout the play.

When a compound subject is joined by *or, nor, either . . . or, neither . . . nor,* the verb is usually in the singular form.

> *One or the other is not telling* the truth.
>
> *Either physics or chemistry satisfies* the science requirement.
>
> *Neither Brian nor Boski is* in condition to play football.

However, if one or both of the subjects are plural, the plural form of the verb is usually used.

> No *bloodshed or riots are expected* by the police.
>
> *Neither guns nor bayonets were given* the new replacements.
>
> *Either students or teachers are* welcome at the dress rehearsal.

When there is a compound subject with one element singular and one plural, and the singular element is nearer the verb, usage in agreement is divided.

> *Neither* the *players nor* the *manager were satisfied* with the team's showing.
>
> *Neither* the *players nor* the *manager was satisfied* with the team's showing.

Sometimes there is a plural meaning to a compound subject joined by *neither . . . nor,* even though the separate members of the compound are singular.

> *Neither difficulty nor tragedy nor adversity stop* the courageous Mr. Blythe.

When the compound subject using *neither . . . nor* consists of pronouns, the plural form of the verb is usually selected.

> *Neither Jane nor I take* sugar in our coffee.
>
> *Neither she nor I are going* to the meeting.

Words ending in *-ics* often give the writer trouble in deciding whether to select the singular or the plural form of the verb. Most of these words are now considered singular and take the singular form of the verb.

> Mathematics *is* a difficult subject.
>
> Physics *is* important to the atomic scientist.
>
> Economics *is* a study that is helpful to the business man.
>
> Civics *includes* the study of state and national government.

Sometimes words ending in *-ics* have a plural usage as well as a singular usage. When they do, they select a plural form of the verb.

> The general's tactics *were* blameless.
>
> Athletics *have been abolished* in Deer Valley High School.
>
> His ethics in the case *were* questionable.
>
> The acoustics in the auditorium *were* poor.

In each of the above sentences the subject is considered a plural form. As such it has a specific definition. The student when using words of this kind should consult a collegiate dictionary to determine whether he is using the word in the singular or in the plural sense.

Structure words which substitute for nouns sometimes cause difficulty in determining number and therefore in securing agreement of subject and verb. This group of words includes *anybody, everybody, somebody, anyone, someone, everyone, no one, nobody, each, neither, some, all, both, few, many, several*, etc.

In standard written English, *anybody, everybody, somebody, anyone, everyone, someone, nobody, each, neither,* and *no one* are considered singular and select a singular verb.

> *Someone is knocking* at the door.
>
> *Everybody loves* Groucho.
>
> *No one loves* Plumkin.
>
> *Each is* incorrect.
>
> *Neither is* the appropriate selection.

Words which are considered plural include *both, several, few,* and *many.*

> *Both* of the problems *are* hard to solve.
> *Several are going* to the convention.
> *Many are called* but *few are chosen.*

The words, *all, some,* and *none* may be used in the singular or plural according to their sense and select the verb form accordingly.

> *All* of the boys *are coming* home for Christmas.
> *All* of the hay *has been cut.*
>
> *Some* of the people *do* not *vote.*
> *Some* of the jelly *has fermented.*
>
> *None* of the men *are going* to work.
> *None* of the work *has been finished.*

Some words which are singular in meaning but plural in form select a plural form of the verb.

> His *trousers are* at the cleaner's.
> *Pliers have* many uses.
> Good *soapsuds make* the clothes clean.
> *Fireworks are* dangerous for children to use.

There are nouns which take a singular form of the verb although plural in meaning.

> The *United States is* a country of opportunity.
> The *news is* very satisfying.
> *Measles is* a child's disease.

Agreement in the Subordinate Clause

A final problem of agreement, for the consideration of the writer, is in the subordinate adjective clause. It will be remembered that an adjective clause is usually connected by some form of *who, which,* or *that.* These words are structure words, connectives, and are called relative pronouns. They perform two functions, that of connective and that of noun substitute. As the substitute for a noun, a relative pronoun may function as the subject of the clause which it connects. It may therefore be bound to the verb in the clause, and the principle of agreement will be operative. Under what conditions will these structure words select a singular verb and under what conditions will they select a plural?

The man *who lives* across the street teaches in the high school.

The word group *who lives across the street* is an adjective clause modifying the noun *man*. The connective is *who*. This word is also the subject of the subject-predicate word group *who lives across the street*. A relative pronoun is a substitute word for a noun — in this case *man*. If the noun is singular, the substitute word is singular in sense and therefore selects a singular form of the verb. Other examples of this selection follow.

I know the boy *who owns* that car.

Mrs. Smith owns a house *that has* ten rooms.

He wrote a novel *which is* widely read.

Each of the relative pronouns in the above sentences is substituted for a noun which is singular in number. Hence it takes a singular form of the verb.

When a relative pronoun is substituted for a noun in the plural number, it selects a plural form of the verb in the adjective clause.

The students *who were dismissed* early were allowed to go home.

In the above sentence, the relative pronoun *who* is a substitute word for the noun *students*, which is plural. The word *who* is subject of the word group *who were dismissed early*. Since *who* is substituted for a plural noun, it selects a plural verb. Other examples of the same kind follow.

They selected the girls *who are going to be sent* to the convention.

They adopted the recommendations *which were made* by the committee.

These are the houses *that were built* by the government.

Each of the relative pronouns in the above sentences is substituted for a noun which is plural in number. The pronoun, therefore, selects a plural form of the verb.

Some difficulty is encountered in sentences using the construction *one of those who*.

He is one of those boys *who are* always willing to help with a tough job.

The question that plagues the writer is whether the pronoun *who* substitutes for the singular *one* or the plural *boys*. It will make a difference in the selection of the verb in the adjective clause. As the sentence is written above, the pronoun substitutes for the plural *boys*, not for the singular *one*, which would take the singular verb form *is*. Standard written English requires, when this construction is used, that the relative pronoun select the plural form of the verb as in the above sentence.

The Subjunctive Mode

An irregularity in agreement occurs with certain sentence constructions in which the almost obsolete subjunctive mode still persists. Traditionally, mode (or mood) is the form of a verb used to indicate an attitude toward the content of the sentence: *indicative* to express statements or questions; *imperative* to express commands or requests; and *subjunctive* to express an action or state of being contrary to fact, a wish, a supposition, or a proposal introduced by a *that* clause. In modern usage, however, the subjunctive mode has tended to merge into or give way to the indicative, and has virtually disappeared as a change in verb form (except in the verb *to be* and in the omission of the *s* inflection in the third-person singular of other verbs). For practical purposes, the student of composition may think of these as idiomatic usages. The following are examples:

> If *I were* you, I would take the make-up examination.
> If *English were* a highly inflected language, we would find a high
>   degree of correspondence between form and function.
> I move that the *meeting be* adjourned.
> I suggest that *he telephone* ahead for a reservation.
> Standard English requires that the *verb agree* with the subject.

Summary

The grammatical principle of agreement is based on the bound relationship between the subject and verb in a subject-predicate word group. In English, the agreement of subject and verb is limited in scope, ordinarily to the present tense or to a verb phrase in which the first auxiliary is a present form of an inflected verb. When a form of the verb *to be* is used either as a verb or as an auxiliary in the first position, the principle of agreement is also operative in the past tense. When personal pronouns are the subject of a subject-predicate word group, agreement is confined to the third person pronoun, unless a form of *to be* is used as the verb or as an auxiliary, when agreement becomes operative for the first person as well. In written composition the student often experiences difficulty in securing agreement of subject and verb because of certain factors which may cloud his immediate awareness of the number of the subject. These factors include an intervening word group between subject and verb; sentence inversion; compound subjects; words ending in *-ics;* words which are plural in form but singular in meaning; and words which have a plural form and a plural meaning. Structure words used as substitutes for nouns, such as *somebody, everyone, all,* and *none,* sometimes pose a problem for the beginning writer who is trying to conform to the conventional patterns of agreement. Finally, there is the relative pronoun in an adjective clause, which selects the appropriate form of its verb, when it is the subject of the clause, according to the number of the noun for which it is substituted.

Exercise A

Select the subject and verb of each subject-predicate word group in the following passage and discuss their bound relationship as illustrated by their agreement in number.

The night was dark and the lights of the harbor were shining far away over the gleaming water. A small cluster of men was standing on the deck of the schooner which was anchored in the bay. There were bells ringing miles away in the suburbs of the city and strange sounds which blended with the music of the bells.

It was one of those nights which come only rarely in the summer. The breeze was gentle and the water was calm. A steamer and a tug pulling it were to be seen in the dim light not too far away. Neither the ship nor the tug was very real to the men on the deck of the schooner; they seemed like dark ghosts gliding through the still waters.

The men who were watching over the bow of the schooner suddenly moved away from the forward part of the boat and began to go below.

They were like shadows moving silently across the deck. A flock of gulls was screaming over a fishing boat which was moving quietly into the harbor not too distant from the schooner. The muffled sounds or the distant lights or the lapping waves were taking turns in ruling the night watch.

There was laughter now coming up from below. The men were drinking heavily. The crew together with some extra passengers was a rough group of men and now they seemed to be making a wild night of it.

Exercise B

In the following sentences, select the verb form which you feel is appropriate according to the principle of agreement.

1. The team (has, have) won fifteen games this season.
2. Mr. Smith, together with his five guests, (has, have) gone out to dinner.
3. What you believe about these matters (doesn't, don't) make a bit of difference.
4. Nora and the children (is, are) waiting for Daddy to come home.
5. There (was, were) a number of players waiting on the bench.
6. Henry and one of the other members (was, were) appointed to the student senate.
7. Plumkin is one of those fellows who (like, likes) to play croquet.
8. The spirit of the letters which we have received (seem, seems) to indicate a desire for reform.
9. The acoustics in the large hall (is, are) very poor.
10. Neither the chairman nor the committee members (was, were) allowed to count the ballots.
11. An interest in people, as well as a sense of humor, (help, helps) to make a successful salesman.
12. The president told me that John and I (am, are) to serve on the committee.
13. Success and happiness (is, are) the goal of almost every American student.
14. Neither Mrs. Flanagan nor I (want, wants) to go back to Hoboken to live.
15. Statistics (is, are) a very difficult subject for the average college student.

16. One of the main reasons for the defeat of the team (was, were) the series of losses of yardage during the second half.

17. All of the dinner (was, were) served before the speeches began.

18. None but the very courageous (dare, dares) to argue with Professor Splatz.

19. Higgins, Brown, and Smith (sell, sells) appliances at discount prices.

20. These are the factors which (account, accounts) for the success or failure of the project.

21. The opinion of the students and also of their parents (determine, determines) the nature of the graduation program.

22. Wisdom, kindness, sympathy (help, helps) the teacher in her daily association with children.

23. He reached for the scissors which (was, were) on the table.

24. There is pleasure and joy that (grow, grows) from an experience of this nature.

25. Economics (include, includes) the study of taxes, of credit, and many other difficult topics.

Exercise C

In the following sentences, make the changes directed and revise as necessary for agreement.

1. Rewrite with a compound subject:
   The corn which was grown in the garden is delicious.

2. Rewrite with a plural subject:
   Here is the man who is to lead our company.

3. Change the second member of the compound subject to the plural form:
   Neither the English exam nor the mental test was difficult.

4. Insert *including students and teachers* after *group:*
   The group is planning to stay for the evening meeting.

5. Change *men* to *man:*
   Where are the men who do not want to work for a better organization?

6. Change *food* to *eggs:*
   None of the food is fit to eat.

7. Change *a student* to *one of those students:*
   George is a student who is eager to study foreign languages.

8. Substitute a noun clause for *Your words:*

      Your words have little meaning to this group of people.

9. Make *what the coach wanted* the subject:

      Strong, active young men were what the coach wanted.

10. Change *one* to *none:*

      One of the best players has left college.

14

Substitution

THE PRINCIPLE of substitution in grammar has two aspects. The first is purely structural. It relates to the quality of our language which permits one to substitute word groups for individual words within the basic sentence patterns. The second is partly structural and partly semantic. It relates to the quality of our language which permits the substitution of one word for another, or perhaps one word for a word group, where identity of meaning is the main consideration. The first aspect of substitution permits greater flexibility of communication. The second permits greater economy of communication.

Structural Substitution

In some of the preceding chapters, we have discussed the first or purely structural kind of substitution. We will summarize here again some of the important facts to be considered by the student of grammar.

Word groups may be substituted for nouns in any of the noun functions. These groups may be subject-predicate word groups or possibly verbal phrases.

SUBJECT

Your *meaning* is hard to determine.

What you mean is hard to determine.

COMPLEMENT

Columbus wanted *adventure*.

Columbus wanted *to find a route to India*.

OBJECT OF A PREPOSITION

Cassidy was hanged for *murder*.

Cassidy was hanged for *murdering his second cousin*.

Cassidy was hanged for *what he did that night*.

APPOSITIVE

The charge, *bigamy*, was dismissed.

The charge, *that he had married two wives*, was dismissed.

The charge, *marrying two wives*, was dismissed.

NOUN ADJUNCT

She had a *demon* look in her eyes.

She had an *I could slay you* look in her eyes.

ADVERBIAL NOUN

Mother will arrive here *Friday*.

Mother will arrive here *when we least expect her*.

Word groups may be substituted for modifiers, adjectival or adverbial.

ADJECTIVAL

The *hungry* elephant ate the gallon of corn meal.

The elephant, *who was hungry*, ate the gallon of corn meal.

The elephant, *starving for food*, ate the gallon of corn meal.

ADVERBIAL

Kelly walked *rapidly* past the graveyard.

Kelly walked past the graveyard *as fast as he could go*.

Structural-Semantic Substitution

The second kind of substitution is word for word, word for word group, or even word group for word group. There is an identity of meaning and a parallelism of form and function.

> Mr. Smith is going to New York. *He* will stay there three days.
> The Johnsons are coming over tonight. *They* want to play bridge.

In the first sentence, *he* substitutes for Mr. Smith. In the second sentence, *they* substitutes for *the Johnsons.* We recognize these words immediately as structure words, pronouns. Meaning little in themselves, they attain meaning in context. They enable the writer to avoid repetition and use language more economically.

> The seniors are going to Washington. A teacher is going with *them.*
> *They* will spend the first day in the Capitol discussing government with *their* instructor.

In the above illustration, we may see that three different words are substituted for *seniors: them, they,* and *their.* We call them inflected forms, inflected according to case. *Them* is used after a preposition and is in the objective case. *They* is the subject and is in the nominative case. *Their* is used as a modifier of the noun *instructor* and is in the possessive case.

> Mrs. Jones has returned home. *She* expects *her* many friends to call on *her.*

In the above illustration, three substitute words are used for *Mrs. Jones.* One is a subject, one is a modifier, and one is the object of a preposition. The nominative form is different from the other two, but the possessive is the same as the objective.

> My mother and I are going to Boston. *We* expect to visit *our* cousins. They are looking forward to seeing *us.*

Here the words *we, our,* and *us* are substitute forms for *my mother and I.* Again we observe inflection for case: nominative, possessive, and objective. In the subject itself the two words *my* and *I* are actually substitute forms for the name of the speaker. We know this by inference, since the speaker does not use his name in discourse. The substitute words have direct reference to the person speaking or writing.

We are all familiar with these substitute words which we call personal pronouns. They are summarized below according to case.

NOMINATIVE

I	you	he	she	it	we	they

POSSESSIVE

my	your	his	her	its	our	their
mine	yours		hers		ours	theirs

OBJECTIVE

me	you	him	her	it	us	them

Another form of substitute word directly related to the personal pronoun is the reflexive pronoun.

> Susie is looking at *herself* in the mirror.
> Mr. Brown is in business for *himself* now.
> I hurt *myself* when I stumbled.
> The girls helped *themselves* to ice cream.

In the first sentence above, *herself* is a substitute word for *Susie;* in the second sentence *himself* is a substitute word for *Mr. Brown;* and so on. There is identity of meaning, and repetition is avoided. There is no ambiguity as there would be if the personal pronoun were used. All the reflexive pronouns are objective in function, although not in form. For example, the pronoun *myself* has the possessive *my*, whereas the pronoun *themselves* has the objective form *them*.

Sometimes the reflexive pronouns are used as intensifiers in the sentence.

> I suppose I will have to do it *myself*.
> George solved the problem *himself*.
> Mary made the dress *herself*.
> You will have to see it *yourself* to appreciate it.

Following is a summary of the reflexive pronouns according to number.

SINGULAR

myself	yourself	himself	herself	itself

Plural

    ourselves   yourselves   themselves

One of the most familiar substitute words is the connective called the relative pronoun. It functions as a connective for adjective clauses and also as a substitute word for a noun.

    I have the book *that* you want.

In the above sentence, *that* is a connective introducing the subordinate adjective clause and including it as a part of the sentence. In the subject-predicate word group *that you want,* *that* is the complement of the verb *want* and substitutes for the word *book.*

    I know the boys *who* are coming here to study.

In the above sentence, *who* is a connective which makes the adjective clause a part of the whole sentence. It is also the subject of the subject-predicate word group *who are coming here to study* and substitutes in this word group for the word *boys.* The fact that *who* selects the plural verb form *are coming* verifies its function as a substitute for the plural noun *boys.*

    This is the boy *whose* father is an actor.

Again the connective, *whose,* introduces the adjective clause, which modifies boy, and makes it a part of the whole sentence. *Whose* also has a function in the clause, serving as a modifier of the word *father.* It is a possessive form and substitutes for the word *boy;* thus we know by means of the statement that "the boy's father is an actor."

    This is the son of *whom* you spoke.

The word *whom* is a connective and a substitute word, a relative pronoun. It serves to make the clause *of whom you spoke* a part of the whole sentence, and it serves to substitute for the word *son* in the clause. As a substitute for *son* it is the object of the preposition *of* and therefore is inflected for the objective case.

The relative pronouns, structure words which serve as connectives and as substitute words for nouns, include *who, that,* and *which.* Only *who* and *which* are inflected.

NOMINATIVE
  who   which

POSSESSIVE
  whose   whose

OBJECTIVE
  whom

Many difficulties occur for the student of writing in the use of pronouns. Since the pronoun is a substitute word, the reader must always be helped to know what word it is being substituted for. If the reader doesn't know or isn't sure, ambiguity results.

> Joe wanted to talk to his brother before *he* left the house.
>
> Mr. Simpson was surprised to see his son Ned driving *his* car down Main Street.
>
> Sarah said she didn't want her sister to go to see *her* girl friend because *she* wanted *her* to stay home with *her* little brother.
>
> Joanne has a cousin living with *her* grandmother *who* owns real estate on Long Island.
>
> Plumkin put the baby in the carriage. *It* was shiny and black with little yellow chickens on *its* sides.

In each of the above sentences, ambiguity results from the fact that the reader is not certain of the reference of the pronoun. The pronoun communicates the full meaning only when the reader knows the word for which it is the substitute.

Another source of difficulty at times lies in the use of a pronoun as a substitute word for such structure words as *anybody, everybody, somebody, nobody,* and so on. As a rule the pronoun *his* substitutes for these words.

> Nobody could find *his* way through this dark alley.
>
> Everybody will seek *his* own path to success.
>
> Anybody can find *his* mistake if he looks long enough.

However, sometimes a word like *everybody* has a plural sense. In this case the substitute word would have to be *they.*

> Everybody may go when *they* are ready.
>
> Everyone should attend to *their* personal problems.

Students very often use the pronouns *you*, *they*, and *it* in a general indefinite context. This kind of writing gives an impression of immaturity, even when it is not actually ambiguous.

> *It* says in the catalog that *you* have to take forty hours of general education. *They* certainly make *it* hard for *you*.

These indefinite substitute words may be eliminated by a more carefully phrased statement.

> According to the catalog, the general education requirement is forty hours. This is rather hard for the average student.

So far we have been considering the use of pronouns (personal, reflexive, and relative) as substitutes for other words in what we may call a one-to-one relationship. The term *antecedent* is used to indicate the word for which a pronoun is substituted.

Sometimes, however, a pronoun or other structure word is substituted for an entire word group. From the standpoint of standard written English, this practice is usually frowned upon. In informal writing, however, it may at times be acceptable.

> He is very friendly, *which* is bound to help him in his business.
>
> He raced the car around the curve, *which* was a very reckless thing to do.
>
> Plumkin ate fried onions before going to bed. *This* often gave him nightmares.
>
> Johnny is teasing the baby. He does *that* all the time.

In none of the above sentences does any single word serve as the antecedent. In each, the structure word (*which*, *this*, *that*) is substituted for an entire group of words.

Sometimes a verb may be substituted for a preceding predicate.

> I have studied English longer than he *has*.

The verb *has* in the above sentence is a substitute word for the whole predicate *has studied English*. Other illustrations follow.

> John plays the piano better than Mary *can*.
>
> Will you go to the store and buy me some milk?
> Yes, I *will*.
>
> Does your mother know that you skipped school?
> Yes, she *does*.

In the last sentence, *does* substitutes for the long predicate *does know that I skipped school.*

> Do you swear that you will tell the truth, the whole truth, and nothing but the truth?
> I *do.*

The word *do* is a substitute word for the long predicate *swear that I will tell the truth, the whole truth, and nothing but the truth.*

Sometimes an adjective is used as a substitute for a word group.

> Mary wants a chocolate ice cream cone, but I want *strawberry.*

The word *strawberry* substitutes for the word group *a strawberry ice cream cone.* Other illustrations follow.

> She would rather have short hair than *long.*
> Smith used the long income tax form, but I used the *short.*
> Henry took the winding path home. I took the *straight.*

Sometimes a preposition substitutes for a word group.

> He likes his coffee without sugar and cream; I like mine *with.*
> He put his books on the desk; I placed mine *under.*

Only a relatively few kinds of substitution have been illustrated in this discussion. The student who searches his reading materials will be rewarded by finding many others.

Summary

Substitution is a useful grammatical device because it permits tremendous structural flexibility in communication. Subject-predicate word groups may be substituted for nouns in any of their functions, and also for adjectival and adverbial modifiers. Verbal phrases may be substituted for nouns, for adjectives, and even for adverbs. Prepositional phrases maybe substituted for adjectival and adverbial modifiers.

Substitution is important also as a grammatical device because it permits greater economy of statement. By use of personal pronouns, nouns already in context can be referred to without monotonous and wordy repetition. Relative pronouns serve both as connectives and as substitute words in adjective clauses.

Words like *this* and *that* may be used to substitute for single words or word groups already in context. Verbs such as *do*, *can*, and *will* are sometimes used as substitutes for preceding predicates. Sometimes an adjective or even a preposition takes the place of a preceding word group.

The student who would improve his writing needs particularly to understand the principle of substitution. When he uses pronouns he must be careful to help his reader know what word the pronoun is substituted for. The careless use of pronouns gives rise to ambiguity and blocks communication.

Exercise A

1. Substitute a noun clause for *the facts* in the following sentence:
     Mr. Smith knows the facts.
2. Substitute an infinitive phrase for *a vacation:*
     Father wants a vacation.
3. Substitute a gerund phrase for *the purchase:*
     Charlie Brown is considering the purchase of a home.
4. Substitute an infinitive phrase for the complement in the following sentence:
     Her only fun is the movies on Saturday night.
5. Substitute an adjective clause for *hungry:*
     A hungry man will enjoy plain food.
6. In sentence 5, substitute a participle for hungry.
7. Substitute an adverbial clause for *soon:*
     We are expecting Grandmother soon.
8. Substitute a gerund phrase for *A brisk climb:*
     A brisk climb up the mountain on a cool morning is healthful exercise.
9. Substitute a noun clause for the subject in the following sentence:
     The news that war has been declared is very ominous.
10. Substitute an infinitive phrase for *art:*
     Art is her great ambition.
11. Substitute an adjective clause for *college:*
     Mary has a very interesting college friend.
12. Substitute a gerund phrase for *an appointment:*
     He never thought of an appointment to that position.

13. Substitute a noun clause for *her friends:*
    She gives presents to her friends.
14. Substitute an adverbial clause for *always:*
    He always enjoys himself at our house.
15. In sentence 14, substitute a noun clause for *himself.*
16. Substitute an infinitive phrase for *favor:*
    I asked him a favor.
17. In sentence 16, substitute a noun clause for *favor.*
18. Substitute a gerund phrase for *The loud noise:*
    The loud noise frightened the baby.
19. Substitute a participial phrase for the adjective clause in the following sentence:
    Emma, who was dressed entirely in red, was the most attractive person at the party.
20. Substitute an infinitive phrase for a modifier word group in the predicate of the following sentence:
    I have come to college for the purpose of studying to become an engineer.

Exercise B

Discuss the use of pronouns and other structure words as substitute words in the following sentences. Indicate where and how ambiguity and lack of clarity may result from the careless use of these words.

1. When George left his father, he didn't realize that he would not see him again for a long time.
2. Everyone likes his own mother's cooking.
3. Just between you and I, I don't think Harry is going to get married.
4. One never realizes the amount of work you have to do in college until it is almost half over.
5. Alice is so excited about dancing the waltz and the rhumba that she is doing it almost all the time.
6. Neither of the boys wants their breakfast.
7. She has a pleasant way with her that puts one at ease as soon as they meet her.
8. Mr. and Mrs. Paul Smith announce the engagement of their daughter Jenny Louise to Mr. Fred Stoneham.

9. Be sure to do your exercises every morning because that will make you healthy.

10. Mrs. Brown gave the needy family a basket of food. This was a very generous act.

11. Hilda gave her mother a big smile when she saw her coming up the drive.

12. When the pitcher struck out Billy Deans, he yelled for joy.

13. The jury filed into the courtroom and gave their verdict to the judge.

14. The boys were quick to tell the girls about their disappointment.

15. It was the brother of the football player who had been taken to the hospital.

16. Nobody came to see her except Mary and me.

17. Neither Father nor the boys had bothered to bring his coat.

18. Everything went well at the party until somebody lost their temper.

19. None of the boys had done their homework.

20. We found the hubcaps of the automobiles that had been stolen.

Exercise C

Indicate and discuss all instances of grammatical substitution in the following passage.

Man, even in the lower stages of development, possesses a faculty which, for want of a better name, I shall call *Number Sense*. This faculty permits him to recognize that something has changed in a small collection when, without his direct knowledge, an object has been removed from or added to the collection.

Number sense should not be confused with counting, which is probably of a much later vintage, and involves, as we shall see, a rather intricate mental process. Counting, so far as we know, is an attribute exclusively human, whereas some brute species seem to possess a rudimentary number sense akin to our own. At least, such is the opinion of competent observers of animal behavior, and the theory is supported by a weighty mass of evidence.

Many birds, for instance, possess such a number sense. If a nest contains four eggs, one can safely be taken, but when two are removed the bird generally deserts. In some unaccountable way the bird can distinguish two from three. But this faculty is by no means confined to birds. In fact the most striking instance we know is that of the insect called the "solitary wasp." The mother wasp lays her eggs in individual cells and provides each egg with a number of live caterpillars on which the young feed when hatched. Now, the number of victims is remarkably constant for a given species of wasp: some species provide 5, others 12, others again as high as 24 caterpillars per cell. But most remarkable is the case of the *Genus Eumenus*, a variety in which the male is much smaller than the female. In some mysterious way the mother knows whether the egg will produce a male or a female grub and apportions the quantity of food accordingly; she does not change the species or size of the prey, but if the egg is male she supplies it with five victims, if female with ten.[1]

[1] From Tobias Dantzig, *Number: The Language of Science.* Copyright 1930, 1933, 1939, and 1954 by The Macmillan Company, and used with their permission.

15

Appositives and
Absolutes

APPOSITION is a grammatical device for gaining more explicitness, more precision in communication. From the standpoint of structure, it is usually a side-by-side relationship between words or word groups having the same function within the sentence. *Appose* means literally "to place beside." Words in apposition, whether nouns, adjectives, verbs, adverbs, or word groups, are usually contiguous in the sentence. They reinforce and supplement each other.

> Our driver *Sam Smith* didn't report for work today.
>
> The novel *Arrowsmith* was written by Sinclair Lewis.
>
> The poet *Wordsworth* was a romanticist.
>
> I saw his son *Michael* this morning.
>
> He told me all about Fred, *his cousin,* and the good times they had together.

The appositives are italicized in the above sentences. Each is in apposition with the word that immediately precedes it. In the first three sentences both the appositive and the preceding word constitute the subject of the sentence. Either word alone could be the subject. The two together supplement and reinforce each other, making the meaning more explicit.

In the fourth sentence, *Michael* is in apposition with *son*. Both words may be thought of as the direct object of the verb *saw*. In the last sentence, *his cousin* is in apposition with *Fred*. Both words are object of the preposition *about*.

The student will note that in each of these illustrative sentences the pattern of apposition is N N (noun, noun). In each, the two nouns have the same function, the same syntactical relationship to the other words in the sentence.

Identifying (Restrictive) Apositives

When nouns are in apposition, their relationship to each other may be identifying or descriptive. In the following sentences the second noun, the appositive, helps to identify the first.

> My neighbor *Dotson* is a very friendly man.
>
> George is an associate of my brother *Phil*.
>
> This symphony is the work of the composer *Beethoven*.
>
> The noun *symphony* is the subject of the preceding sentence.
>
> I saw the widow *MacPherson* at the beauty parlor.

There is a very close relationship between the words in apposition in each of these sentences. Some grammarians call them close appositives or restrictive appositives. The student will note that no punctuation is used between two words so intimately associated. They approach a compound relationship.

Descriptive (Nonrestrictive) Apositives

Nouns in apposition may have a descriptive relationship to each other. They are not then so closely associated as in the identifying relationship.

> The prisoner, *a youth of seventeen*, was led from the room.

Charles Simpson, *the famous author*, was found dead early this morning.

And there we met Jack's mother, *a lady with white hair and black eyes*.

His youngster, *a bright little fellow*, was playing on the front lawn.

In the above sentences the appositive relationships are less close than those in the preceding list. Here the second noun describes but does not necessarily identify the first. This relationship is called by some grammarians a loose or a nonrestrictive apposition. The student will observe that commas set off the noun used as appositive, along with its modifiers.

Two nouns in apposition are sometimes separated by an introductory or transitional word. Grammatically, they are still in apposition although not actually contiguous.

I should like to refer to an authority, namely *Dr. Henry Brown*.

May I present to you my cherished spouse, in other words, *my dear husband*.

In discussing the resources of our language — for example, *subordination* — we will need to give many illustrations.

Two of my old friends, specifically *Kelly and O'Brien*, were at the bus terminal to meet me.

The pathos — that is, *the element of sadness which is developed throughout the play* — makes *Cyrano* a very moving drama.

Variety of Forms Used as Appositives

So far we have considered only nouns in apposition. We may now consider a variety of forms of apposition. The following sentences illustrate the use of substitute words for nouns as appositives.

The Maguire sisters, *all of them*, will appear in the last act.

Mary and I, *both of us*, want to go with father.

In fact, we would *all* like to go along.

I told them *each* a story before they went to bed.

You won't see the Smith brothers at the show, *neither of them*.

In the third sentence above, *we* and *all* are in apposition even though separated by an auxiliary verb. In the last sentence, *neither of them* is in apposition with *Smith brothers*.

When personal pronouns are used as appositives, the student is sometimes bothered by the problem of the appropriate case form, since the personal pronoun is inflected for case. Since the case of the pronoun is determined by its function in the sentence or word group in which it occurs, conventional usage follows this principle when the pronoun is an appositive.

> Two of us — *Mr. Cooke and I* — will go to San Francisco next week.

Since *Mr. Cooke and I* is in apposition with the subject of the sentence, it is technically a part of the subject and in fact may be substituted for it:

> *Mr. Cooke and I* will go to San Francisco next week.

The pronoun *I*, then, is used because it is the inflected form for the nominative case. The inflected form *me* would not be appropriate in this instance, since its function requires the objective case. Other illustrations of pronouns used as appositives follow.

> Miss Smith had told us — *John and me* — to go to the library.
> (Miss Smith had told John and me to go to the library.)
>
> The Browns have gone on separate vacations, *he to Canada and she to Mexico.*
> (He has gone to Canada and she has gone to Mexico.)
> or
> (He and she have gone on separate vacations.)

Occasionally, to make or emphasize a point, a writer will use a noun in apposition with a whole subject-predicate word group.

> The manager appointed Simpson superintendent of the whole plant — *a splendid decision indeed.*
> Ashfork defeated Pinetop today by a score of 12 to 6, *the first victory for the Lumberjacks in the current football season.*

We have said that apposition is a side-by-side relationship, the purpose of which is to make communication more precise, more explicit. The words in apposition supplement and reinforce each other, both having the same function in the sentence and approximately the same meaning. Although adjectives are not usually considered as appositives when used contiguously before a noun, they secure the same rhetorical effect as the more conventionally

termed appositives when used deliberately by the writer to secure
this reinforcement of communication.

> This has been a *long, long* winter.
>
> Winter in Ohio is a *dreary, gloomy* season.
>
> All we could see were the *dwarfed, stunted* trees rising out of the
> sand.
>
> The *exciting, stirring* music of the band came to us from the
> parade ground.

In much the same way, verbs may be in apposition.

> He was *pushed, shoved, crowded* to the wall.
>
> Alice *danced, pirouetted, glided* across the stage.
>
> Sleigh bells *rang, jingled, tinkled* through the frosty night.
>
> The silver *shone, glistened, gleamed* under the bright chandelier.

Similarly adverbs may be in apposition, as the following sentences illustrate.

> He fought *doggedly, stubbornly* for ten rounds.
>
> He was *recklessly, indiscreetly* generous with his gifts.
>
> The raiding party made its way through the long grass *silently,
> very silently*.
>
> The prisoner will be executed *immediately — tomorrow at dawn*.

Verbals and verbal phrases may be in apposition.

> He liked *flying a plane, moving swiftly above the soft clouds*.
>
> Helen wanted *to scream, to cry out in anger at the injustice*.
>
> Joe talked in a *stumbling, blundering* manner.
>
> *Saving your money, putting it away for a rainy day* helps you to
> gain independence.
>
> The sergeant ordered his men *to police the grounds, to pick up all
> the cigarette butts and papers*.

Prepositional phrases may be in apposition.

> He told me *about his good luck, about his success in the lottery*.
>
> Jim has come home *from Alaska, from the forty-ninth state*.
>
> He left all his money *to his daughter, to the one who had loved him
> best*.
>
> Mrs. Smith is sailing next week *to the Orient, to China and Japan*.

Subordinate clauses are sometimes used in apposition.

This is *what he told me, what he swore was the gospel truth.*

You can see *that he is stubborn, that he balks at everything you tell him to do.*

Jim plans to start out *when the spring comes, when the warm sun begins to melt the snow and ice.*

This is the village *where Aunt Agatha spent her life, where she worked and played for many long years.*

Noun clauses may be used in apposition with a noun.

The fact *that Helen is coming home* shouldn't upset our plans.

He admitted the truth, *that he had stolen a large sum of money.*

Peterson predicted the inevitable result, *that he would go bankrupt.*

The workers agreed to a compromise, *that they would receive a ten per cent pay increase.*

Verbals and verbal phrases may also be used in apposition with a noun.

He seemed to be in some kind of a dream, *slipping farther and farther into the world of fantasy.*

Mrs. Fay had one last wish, *to see her son before she died.*

Henry Brown's great fault, *playing the market,* almost drove him into bankruptcy.

Thompson's request, *to pitch the first game,* was refused by the coach.

A construction common in writing is the sentence which begins with *it* and ends with a verbal or verbal phrase.

It is wrong *to tell a lie.*

It is fun *to slide on the ice.*

In the above sentences, the infinitive phrase may be considered in apposition with the subject *it.* We may substitute the infinitive phrase for *it* in each sentence.

To tell a lie is wrong.

To slide on the ice is fun.

This same kind of construction is sometimes used with a gerund phrase or even with a subordinate noun clause.

It is very interesting, *visiting all of the great art galleries.*

It is very dull, *spending the day with Plumkin.*

It was a very important achievement, *that Henderson was able to graduate the number one man in his class.*

Summary: Apposition

Apposition is a grammatical device which makes communication more explicit. Words in apposition most often occur consecutively, although sometimes transitional phrases such as *that is, for example, in other words,* and *namely* intervene. When nouns are in apposition, the relationship may be restrictive or nonrestrictive. If the relationship is nonrestrictive, commas are used to set off the appositive. The relationship in this case is more descriptive than identifying.

In this chapter we have considered several kinds of appositional relationships: nouns with nouns, adjectives with adjectives, verbs with verbs, adverbs with adverbs, and so on through verbals and verbal phrases, prepositional phrases, and subordinate clauses. We have seen that substitutes for nouns may be used in apposition with nouns; that when a personal pronoun is so used it is inflected for case according to its function in the sentence. We have seen, too, that nouns may also be used appositionally with verbals and verbal phrases, noun clauses, and even independent subject-predicate word groups. Sometimes the pronoun *it* is used as the subject of a sentence in place of an appositive verbal phrase or a noun clause which comes at the end of the sentence.

Absolute Constructions

Absolute constructions in our language are word groups which do not have the usual syntactical relationships to other parts of the sentence. They may not be classified as subjects, verbs, complements, or modifiers. Though these constructions are termed absolute (independent), they are not truly so, for semantically they are in coherent connection to the statement to which they are joined.

The sea being calm, we pulled up anchor and set sail.

Weather permitting, we leave for New York tomorrow.

His work finished, the President left for Gettysburg.
The field having been ploughed, the farmer unhitched the mules.
She stalked into the room, *her eyes burning with hatred.*
Dinner ready, the cook called the men in from the fields.
They kept the boat balanced, *each sitting on opposite sides.*

The most common construction used as an absolute is what has long been conventionally called the nominative absolute. The name is not well chosen since usually there is no inflection for case, nouns instead of pronouns almost always being used. The construction consists of a noun and a participle, usually with modifiers of one or both; the noun is considered the subject of the participle.

The weather being clear, we set sail for Montauk Point.
The pitcher having been broken, Mother poured the milk into bottles.
The students having left the room, the janitor began to clean up.
My studies completed, I decided to go to bed.

If a pronoun is used as the subject of the participle (this is not a common usage), the case of the pronoun is nominative.

He being such a close friend, I had to lend him the money.
They having purchased our house, we decided to try to sell them the furniture.

Sometimes the absolute word group is stated as though the word order were inverted.

Given enough rope, the man will hang himself. (*Enough rope being given,* the man will hang himself.)
Conceded that your premise is sound, I still do not admit that your plan will work.
Granted that your attendance was regular, you still cannot pass the course.

Prepositional phrases are sometimes used as absolute constructions.

Your promotion, *in the final analysis,* will depend on your service to the company.

> *In my opinion*, the prisoner should be discharged.
>
> *Notwithstanding his heavy program*, Charley Brown made the honor roll.

Infinitive phrases and participial phrases are used occasionally as absolute constructions.

> *To state the case midly*, you have been guilty of copying other people's writing.
>
> I am going to the convention, *to be sure*.
>
> *To make my meaning perfectly clear*, I am certain that you will never succeed in this business.
>
> Lincoln's decision, *viewing it in the perspective of time*, was an intelligent one.
>
> The burden of responsibility, *putting it very briefly*, is entirely yours.
>
> The boy's achievement, *considering his youth*, is very remarkable.

EXERCISE A

Identify all the nouns used in apposition and describe their function within framework of the sentence.

1. My father spoke often of his old friend Mr. Baxter.
2. I have told Jim, the gardner, that he is to report to work every day.
3. Batson, the old fellow who lives on the next street, has a very nice rose garden.
4. When I arrived at the station this morning, whom should I meet but your old friend Milligan.
5. This painting is the work of the artist El Greco.
6. The professor discussed the denouement, in other words, the solution of the plot complications.
7. He is the third person this morning who wished to see our manager Mr. Simpson.
8. Albany, the capital of New York State, is situated on the Hudson River, one of America's scenic waterways.
9. In some of our great universities, for example Yale and Chicago, gifted students are allowed to carry on independent study in their undergraduate years.
10. Phoenix, the sunshine capital of the United States, is located in Arizona, the third youngest state.

11. May I present to you my junior partner, Mr. Henry Schiller.

12. The theme of the novel — that is, the underlying thought which shapes the story — is the spiritual poverty of Henry Smith, the clergyman.

EXERCISE B

Identify the appositives in the following sentences and explain their function within the sentence.

1. Our family would all like to get together this year for a reunion.

2. I am writing to both of you, Jim and Edna, to enlist your co-operation in this project.

3. To become successful, the ambition of most of our students, is not a simple matter in the world of today.

4. She scolded the children, each of them, and sent them into the house.

5. They selected Smithson for the job, clearly an intelligent appointment.

6. My power of attorney, this is what he has been after all the time.

7. She is extremely frightened, afraid to go back to her home, a gloomy, desolate cottage on the shore.

8. They expedited the process, hurried it to its conclusion.

9. In an excited, impassioned speech Connelly pleaded for fair play.

10. Tompkins rushed wildly, recklessly out of the hall.

11. To hear the compliments, to listen to the praise of others, was the great delight of Agatha Anne.

12. This, students, is the duck-billed platypus, an egg-laying monotreme mammal *Ornithorhynchus anatinus* of Australia and Tasmania.

EXERCISE C

Write sentences to illustrate:

1. A noun in apposition with: (*a*) a noun used as subject of the sentence; (*b*) a noun used as direct object; (*c*) a noun used as object of a preposition; (*d*) a noun used as subject of an infinitive; (*e*) a noun used as indirect object.

2. A noun substitute in apposition with a noun.

3. A personal pronoun in apposition with a noun.

4. Two nouns in loose apposition.

5. Two nouns in close apposition.

6. Two adjectives in apposition.
7. Two adverbs in apposition.
8. Two verbs in apposition.
9. Two nouns in apposition separated by a transitional phrase.
10. A noun in apposition with a subject-predicate word group.
11. Two infinitive phrases in apposition.
12. Two gerund phrases in apposition.
13. Two prepositional phrases in apposition.
14. Two participles in apposition.
15. Two adverbial clauses in apposition.
16. A noun clause in apposition with a noun.
17. An absolute construction consisting of a noun and a participle.
18. An absolute construction with word order inverted.
19. A prepositional phrase used as an absolute construction.
20. An infinitive phrase used as an absolute construction.

Exercise D

Identify all the appositives in the following selection. Discuss their grammatical function within their respective sentences.

Becoming an inhabitant of a great English town, I often turned aside from the prosperous thoroughfares (streets where the edifices, the shops, and the bustling crowd differed not so much from scenes with which I was familiar in my own country), and went designedly astray among precincts that reminded me of some of Dickens's grimiest pages. There I caught glimpses of a people and a mode of life that were comparatively new to my observation, a sort of sombre phantasmagoric spectacle, exceedingly undelightful to behold, yet involving a singular interest and even fascination in its ugliness.

Dirt, one would fancy, is plenty enough all over the world, being the symbolic accompaniment of the foul incrustation which began to settle over and bedim all earthly things as soon as Eve had bitten the apple; ever since which hapless epoch, her daughters have chiefly been engaged in a desperate, hopeless struggle to get rid of it. But the dirt of a poverty-stricken English street is a monstrosity unknown on our side of the Atlantic. It reigns supreme within its limits, and is inconceivable everywhere beyond them. We enjoy the great advantage, that the brightness and dryness of our atmosphere keep everything clean that the sun shines upon, converting the larger portion of our impurities into transitory — that is, temporary dust which the next wind can sweep away, in contrast with the damp, adhesive grime that incorporates itself with all surfaces (unless continually and painfully cleansed) in the chill moisture of the English air. Then the all-pervading smoke of the city, abundantly intermingled with the sable snowflakes of bituminous coal, hovering overhead, descending and alighting on pavements and rich architectural fronts, on the snowy muslin of the ladies, and the gentlemen's starched collars and shirt-bosoms, invests even the better streets in a half-mourning garb, in the gray clothing of sorrow. It is beyond the resources of Wealth to keep the smut away from its premises or its own fingers' ends; and as for Poverty, it surrenders itself to the dark influence without a struggle. Along with disastrous circumstances, pinching need, adversity so lengthened out as to constitute the rule of life, there comes a certain chill depression of the spirits which seems especially to shudder, to tremble at cold water. In view of so wretched a state of things, we accept the ancient Deluge not merely as an insulated phenomenon, but as a periodical necessity, and acknowledge that nothing less than such a general washing-day could suffice to cleanse the slovenly old world of its moral and material dirt.[1]

Exercise E

Identify the absolute constructions in the following selection and discuss their structure.

The student of English literature usually develops a love of fine poetry. One of the favorite modern poets, of course, is William Butler Yeats. Yeats being a romantic, the student sometimes finds it difficult to sympathize with his great interest in the supernatural. To be sure, Yeats has drawn much of his material from the early Celtic legends of gods and heroes, many of whom have been later transported to fairyland.

In "The Wanderings of Oisin" the poet tells of the meeting of Oisin with Niam, the beautiful young woman of the fairy world. Oisin being one of the Fianna, a company of courageous Irish warriors, is at first loath to leave his valiant comrades. However, Niam is able to overpower him with her great charm, and he leaves the world of men to spend three centuries in fairyland. Here time stands still, change and death belonging only to the experience of humankind.

But Oisin, still a mortal, grows restless. He longs to return to his comrades, to the hunt and chase and the thrill of battle. Niam, notwithstanding her great love for Oisin, permits him to go, but warns him

[1] Adapted from Nathaniel Hawthorne, "Outer Glimpses of English Poverty."

not to dismount from the horse he will ride or touch the ground in any way upon his return to the land of men. Oisin finally gets back to his homeland only to find all his old comrades dead. Niam's warning forgotten, in an effort to help two men carry a sack of sand, he falls from his horse and his body touches the ground.

> "And my years three hundred fell on me, and I rose, and walked on
>   the earth,
>   A weeping old man, full of sleep, with the spittle on his beard
>   never dry."

Oisin, now in Ireland, meets St. Patrick, who urges him to repent and be saved. But Oisin, still the pagan, refuses. He scorns the offers of prayer and forgiveness. As the poem comes to an end he tells St. Patrick that he will "dwell in the house of the Fenians, be they in flames or at feast."

16

Composition
and Affixation

Two GRAMMATICAL DEVICES that add to the richness, flexibility, and force of the English language are composition and affixation. But though these devices contribute immeasurably to the writer's resources, they also add to his problems.

Composition

The process of developing new words by joining separate words to form compounds is called composition. Sometimes the meaning of the compound is the same as the combined meaning of the separate words, for example, *saddlebag*. Sometimes the compound is used to develop a figurative meaning, for example, *carpetbagger*. And sometimes the compound acquires an entirely new meaning and connotation of its own after it has been used for a long time, for example, *nightmare*.

Compound words are written in three different ways: as discrete words, such as *fruit jar;* as a hyphenated word, such as *half-wit;* and as one word, such as *hallmark*. Usually a compound consists of a combination of two words, but we have also such compounds as *mother-in-law*, *ducks and drakes*, *jack-of-all-trades*, and *Johnny-on-the-spot*.

Compounds come into our language in various ways and for various reasons, but always in response to a need which no single word in the existing vocabulary can fill in itself. They are thus a source of language enrichment and a means of more complete, exact, and graphic communication. Poets derive from the principle of composition an added power of metaphor, as when Keats writes of the tongueless nightingale dying *heart-stifled* in her dell, or Hopkins of the *dapple-dawn-drawn* falcon. In less personal and private contexts, writers and speakers of all kinds coin compounds to fit the occasion. Scientists need new terms to keep pace with their own discoveries, and we now speak glibly of *atom bombs*, *launching pads*, and *spaceships*. Sports writers add color and life to their style with such combinations as *Sunday punch*, *double-header*, and *portsider*. Technological and social phenomena give rise to compounds like *countdown* and *rock-and-roll*, unknown to the dictionaries of only a few years ago. When a compound passes into common use in speech and in print, it will be included in new editions of dictionaries, in this way becoming established in our recorded language.

For the average student of writing, however, compounds mean nothing but a headache. He usually has to make one of four guesses. First, he doesn't know whether his compound is an acceptable word in the language. Second, he doesn't know whether to use a hyphen. Third, he doesn't know whether to write the compound as two words. Fourth, he doesn't know whether to write the compound as a single word. All too often he makes the wrong guess and his paper comes back with a neat little red mark emphasizing his ignorance of this subtle problem of usage.

Now the fact is that while there is considerable lack of uniformity with respect to compounds in newspaper style, in magazine style, and even in dictionaries, there is also a large amount of agreement. In this chapter we will show how the student can help himself materially by becoming familiar with this core of consistency and exploiting it.

Compound Nouns

Compound nouns long in use that have the stress heavy on the first element are usually written as a single word.

backache	iceberg
campfire	jawbone
deathbed	landlord
eyebrow	makeshift
grandson	plowman

In most compound nouns written as one word, the stress is on the first element, the important part to be communicated. On pages 235–243 there are listed over eleven hundred compound nouns written as single words. A few examples are given here.

schoolboy	watchdog
shopgirl	workshop
silkworm	brownstone
taxpayer	collarbone
wineglass	churchgoer

When a compound noun is written as two words, the emphasis is often on the second word, reinforcing the relative importance of the second element of the compound. On pages 244–253 there is a list of over twelve hundred compound nouns written as two words. In most of these, the word communicates the importance of both parts or principally the second part of the compound. A few examples are given here.

black eye	dust bowl
cane sugar	first baseman
child labor	green light
day laborer	half brother
depth charge	major general

Compound nouns are sometimes hyphenated. However, of the 2,658 compound nouns listed on pages 235–255 — nouns commonly used in everyday communication and selected from a current revision of a collegiate dictionary[1] — only 163, or 6 per cent of the total, are hyphenated. This is a relatively small proportion to be concerned about. A few examples are given here.

at-home	one-step
four-poster	safe-conduct
great-grandfather	standard-bearer
higher-up	walkie-talkie
man-hour	well-wisher

No single characteristic feature distinguishes these hyphenated compound nouns to the writer. It is simply a matter of past and current usage, and the writer will know them only through use or memorization. A handy list of 138 hyphenated two-word compound nouns is given on pages 254–255, as also a list of multiple compound nouns including 25 that are hyphenated. A few examples of multiple compound nouns follow below.

bill of rights	hot cross bun
attorney at law	officer of the day
boom-and-bust	right of way
coat of arms	rock-and-roll
middle-of-the-roader	wear and tear

Compound Adjectives

After nouns, adjectives comprise the largest class of words formed by compounding. A list of 525 compound adjectives commonly used in communication (approximately one-fifth the number of compound nouns listed) is given on pages 256–260. The compound adjective is usually hyphenated; 423 out of the 525 listed have the hyphen. This means that four out of every five commonly used compound adjectives are hyphenated. A few examples of compound adjectives are given here.

all-American	headstrong
barefaced	high-spirited
double-jointed	plain-spoken
empty-handed	second-hand
good-natured	sunlit

[1] *The American College Dictionary* (New York: Random House, 1958).

In addition, compound numbers through ninety-nine and compound fractions used as adjectives are hyphenated. All two-word compound adjectives are hyphenated.

The number of multiple compound adjectives is relatively small. Only 26 are listed in this chapter, and all but one of these are hyphenated. A few examples are given here.

black-and-blue	open-and-shut
happy-go-lucky	out-of-date
heart-to-heart	ready-to-wear
lighter-than-air	two-by-four
matter-of-fact	hard and fast

Compound Verbs

Compound verbs are written either as a single word or as two words with a hyphen between. More than half of the compound verbs are hyphenated. There seems to be no way of determining whether a compound verb should be hyphenated; it is purely a matter of usage. A list of 88 compound verbs commonly used in communication is given on pages 260–261. A few examples follow below.

air-cool	jaywalk
barnstorm	pinch-hit
brain-wash	skin-dive
cross-examine	typewrite
henpeck	window-shop

Compound Adverbs

Compound adverbs are a very small group indeed, only 23 being listed in this chapter. Relatively few compound adverbs are hyphenated and these may be memorized. A few examples of compound adverbs are given here.

beforehand	nevermore
downstream	piecemeal
fifty-fifty	piggyback
headfirst	sideways
henceforth	topsy-turvy

Summary: Composition

Compounds are mainly nouns. Of the compounds listed in this chapter, 81 per cent are nouns, 16 per cent are adjectives, and 3 per cent are verbs and adverbs.

Most compound nouns are made up of two words. Those in which the stress is on the first element are usually written as one word. Those in which the stress is about the same on both elements, or heavier on the second, are usually written as two words. The use of the hyphen with two-word compound nouns is irregular and relatively infrequent. Since only about ten per cent of these are hyphenated, the student who guesses not to use a hyphen has a nine-to-one chance of being right. Many two-word hyphenated compound nouns are best looked up in a dictionary and memorized as used.

Compound nouns of three or more words are not usually hyphenated — the probabilities are better than four to one against the hyphen. Hyphenated multiple compound nouns may be looked up and memorized as used.

Two-word compound adjectives are written either as one word or as two words with a hyphen. Most of them are hyphenated, more than 80 per cent in the list in this chapter. Practically all multiple compound adjectives are hyphenated.

Compound numbers up to ninety-nine and compound fractions used as adjectives are hyphenated.

Compound verbs and adverbs comprise such a small group that they are best looked up in a dictionary when used, and memorized.

Compound Nouns (One Word)

afternoon	beanstalk	bowleg
afterthought	bearbaiting	boxwood
aircraft	bearskin	brakeman
airplane	bedbug	breadwinner
alpenglow	bedfellow	breakthrough
alpenstock	bedpost	breastpin
angleworm	beefeater	brickyard
anteater	beehive	bridegroom
applesauce	beeline	bridgehead
armchair	beetlehead	brimstone
armorbearer	bellyband	broadcast
arrowhead	bighead	broadside
autotruck	billboard	brownstone
axman	billfold	buckeye
backache	birdman	buckshot
backfield	birthday	bulldog
backwoods	blackball	bullfrog
backwoodsman	blackboard	bushman
bagpipe	blackberry	bushranger
bailsman	blackbird	businessman
bakehouse	blackguard	businesswoman
baldhead	blackmail	busybody
ballroom	blacksmith	butterfly
bandbox	blockbuster	buttermilk
bankbook	blockhead	butterscotch
bargeman	bloodhound	buttonhole
barleycorn	bloodstain	bylaw
barmaid	blowgun	bygone
baseball	blowtorch	byword
baseboard	bluebird	byway
bathhouse	bluejay	cabinetmaker
bathroom	blueprint	cabinetwork
bathtub	boardwalk	cabman
batman	boathouse	cakewalk
batsman	bombsight	calfskin
battlefield	bondman	callboard
battleship	boneblack	callboy
beachcomber	bookcase	cameraman
beachhead	bookkeeper	campcraft
beadwork	bootblack	campfire
beanbag	bottleneck	campground

campstool
candleholder
candlelight
candlewick
canvasback
cardboard
carload
carpetbag
carpetbagger
carryall
cashbook
castaway
castoff
catboat
catcall
catchall
catchword
cattleman
centerboard
centerpiece
cesspool
chainman
chainwork
chairman
chairwoman
chambermaid
chatterbox
checkbook
checkerboard
checkmate
checkoff
checkroom
checkup
cheekbone
cheesecake
cheesecloth
chessman
childbirth
choirboy
choirmaster
chophouse
chopstick
churchgoer
churchman

churchwarden
churchyard
citystate
clamshell
classbook
classroom
cleanup
clergyman
clockmaker
clockwork
clotheshorse
clothesline
clothespin
cloudburst
clubfoot
clubhouse
clubman
clubroom
coachman
cobweb
cockpit
cockroach
cocktail
collarbone
colorbearer
comeback
cookbook
copperhead
copybook
copyreader
copyright
corkscrew
corncob
corncrib
cornerstone
cornhusk
cornstalk
cornstarch
cottonseed
councilman
countryside
courthouse
courtroom
cowbell

cowcatcher
cowboy
crankcase
crapshooter
crossbones
crossbow
crossroad
crybaby
cupboard
cupcake
curbstone
cutthroat
dairymaid
dairyman
darkroom
dashboard
daydream
daylight
daytime
deadfall
deadhead
deadline
deadlock
deathbed
deathblow
deathwatch
deckhouse
deerskin
diamondback
dishcloth
dishtowel
dishwater
Dixieland
dockyard
doeskin
dogcart
dogfight
dogtrot
doomsday
doorbell
doorjamb
doorkeeper
doorknob
doorman

doorstep
doorway
dooryard
doughboy
doughnut
dovetail
downfall
downpour
draftsman
drainpipe
drawback
drawbridge
dreadnought
dreamland
dressmaker
driftwood
drillmaster
driveway
droplight
drumbeat
drumstick
duckpin
dugout
dumpcart
dustpan
dyestuff
earache
eardrum
earmark
earmuff
earphone
earthquake
earthwork
earthworm
eggnog
eggplant
eggshell
evensong
evergreen
evildoer
eyeball
eyebrow
eyecup
cyeglass

eyelash
eyesight
eyestrain
eyetooth
eyewash
eyewitness
fairground
fairway
fancywork
farmhouse
farmyard
fathead
fatherland
faultfinder
featherweight
feedbag
ferryboat
fiberboard
fiddlestick
fieldwork
figurehead
fingernail
fingerprint
firearm
fireball
fireboat
firebox
firebrand
firebreak
firebrick
firebug
firefly
firehouse
fireman
fireplace
fireplug
fireside
firetrap
firewarden
firewood
fishhook
fishline
fishworm
flagman

flagship
flagpole
flagstone
flareback
flashback
flashlight
flatboat
flatcar
flatiron
flattop
fleabite
fleshpot
flintlock
floodgate
floodlight
floorwalker
flophouse
flyleaf
flypaper
flyweight
foghorn
folklore
folkways
foodstuff
foolscap
football
footbridge
footfall
foothill
foothold
footlights
footman
footnote
footpath
footprint
footrest
footstep
footstool
fortuneteller
foursome
foxhole
foxhound
framework
freebooter

freshman
friedcake
frogman
frostbite
fullback
gamecock
gasbag
gamekeeper
gaslight
gatehouse
gatekeeper
gatepost
gateway
gearshift
gentleman
gingerbread
gingersnap
glasshouse
glassware
glasswork
glassworker
glassworks
globetrotter
glowworm
goalkeeper
goatskin
godchild
godfather
godmother
goldfish
goldsmith
gooseneck
grandchild
granddaughter
grandfather
grandmother
grandstand
grandson
graniteware
grapefruit
grapevine
grasshopper
gravestone
graveyard

greenback
greenhorn
greenhouse
griddlecake
gridiron
grindstone
grogshop
groomsman
groundwork
grownup
grubstake
guardhouse
guardsman
guesswork
guidebook
guidepost
gumboil
gumdrop
gunboat
guncotton
gunfire
gunman
gunpowder
gunshot
gunsmith
hairbrush
haircut
hairdo
hairdresser
hairline
hairpin
halfback
hallway
handbag
handball
handbill
handbook
handcuff
handspring
handwriting
hangman
hangnail
hangout
hangover

hardpan
hardship
hardtack
hardware
harelip
hatband
hatbox
hayfield
hayfork
hayloft
haymaker
hayseed
headache
headband
headdress
headlight
headline
headmaster
headquarters
headrest
headset
headstone
headway
heartache
heartbeat
heartbreak
heartburn
hearthstone
heatstroke
heavyweight
hedgehog
hedgerow
heirloom
hellcat
helmsman
helpmate
herdsman
highball
highbrow
highland
highway
highwayman
hillside
hilltop

hipbone
hoarfrost
hobbyhorse
hobnail
hodgepodge
hoecake
hogshead
holdup
homeland
homework
honeybee
honeycomb
honeymoon
hookup
hookworm
horseback
horsecar
horsefly
horsehair
horsehide
horselaugh
horseman
horseplay
horsepower
horseradish
horsewhip
hotbed
hotfoot
hothead
hourglass
houseboat
housedress
housefly
housekeeper
housemaid
housemother
housetop
housewarming
housewife
housework
humpback
iceberg
iceboat
icebox

icebreaker
icecap
icehouse
iceman
incurve
inkwell
inroad
ironwork
jackknife
jawbone
jawbreaker
journeyman
keepsake
keyboard
keyhole
keynote
keystone
kickoff
kingpin
knockout
knothole
ladybug
ladyfinger
lampblack
lamplight
lamplighter
lamppost
landholder
landlady
landlord
landmark
landowner
landscape
landslide
latchstring
latchkey
latticework
laughingstock
laundryman
lawbreaker
lawmaker
lawsuit
layman
layoff

layout
lazybones
leadoff
leasehold
leaseholder
leatherneck
letterhead
lifeblood
lifeboat
lifeguard
lifesaver
lifetime
lifework
lighthouse
lightship
lightweight
limekiln
limelight
limewater
lineman
liveryman
livestock
lockjaw
lockout
locksmith
logbook
longbow
longboat
longhand
lookout
loophole
lowbrow
lowland
lumberjack
lumberman
lumberyard
lunchroom
madhouse
madman
mailbox
mainland
mainmast
mainspring
mainstay

makeshift	neckband	packsaddle
manhole	neckcloth	paintbrush
mankind	necklace	pallbearer
manservant	necktie	paperback
manslaughter	needlework	paperweight
markdown	newsboy	parlormaid
markup	newscast	password
marrowbone	newsdealer	patchwork
masterpiece	newsman	patrolman
masthead	newspaper	pawnshop
matchmaker	newsprint	payday
mealtime	newsreel	payload
merchantman	newsstand	paymaster
milepost	nightcap	peacemaker
milkmaid	nightdress	peacetime
milkman	nightfall	penknife
millpond	nightgown	pickaxe
millstone	nightmare	pickpocket
millstream	nightshirt	pickup
millwork	nighttime	piecework
mincemeat	nightwalker	pigeonhole
minuteman	nobleman	pigtail
mixup	noisemaker	pillbox
molehill	noontide	pillowcase
moleskin	noontime	pilothouse
moneybag	northland	pinball
moneychanger	nosebleed	pineapple
moneylender	nosepiece	pinfeather
moonbeam	notebook	pinhole
moonlight	nursemaid	pinup
moonshine	nurseryman	pinwheel
moonshiner	nutpick	pitchfork
mortarboard	oarlock	pitchman
motherland	oarsman	pitfall
motorcycle	oatmeal	plainsman
motorboat	officeholder	plasterboard
motorbus	offshoot	playback
motorcar	offshore	playboy
motorman	offspring	playgoer
mouthpiece	oilcloth	playground
mudguard	oilskin	playhouse
muskmelon	onionskin	playpen
muzzleloader	oxtail	plaything

playtime	ringside	schoolhouse
plowboy	roadbed	schoolman
plowman	roadblock	schoolmaster
plowshare	roadhouse	schoolmate
plywood	roadway	schoolmistress
pocketbook	rollback	schoolroom
pocketknife	roommate	schoolteacher
polecat	ropedancer	schoolyard
policeman	rosebud	scoutmaster
poorhouse	rosebush	scrapbook
popover	roughhouse	screwball
porthole	roughneck	screwdriver
potbelly	roughrider	seacoast
potboiler	roundhouse	seafarer
potluck	roundup	seafowl
poundcake	rowboat	sealskin
powerboat	rubdown	seaman
powerhouse	runabout	seaplane
pressman	runaway	seaport
pressroom	sackcloth	searchlight
pulpwood	saddlebag	seashore
pushcart	safebreaker	seaweed
quarterback	safeguard	serviceman
quartermaster	safekeeping	setback
quicksand	sailboat	sharecropper
radiobroadcast	salesclerk	shareholder
radiofrequency	salesgirl	sharpshooter
ragpicker	saleslady	sheepfold
ragtime	salesman	sheepherder
railroad	saltcellar	sheepskin
railway	sandbag	shellfire
rainbow	sandbox	shellfish
raincoat	sandman	shipboard
raindrop	sandstorm	shipbuilder
rainfall	saucepan	shipload
ramrod	sawdust	shipmate
rangefinder	sawhorse	shipowner
rattlebrain	sawmill	shipwreck
rawhide	scapegoat	shipyard
razorback	scarecrow	shirtwaist
redskin	scatterbrain	shoeblack
ridgepole	schoolboy	shoehorn
ringleader	schoolgirl	shoelace

shoemaker	smokehouse	stationmaster
shoestring	smokestack	steamboat
shoetree	snapshot	steamship
shopgirl	snowball	steelwork
shopkeeper	snowdrift	steelworks
shoplifter	snowflake	steelyard
shopwindow	snowplow	steeplechase
shoreline	snowstorm	steeplejack
shortbread	snowsuit	stickpin
shortcake	soapbox	stockroom
shortcoming	soapsuds	stockyard
shorthand	softball	stonecutter
shortstop	songbird	stonemason
shotgun	soothsayer	stonewall
showboat	sorehead	stonework
showcase	sourdough	stopgap
showdown	soybean	stoplight
showman	spaceship	stopover
showroom	spadework	storehouse
shuffleboard	spearhead	storekeeper
shutdown	speedboat	storeroom
shutoff	speedway	storyteller
shutout	spendthrift	stovepipe
sickbed	spillway	straphanger
sideboard	spitball	streetcar
sideburns	sportsman	stretcherbearer
sidecar	spotlight	strikebreaker
sidehill	springboard	strongbox
sidewalk	spyglass	strongroom
signalman	squarehead	stylebook
signboard	stableboy	suitcase
silkworm	stagecoach	summerhouse
silversmith	stagecraft	sunbonnet
sinkhole	stagehand	sunburn
sketchbook	staircase	sundown
skullcap	stairway	sunglass
skylight	stakeholder	sunlight
skyrocket	stalemate	sunrise
slapstick	standout	sunset
slaughterhouse	standpoint	sunshade
sleepwalking	starlight	sunshine
slipknot	stateroom	sunspot
slowdown	statesman	sunstroke

sunup
surfboard
sweatshop
sweepstakes
sweetheart
switchboard
swordplay
tablecloth
tablespoon
taillight
taskmaster
taxicab
taxpayer
teacart
teacup
teakettle
teammate
teapot
teardrop
tearoom
teaspoon
telltale
tenderfoot
textbook
thickhead
thoroughfare
throwback
thumbnail
thumbtack
thunderbolt
thundercloud
thunderhead
thundershower
thunderstorm
tideland
tidewater
tightrope
tightwad
timecard
timekeeper

timepiece
timetable
tinderbox
tiptoe
toadstool
toastmaster
toenail
tollgate
tomboy
tomcat
toothbrush
toothpaste
toothpick
topknot
tossup
touchdown
towrope
trackwalker
trademark
trainman
treadmill
troopship
troublemaker
truckman
truelove
tugboat
turncoat
turnover
typesetter
typewriter
uppercut
viewpoint
volleyball
wagonload
waistline
wallboard
wallflower
warhead
warpath
washboard

washbowl
washcloth
washday
washroom
washtub
wastebasket
watchdog
watchmaker
watchword
watermelon
weatherman
weekday
whaleboat
whalebone
wheelbarrow
wheelbase
whirlpool
wildcat
windbag
windbreaker
windowpane
windshield
windup
wineglass
wishbone
woodland
woodwork
wordbook
workbench
workbook
workhouse
workman
workout
workroom
workshop
worktable
yardmaster
yardstick
yearbook

Compound Nouns (Two Words)

air alert	bank rate	blood bank
air brush	barley sugar	blue book
air castle	barn swallow	blue laws
air brake	barrel roll	boarding house
air lift	basket weave	boarding school
air line	bass clef	bomb rack
air raid	bass drum	bond paper
alimentary canal	bass horn	bone meal
alpha particle	bass viol	booby trap
alpha ray	battle cry	book club
altar boy	battle fatigue	book end
animal kingdom	battle royal	book review
anthropoid ape	battle wagon	bowling alley
arithmetic mean	bay rum	box kite
army worm	beach flea	box office
artesian well	beach wagon	boy scout
assembly line	bean tree	brain washing
athlete's foot	beauty spot	brake drum
atom bomb	beef tea	bread line
atomic bomb	beet sugar	breast stroke
atomic power	bell jar	brief case
atomic weight	bench warrant	broad jump
attorney general	best man	brown bread
Australian ballot	best seller	buck fever
baby sitter	beta ray	bulletin board
baccalaureate sermon	bevel gear	bull pen
back number	big game	bull ring
back talk	bird dog	bull snake
back yard	birth control	bull tongue
balance sheet	black book	burnt offering
bald eagle	Black Death	bus boy
ball bearing	black eye	buzz bomb
balloon tire	black lead	buzz saw
band saw	black list	cabin boy
band wagon	black widow	cáble railway
bank account	blank check	calendar year
bank clerk	blank verse	calendar month
bank discount	blindman's buff	calendar day
bank note	block letter	calf love

call rate
call slip
camel's hair
camp follower
camp chair
canal boat
candy pull
cane sugar
cannon ball
can opener
capital account
capital gain
capital stock
capital ship
carbon paper
card case
carload lot
cartridge belt
cartridge clip
case history
case record
cash discount
cashier's check
cash register
cast iron
catch phrase
cauliflower ear
center bit
certified milk
chafing dish
chain gang
chain lightning
chain reaction
chain stitch
chain store
chair car
chamber music
channel iron
chapter house
charcoal burner
charnel house
charter member

check list
cheese cake
chewing gum
chicken breast
chicken feed
chicken hawk
chicken pox
chief justice
child labor
chipped beef
chip shot
choir loft
chuck wagon
cider press
cinder track
circuit breaker
circuit court
city editor
city father
city hall
city manager
civil engineer
civil law
civil liberty
civil rights
civil servant
civil war
claiming race
clasp knife
class day
class struggle
claw hammer
clay pigeon
cliff dweller
clog dance
close call
closed shop
close quarters
clothes pole
club car
club sandwich
club steak

coach dog
coach horse
coal car
coal gas
coal tar
coast guard
cocoa butter
coffee break
cold cream
cold front
cold sore
cold war
color blindness
color sergeant
color guard
commission plan
common carrier
common council
common law
common noun
common sense
common stock
compound interest
compound sentence
confidence man
connecting rod
conning tower
consul general
conveyor belt
copy desk
corn bread
corn syrup
corporal punishment
cost accounting
cottage cheese
cotter pin
cotton gin
cotton picker
cough drop
counting house
country club
country gentleman

county court
county seat
court plaster
cover charge
cow hand
cow pony
crab apple
crab grass
crazy quilt
cream cheese
cross fire
cross section
cross street
crown colony
crown prince
cube root
cub reporter
cuckoo clock
cue ball
cuff button
curling iron
curtain call
custom house
cut glass
dairy cattle
dairy farm
dangling participle
dark horse
dark lantern
darning needle
date line
date palm
day bed
day coach
day laborer
day letter
day nursery
day school
dead beat
dead end
dead heat
dead pan

dead reckoning
dead weight
death house
death rate
death warrant
decimal fraction
decimal system
deck hand
definite article
demolition bomb
department store
depth bomb
depth charge
dew point
dial telephone
dial tone
diet kitchen
dill pickle
dinner coat
dinner jacket
direct current
direct action
direct object
discount rate
disk jockey
distaff side
district attorney
district court
ditto marks
dive bomber
diving bell
diving suit
divining rod
dog days
dog tag
dollar diplomacy
donkey engine
dorsal fin
double boiler
double chin
double cross
double date

double eagle
double entry
double play
double standard
double take
double talk
double time
down town
drawing account
drawing card
drawing room
draw string
dream world
dressing gown
dressing room
dressing table
dress rehearsal
dress suit
drift ice
drill press
drop kick
drop leaf
drug store
drum corps
drum major
dry cell
dry dock
dry law
dry measure
dry nurse
dry rot
dude ranch
duffel bag
dust bowl
dust storm
Easter egg
elder statesman
electoral college
electric chair
electric eye
end man
end product

evening dress
evening gown
evening star
evil eye
excursion ticket
exhaust fan
extension course
eye opener
face card
face lifting
face value
fair catch
fairy tale
faith cure
false bottom
family circle
family name
family tree
fancy ball
fancy dress
far cry
farm hand
fashion plate
father confessor
fatigue clothes
feature story
fellow creature
fellow traveler
fever sore
fiddle bow
field artillery
field corn
field day
field glasses
field goal
field marshal
field mouse
field ration
field trip
field work
fiery cross
fifth column

fighting chance
filling station
film library
finger bowl
finger wave
fire alarm
fire company
fire control
fire department
fire engine
fire escape
fire extinguisher
fire insurance
fireless cooker
fire sale
firing squad
first aid
first base
first baseman
first lady
first lieutenant
first mortgage
first person
fiscal year
fish cake
fishing rod
fishing tackle
fish story
flame thrower
flash bulb
flash flood
flash point
flesh wound
flight deck
flint glass
floating island
floating stock
flood control
flood tide
floor leader
floor show
flying boat

flying field
flying fish
flying machine
foam rubber
fog bank
folding doors
folk dance
folk music
folk song
folk tale
fool's cap
fool's errand
fool's paradise
foot brake
foot soldier
foot warmer
forced march
foreign office
foreign legion
form class
form letter
fortune hunter
foster brother
foster child
foster father
foul ball
foul line
foul play
foul shot
foul tip
fountain pen
four flush
fourth estate
fox hunt
fox terrier
fox trot
frame house
free city
free delivery
free enterprise
free hand
free lance

free love

free lunch

free throw

free trade

free verse

free will

freight car

freight house

front foot

fruit cake

fruit cup

fruit jar

full house

full moon

future life

gable roof

gable window

galley slave

game bird

game fish

game fowl

game law

gas attack

gas burner

gas engine

gas fixture

gas mask

gas meter

gas range

gas shell

general staff

general strike

gentle reader

ghost writer

ginger ale

gin rummy

goal line

goal post

gold brick

gold digger

gold dust

golden age

golden rule

golden wedding

gold field

gold mine

gold reserve

gold standard

golf club

golf links

good nature

good will

goose flesh

goose step

grade crossing

grade school

grain alcohol

grain elevator

grammar school

grand duke

grand opera

grand piano

grape sugar

grass widow

graven image

gravy boat

gray matter

great circle

green light

green tea

grizzly bear

ground crew

ground floor

ground glass

ground hog

ground plan

ground swell

group insurance

growing pains

growing season

guard duty

guest room

guided missile

guide rope

guinea pig

gun carriage

gun metal

hair trigger

half brother

half dollar

half hose

half sister

half sole

hand brake

hand grenade

harbor master

hard cider

hard sauce

harvest moon

hatchet face

hay fever

head gate

head pin

health insurance

hearing aid

heart disease

heat wave

heir presumptive

high comedy

high explosive

high hat

high jump

high priest

high school

high sea

high tide

high treason

hip joint

hip roof

hitching post

hobble skirt

holding company

holy water

home economics

home rule

home run

homing pigeon
honor system
hoop skirt
hope chest
horse chestnut
horse sense
hot dog
hot plate
hot rod
hour hand
house coat
house party
human nature
hunger strike
hunting case
hunting knife
hurricane lamp
hush money
husking bee
hydraulic brake
hydrogen bomb
ice age
ice bag
ice cream
ice field
ice pick
ice skate
ill humor
ill temper
inclined plane
income tax
Indian giver
Indian summer
interior decorator
iron curtain
iron lung
island universe
ivory tower
jack pot
jack rabbit
jazz band
jet plane

jig saw
joy ride
judgment day
juke box
jump ball
jump bid
kangaroo court
kidney bean
kitchen cabinet
knee action
knife edge
knitting needle
knuckle ball
labor market
labor union
lady's maid
lame duck
land bank
land grant
landing gear
land mine
land office
lantern slide
lateral pass
laughing gas
lawn mower
lawn tennis
lay brother
layer cake
leading article
leading edge
leading question
lead pencil
leap frog
leap year
lee shore
left wing
legal reserve
legal tender
letter box
letter carrier
liberal arts

library science
lieutenant colonel
life belt
life buoy
life cycle
life expectancy
life history
life insurance
life line
life net
life preserver
life span
light heavyweight
lightning rod
liquid air
liquid fire
listening post
little theater
livery stable
live wire
living room
living wage
loan office
loan shark
lobster pot
local color
lock step
lodging house
long distance
looking glass
lost cause
loving cup
lower case
low tide
machine gun
machine shop
machine tool
magic lantern
maiden name
mailing machine
main clause
major general

major league

manual training

marble cake

market place

market price

martial law

mass meeting

master builder

master hand

master key

master mechanic

master sergeant

match play

match point

maternity hospital

meeting house

merchant marine

mercy killing

middle age

middle class

milk bar

milking machine

milk punch

milk shake

mill wheel

mind reading

mind's eye

mine field

mine layer

minute hand

miracle play

missing link

modern dance

money order

mooring mast

morning star

mosquito net

moth ball

mother lode

mother superior

mother tongue

motion picture

motor scooter

motor ship

motor truck

motor van

mountain range

mountain sheep

mouth organ

mowing machine

mud hen

mud turtle

mule skinner

musical comedy

music box

music hall

mutton chop

nail file

nail set

national bank

national income

natural gas

natural history

nature study

naval academy

needle point

nerve center

nervous system

nest egg

new moon

new year

nickel plate

night clothes

night club

night letter

night school

night stick

night watch

note paper

nuisance tax

nursery rhyme

nursery school

nursing home

nut cake

office boy

office hours

office seeker

oil color

oil field

oil well

old age

old maid

olive branch

olive oil

open air

open door

open house

open shop

opera hat

opera house

organ grinder

other world

oyster bed

oyster cracker

paddle wheel

panel discussion

paper hanger

paper money

parcel post

parlor car

party line

passed ball

passion play

patent leather

patent medicine

patrol wagon

peace offering

peace officer

peanut butter

peep sight

pen name

personal pronoun

petty cash

petty jury

petty larceny

petty officer

physical science

picture tube

picture window

pig iron

pile driver

pilot light

pinch bar

pinch hitter

pine needle

pine tar

pin money

pipe dream

pipe line

pitch pipe

place kick

plane geometry

plate glass

playing card

playing field

plum pudding

pocket money

pocket veto

poet laureate

poison gas

poker face

pole jump

pole vault

police court

police dog

pony express

poop deck

poor law

poor white

poppy seed

pork barrel

postal card

post office

post road

potato chip

pot cheese

pot roast

pot shot

potter's field

powder puff

practical nurse

prairie schooner

prayer book

precious stone

press agent

pressure cooker

pressure group

prime minister

prince consort

prince regent

printer's devil

print shop

prize fight

prize money

prize ring

promissory note

proof sheet

proper noun

prowl car

public school

public servant

public utility

public works

punch bowl

punching bag

purse strings

push button

quarter note

quarter section

queen mother

quick fire

quick time

quick trick

quotation mark

rabbit punch

rabbit's foot

race horse

race riot

race suicide

race track

radio station

radio tube

radio wave

rain check

rain water

raw material

reading room

real estate

rear admiral

rear guard

red light

red man

red tape

relief map

reserve bank

return ticket

rifle range

right hand

rock bottom

rock candy

rock crystal

rocking chair

rocking horse

rock wool

roll call

roller coaster

roller skate

rolling pin

rooming house

root beer

rotary plow

rotary press

round steak

round trip

royal flush

rubber stamp

running board

running gear

sacrifice hit

saddle horse

saddle soap

safe hit

safety belt
safety glass
safety match
safety pin
safety razor
safety valve
salad dressing
sales resistance
sales tax
salt marsh
sand bar
savings bank
school board
school year
science fiction
scrap iron
sea captain
sea gull
sea level
sea power
search warrant
sea shell
season ticket
sea wall
second childhood
second fiddle
second lieutenant
second mortgage
second nature
sense organ
sergeant major
serial number
service club
service man
service station
seven seas
seventh heaven
sewing circle
sewing machine
shade tree
sheath knife
sheep dog

sheet iron
sheet metal
sheet music
shell shock
ship canal
shipping clerk
shipping room
shock absorber
shock troops
shooting star
shop assistant
shopping center
short circuit
short wave
shoulder blade
shoulder strap
shower bath
show window
side dish
side line
side show
side step
side whiskers
sign language
silent partner
silver standard
silver wedding
simple interest
single entry
single file
single tax
skeleton key
slave driver
sledge hammer
sleeping bag
sleeping sickness
slide rule
slide trombone
slip cover
small change
small talk
smart set

smelling salts
smoke screen
sneak thief
soap opera
social security
soda cracker
soda fountain
soda water
soft coal
soft drink
soft pedal
soft soap
soil bank
soil pipe
solar system
sound barrier
sounding board
sound track
sour grapes
space time
spark coil
spark plug
special delivery
spending money
spinal cord
spinning wheel
spoils system
sponge cake
spoon bread
sports car
spread eagle
square dance
square deal
square shooter
squeeze play
staff sergeant
stage fright
stage whisper
stainless steel
stamping ground
standing army
station house

station wagon	tail spin	trench mouth
steam boiler	tail wind	trial balloon
steam engine	tap dance	trolley car
steam fitter	task force	truck farm
steam heat	taxi dancer	turning point
steam roller	tax rate	ugly duckling
steam shovel	tea ball	unwritten law
steering wheel	tear bomb	upper hand
stepping stone	tear gas	utility man
sticking plaster	tea wagon	vacuum cleaner
still life	teen age	vacuum tube
stock certificate	tenement house	voting machine
stock market	term insurance	wage earner
stock pile	theme song	wage scale
stomach ache	third degree	wagon train
stool pigeon	third estate	waiting room
stop order	third person	walking stick
stop watch	third rail	war cry
storage battery	time clock	war dance
storm cellar	time exposure	war game
storm center	time out	war paint
storm door	tin foil	washing machine
storm window	tin plate	water wave
straight flush	title page	wave length
strait jacket	title role	weather map
straw vote	toe dance	weather strip
string bean	toe hold	week end
strip tease	toll bridge	wheel chair
study hall	toll call	whip hand
stumbling block	top kick	whisk broom
sugar cane	top sergeant	white heat
sun bath	torpedo boat	white lie
sun lamp	torpedo tube	whooping cough
sun parlor	totem pole	wild flower
swagger stick	town clerk	window box
swan song	town hall	wine press
sweet cider	town meeting	wire cutter
swing shift	track meet	wood pulp
swivel chair	trade union	word order
symphony orchestra	trade school	wrist watch
table linen	trench coat	yeast cake
table tennis	trench foot	zero hour

Compound Nouns (Hyphenated)

ampere-hour	follow-through	jew's-harp
at-home	follow-up	knight-errant
battle-ax	forty-niner	knock-knee
beam-ends	four-cycle	know-how
boogie-woogie	four-poster	know-nothing
bull's-eye	frame-up	lady-killer
by-election	good-by	lean-to
by-line	great-grandchild	light-year
by-play	great-granddaughter	line-up
by-product	great-grandfather	looker-on
by-work	great-grandmother	loud-speaker
carry-over	great-grandson	make-up
cat's-paw	great-niece	man-eater
cease-fire	great-nephew	man-hour
city-state	great-uncle	make-believe
close-up	great-aunt	mischief-maker
come-on	hanger-on	mock-up
court-martial	has-been	old-timer
cross-eye	hair's-breadth	one-step
crow's-foot	half-breed	passer-by
cross-purpose	half-caste	put-out
cross-stitch	half-hour	run-around
crow's-nest	half-mast	runner-up
cure-all	half-tone	run-off
deaf-mute	half-track	run-through
dim-out	half-truth	safe-conduct
ding-dong	half-wit	save-all
dog-ear	head-hunting	say-so
double-dealing	hide-out	seven-up
double-dealer	higher-up	shake-down
double-decker	hocus-pocus	selling-plater
double-header	home-brew	send-off
drive-in	hugger-mugger	show-off
fade-out	hula-hula	shot-put
fall-out	hurly-burly	six-shooter
fighter-bomber	hundred-percenter	slip-up
fire-eater	hurdy-gurdy	smash-up
first-nighter	hurry-scurry	speed-up
flare-up	in-group	stem-winder

stick-up
standard-bearer
stand-by
stand-in
stand-off
stretch-out
take-in

take-off
take-up
tape-recorder
teen-ager
tie-up
tip-off
trade-in

trouble-shooter
tune-up
two-step
walkie-talkie
well-being
well-wisher
write-up

Compound Nouns (Multiple)

angel food cake
angle of attack
apple of discord
apple of the eye
assault and battery
attorney at law
balance of power
beast of burden
bill of rights
bill of sale
bird of passage
bird of prey
block and tackle
board of trade
boom-and-bust
Boston brown bread
bread and butter
break of day
brother-in-law
burden of proof
cakes and ale
call to quarters
cat-o'-nine-tails
center of gravity
center of mass
chamber of commerce
change of life
change of venue
cheek by jowl
Chief of Staff
circuit court of appeal

citizen of the world
coach-and-four
coat of arms
coat of mail
commander in chief
council of war
crack of doom
dance of death
days of grace
debt of honor
divine right of kings
fly in the ointment
father-in-law
field of honor
figure of eight
figure of speech
fish and chips
five-and-ten
flag of truce
flesh and blood
fly-by-night
fly in the ointment
four-in-hand
freedom of the press
freedom of the seas
friend at court
give-and-take
good-for-nothing
half-and-half
hand-to-hand
hare and hounds

hide-and-seek
high-low-jack
hot cross bun
jack-in-the-box
jack-of-all-trades
jack-o'-lantern
justice of the peace
kith and kin
letter of credit
man about town
man of the world
man on horseback
master-at-arms
man in the street
matron of honor
middle-of-the-roader
mother-in-law
mother-of-pearl
next of kin
officer of the day
officer of the guard
oil of vitriol
part of speech
poor white trash
port of entry
power of attorney
rank and file
rate of exchange
right of way
rock-and-roll
round of beef

rule of thumb
sergeant at arms
sergeant first class
ship of the line
skull and crossbones
sleight of hand
soldier of fortune

standard of living
stations of the cross
struggle for existence
survival of the fittest
thing-in-itself
tick-tack-toe
tree of life

tug of war
two-by-four
ways and means
wear and tear
wing back formation

Compound Adjectives

air-borne
air-bound
air-line
airtight
all-American
all-around
almond-eyed
Anglo-American
backbreaking
bandy-legged
barefoot
barefaced
barehanded
barelegged
barrel-house
battle-scarred
beetle-browed
beetleheaded
bell-mouthed
big-headed
big-hearted
bird's-eye
bittersweet
blear-eyed
bloodguilty
blood-red
bloodstained
bloodthirsty
blue-coated
blue-green
bone-dry

bow-legged
brand-new
broad-minded
broken-down
built-in
bulletproof
bullheaded
bull-necked
camel's-hair
cast-iron
chicken-hearted
chock-full
clear-cut
clear-eyed
clear-headed
close-fisted
close-mouthed
cold-blooded
color-blind
commonplace
crackbrained
cream-colored
crop-eared
cross-country
cross-eyed
cross-legged
cross-town
custom-made
cutglass
daylight-saving
dead-beat

dead-end
dead-pan
dead-stick
deep-dish
deep-laid
deep-rooted
deep-sea
deep-seated
dirt-cheap
dog-tired
double-acting
double-barreled
double-breasted
double-edged
double-faced
double-jointed
double-quick
downcast
downhearted
downright
eagle-eyed
ear-minded
eastbound
easygoing
egg-shaped
empty-handed
empty-headed
even-minded
even-tempered
everlasting
evil-minded

face-saving
fact-finding
fair-minded
fair-spoken
fair-trade
fair-weather
false-hearted
fancy-free
far-off
far-seeing
faultfinding
fine-drawn
fine-spun
fireproof
first-born
first-class
first-hand
first-rate
flea-bitten
fleet-footed
foot-loose
footsore
footworn
foul-minded
foul-mouthed
four-footed
four-masted
fourscore
foursquare
four-wheel
freeborn
freehand
free-handed
free-hearted
free-soil
free-spoken
freewill
fresh-water
full-blooded
full-blown
full-bodied
full-grown

general-purpose
gilt-edged
goggle-eyed
gold-filled
good-humored
good-looking
good-natured
good-tempered
grass-roots
gray-headed
green-eyed
grown-up
hairbreadth
hair-raising
half-baked
half-blooded
half-hearted
half-hourly
half-witted
hangdog
hard-bitten
hard-boiled
hard-fisted
hard-headed
hard-hearted
hard-shell
head-on
headstrong
heartbroken
heartfelt
heart-free
heart-rending
heart-shaped
heartsick
heaven-born
heavy-armed
heavy-duty
heavy-handed
heavy-laden
hidebound
highborn
highbred

high-colored
high-fidelity
highflown
highflying
high-frequency
high-handed
high-minded
high-pressure
high-priced
high-proof
high-sounding
high-spirited
high-strung
high-tension
high-test
high-toned
homebred
homesick
homespun
honey-sweet
hot-blooded
hot-headed
housebroken
humpbacked
icebound
ice-cold
ill-bred
ill-founded
ill-gotten
ill-mannered
ill-natured
ill-starred
ingrown
ironclad
iron-gray
jet-black
kindhearted
king-size
knee-deep
knee-high
knife-edged
knockdown

labor-saving
landlocked
land-poor
large-minded
large-scale
latter-day
law-abiding
left-hand
left-handed
letter-perfect
level-headed
lifelong
life-size
light-fingered
light-footed
light-headed
light-hearted
light-minded
light-struck
lily-livered
lion-hearted
livelong
long-drawn
long-headed
longshore
longstanding
long-suffering
long-winded
lop-eared
loud-mouthed
lovesick
lowborn
lowbred
low-down
low-minded
low-necked
low-pitched
low-pressure
low-spirited
low-tension
low-test
lukewarm

made-up
make-believe
makeshift
many-sided
mealy-mouthed
middle-aged
middle-class
milk-white
mock-heroic
moonlit
moon-struck
moss-grown
moth-eaten
narrow-gauge
narrow-minded
nation-wide
native-born
needle-point
newfangled
new-fashioned
no-par
northernmost
nutbrown
offbeat
off-color
off-chance
offside
off-stage
off-white
old-fashioned
old-line
old-time
old-world
olive-green
one-sided
one-time
one-track
one-way
open-air
open-eyed
open-faced
open-handed

open-hearted
open-minded
open-mouthed
paid-in
painstaking
peg-top
pell-mell
penny-wise
pent-up
pigeon-toed
pigheaded
pitch-dark
plain-spoken
point-blank
poverty-stricken
praiseworthy
public-spirited
punch-drunk
purse-proud
push-button
quarter-final
quick-fire
quick-tempered
quick-witted
rapid-fire
rawboned
ready-made
red-blooded
red-letter
right-hand
right-minded
rock-bottom
rock-bound
rock-ribbed
roly-poly
rose-colored
roughshod
roundabout
round-shouldered
run-down
run-on
rust-colored

rustproof
safe-deposit
salt-water
saw-toothed
seasick
second-class
second-hand
second-rate
seventh-day
shamefaced
sharp-set
sharp-witted
shellproof
ship-rigged
shipshade
shopworn
short-handed
short-sighted
short-tempered
short-term
short-winded
shut-in
side-wheel
silk-stocking
simple-minded
single-action
single-breasted
single-handed
single-hearted
single-minded
single-phase
skin-deep
skin-tight
slip-on
slipover
slow-motion
small-minded
smoothfaced
snow-blind
snowbound
snow-capped
snow-clad

snow-white
sober-minded
so-called
soft-headed
soft-hearted
soft-spoken
soundproof
space-time
spellbound
spoon-fed
square-rigged
squint-eyed
stage-struck
stem-winding
stiff-necked
stone-blind
stone-broke
stone-deaf
stony-hearted
stormproof
stout-hearted
straightforward
strait-laced
strong-arm
strong-minded
strong-willed
stuck-up
sun-dried
sunlit
sun-struck
sure-footed
sway-backed
swift-footed
tailor-made
telltale
teen-age
tender-hearted
thick-headed
thick-set
thick-skinned
thin-skinned
third-rate

thoroughbred
thoroughgoing
threadbare
three-dimensional
thumbnail
thunderstruck
tight-fisted
tight-lipped
time-honored
time-saving
timeworn
top-secret
true-blue
tumble-down
turndown
twice-told
twinborn
twin-screw
two-ply
uncalled-for
upper-class
walleyed
warm-blooded
warm-hearted
washed-out
washed-up
water-logged
waterproof
weak-kneed
weak-minded
weather-beaten
weatherproof
week-end
well-balanced
well-behaved
wellborn
well-bred
well-disposed
well-fed
well-founded
well-groomed
well-informed

well-known
well-mannered
well-meaning
well-off
well-preserved
well-read
well-spoken
well-timed
well-worn
white-hot

white-livered
whole-wheat
wide-awake
wide-open
widespread
wild-eyed
wind-blown
wind-broken
wind-swept
wing-footed

wire-haired
word-blind
worldly-minded
world-weary
world-wide
write-in
wrong-headed
wrought-up

Compound Adjectives (Multiple)

black-and-blue
fly-by-night
happy-go-lucky
hand-to-hand
hand-to-mouth
hard and fast
heart-to-heart
ill-at-ease
leg-of-mutton

lighter-than-air
matter-of-course
matter-of-fact
milk-and-water
open-and-shut
out-and-out
out-of-date
out-of-doors
out-of-the-way

ready-to-wear
rough-and-ready
rough-and-tumble
to-and-fro
touch-and-go
two-by-four
well-thought-of
well-to-do

Compound Verbs

air-condition
air-cool
backbite
backslide
backfire
barnstorm
blackball
black-list
blackmail
blindfold
blueprint
brain-wash
bulldoze
bull-tongue
cross-examine
cross-fertilize
cross-question
deep-fry

double-check
double-date
double-park
double-time
double-tongue
dovetail
drop-kick
dry-clean
dry-dock
dry-nurse
eavesdrop
earmark
face-harden
four-flush
fox-trot
freeboot
free-lance
gold-brick

goose-step
grubstake
half-sole
hedgehop
henpeck
high-hat
highlight
hitchhike
horsewhip
ice-skate
jaywalk
keelhaul
lower-case
machine-gun
mastermind
nickel-plate
pinch-hit
pole-jump

pole-vault
pooh-pooh
proofread
quick-freeze
roller-skate
rough-dry
rough-hew
rubber-stamp
short-change
short-circuit
side-step
sideswipe

sidetrack
skin-dive
sledge-hammer
soft-pedal
soft-soap
spellbind
spread-eagle
steam-roller
stock-pile
straight-arm
sugar-coat
sunburn

tape-record
tin-plate
tiptoe
toe-dance
top-dress
typewrite
water-wave
waylay
weather-strip
window-shop

Compound Adverbs

beforehand
downhill
downstage
downstream
downtown
evermore
fifty-fifty
halfway

headfirst
headlong
henceforth
herein
hereof
heretofore
hitherto
midway

nevermore
pell-mell
piecemeal
piggyback
sideways
topsy-turvy
will-nilly

Affixation: Prefixes

The grammatical device of affixation consists in adding or joining a prefix or a suffix to a word or a word stem. Since we have considered suffixes in their structural functions in previous chapters, we shall discuss affixation here in terms of prefixes.

As we have seen, suffixes are useful principally in the marking of word classes — nouns, verbs, adjectives, and adverbs. They facilitate communication because they help the reader or listener identify the word as it is used. Prefixes, on the other hand, do not usually serve as structural signals. Their function is lexical. They change the meaning of the word or stem to which they are joined:

happy	unhappy
connect	disconnect
normal	abnormal
market	supermarket
weekly	biweekly

One may quickly perceive, therefore, how the use of prefixes with many different words and stems enhances the flexibility and power of communication. An understanding of prefixes and practice in using them should be of considerable help to the student who wishes to write more effectively.

In the following pages, lists of prefixes are given, together with their meanings and illustrations of their use. These lists — common Latin prefixes, Greek forms used as prefixes, and English prefixes — should be studied carefully.

Latin Prefixes

ab-	from, away from	abnormal abduct
ad-	to, toward	adhere adjoin
ante-	before in time or place	antedate antecedent
bi-	two	bimonthly bisect
circum-	around	circumnavigate circumscribe
com-	with	compassion combat
contra-	against	contradict contraband
de-	separation, negation, reversal, descent	degrade dehydrate
dis-	away, separation, reversal, negation	disassemble dishonest
ex-	out of, former	excavate ex-president
extra-	outside, beyond	extracurricular extrasensory
in-	in, into	inflow indoors
in-	not	insane incorrect
inter-	between, among	interscholastic interfere

intra-	within	intramural
		intravenous
intro-	inward, within	introspection
		introvert
non-	not	nonresident
		nonessential
ob-	against	object
		obstruct
per-	through, throughout	perennial
		perspire
post-	after	postgraduate
		postwar
pre-	before	prefix
		prehistoric
pro-	in favor of, for, forward	proslavery
		promote
re-	back, again	recall
		rebuild
retro-	backwards	retrograde
		retrospect
se-	aside, withdrawal	secede
		seclude
semi-	half	semimonthly
		semicircle
sub-	under	submarine
		subway
super-	over	supersensitive
		supersaturate
trans-	across, over, through	transcontinental
		transparent
ultra-	beyond	ultraviolet
		ultramodern

Greek Prefixes and Combining Forms

an-	not, without, lacking	anarchy
		anhydrous
anti-	against, opposed to	antibiotic
		antifreeze

anthropo-	man, human being	anthropology anthropomorphic
arch-	first, chief	archbishop architect
auto-	self, same	autobiography autosuggestion
bio-	life	biology biochemistry
cata-	down, against	catalog catastrophe
chron-	time	chronometer chronology
di-	twice	dichotomy diatomic
epi-	on, to, against	epigram epiglottis
eu-	good, well	eulogy euphoria
hemi-	half	hemisphere hemistitch
hetero-	different, other	heterogeneous heteronym
homo-	the same	homogeneous homonym
hyper-	over	hypersensitive hypertension
hypo-	under	hypodermic hypocotyl
meta-	among, after, behind	metaphysics metamorphosis
micro-	very small	microscope microcosm
mono-	one, alone	monogram monotone
neo-	new	neologism Neoplatonism
neuro-	nerve, tendon	neuropathic neurology
pan-	all	panacea Pan-American

phil-	loving	philosophy
		philharmonic
phon-	sound, voice	phonograph
		phonology
photo-	light	photograph
		photometer
poly-	much, many	polychrome
		polytechnic
para-	near, beyond, beside	parable
		parallel
pseudo	false	pseudonym
		pseudoclassic
syn-	with, together	synchronize
		synthesis
tele-	distant	telephone
		telescope

English Prefixes

a-	on, in, to, towards	afoot
		ashore
be-	about, around,	belay
	(intensifier)	befriend
by-	secondary,	by-product
	out of the way	byway
for-	away, off,	forgive
	(negative)	forbid
fore-	front, ahead of	forefoot
	time	foretell
mid-	middle	midday
		midstream
mis-	ill, wrong,	misapply
	(negative)	mistrust
out-	out,	outcast
	(a going beyond)	outlast
over-	over, excess	overthrow
		overact
self-	self,	self-defense
	(reflexive)	self-control
un-	not	unfair
		unseen

under-	under, of lesser degree	undermine underpay
up-	up, to a higher degree	upstream uplift
with-	separative, opposing	withdraw withstand

Hyphenation of Prefixes

Ordinarily, prefixes are not hyphenated to the stem of the word or to the word itself. There are a few exceptions, however, as follows.

1. When the last letter of the prefix is the same as the first letter of the stem or word:

co-operate	semi-independent
pre-election	pre-establish
re-enter	micro-organism

2. When confusion would otherwise result between similar words of different meaning:

re-cover	"to put on a new cover"
recover	"to get well"
re-act	"to perform again"
react	"to respond to a stimulus"
re-form	"to form again"
reform	"to change one's character for the better"

3. When the prefix *self* is used:

self-control	self-respect
self-evident	self-service
self-educated	self-taught

4. When the prefix *pan* is used before a proper noun or adjective:

Pan-American	Pan-Slavism
Pan-Germanic	Pan-Islamism

5. When the prefix *ex* is used before a noun:

ex-wife	ex-soldier
ex-governor	ex-president

EXERCISE A

1. Make a list of compound nouns and adjectives that you find in a current magazine or newspaper. Continue your reading in this particular periodical (various issues) until you have one hundred compound words. Now list the compound nouns under three headings: one word, two words, hyphenated. Make a separate list of multiple compound nouns. Compile also a list of compound adjectives; count the number hyphenated, the number unhyphenated. Compare your findings, for percentage and usage, with those reported in this chapter. Similarly compare your lists with those compiled by other students from different magazines and newspapers.

2. From the list of one-word compound nouns on pages 235–243, list those which have the accent on the second element. What proportion of the whole list would you estimate this group of words to be?

3. From the list of two-word compound nouns on pages 244–253, list those which definitely have the stress on the first element. What proportion of the whole list would you estimate this group of words to be?

4. Compile lists of compound nouns and adjectives taken (a) from nineteenth-century prose, (b) from twentieth-century prose. Compare for frequency of usage of compounds. Do you find any evidence of language change in usage of compounds? Illustrate with specific examples.

5. Repeat item 4, selecting the compounds from poetry instead of prose.

EXERCISE B

1. List ten words using each of the Latin prefixes on pages 262–263.

2. List as many words as you can for each of the Greek prefixes and forms on pages 263–265.

3. List ten words for each of the English prefixes on pages 265–266.

4. The following words contain many of the prefixes which you have studied. Identify both the prefix and the word root, using the dictionary for this purpose. State the meaning of the prefix and the root, as well as the meaning of the word.

polygamy	college	postscript
destruction	agitate	epidermis
expel	subsequent	monarch

imponderable	depend	detract
proponent	perform	perspire
recur	edict	periscope
incline	impetus	dissent
retrograde	presume	transfusion
intermittent	implore	restrain
inspect	monotone	conduct
recollect	emit	secede
obstruct	transact	introduce
propel	automobile	immoral
explore	adjunct	ascribe
convince	suppress	symphony
expire	advertisement	aggression
dismiss	seduce	illegal

Exercise C

1. Compile a list of words with Latin prefixes taken from newspaper material. Compare news stories, editorials, and special features for frequency of Latin-prefix words.

2. From your general reading, compile a list of words using Greek prefixes and combining forms. Discuss the words you find in relation to what they communicate, the function they have in our language.

3. From your general reading, compile a list of words in which the prefix is joined to the stem with a hyphen. What prefixes are most generally hyphenated? Discuss special uses of the hyphen when it occurs with a prefix.

4. From your general reading, compile a list of words in which English prefixes are used. Discuss the relative frequency of use of Latin, Greek, and English prefixes.

5. Examine your themes which have been returned to you. From them, make up a list of words which contain Latin prefixes, Greek prefixes, English prefixes. Compare your use of Latin-prefix words with that of journalism, as studied in item 1.

17

Phonemics and Spelling

MANY STUDENTS have difficulty with spelling. There are two very important reasons for this difficulty. In the first place, if the student has not done much reading, he is likely to be unfamiliar with the pattern of letters forming a word. He cannot visualize this pattern when he wants to write the word. He will often represent the word with an approximate letter pattern which is unconventional and therefore "incorrect" in terms of standard written English. And as he quickly learns in the Freshman English class, the conventions of standard written English are nowhere more rigid than in the spelling of words. Although we may pronounce words differently, we all have to spell them the same when we write. Written English is a standardized dialect.

The second reason for difficulty in spelling is that there is no absolute one-to-one correspondence between the spoken sound and the written letter or letters. A given sound in the spoken language may be represented by different letter or letter combinations in the written language; the same letter may represent different sounds in speech; and some letters used in the written word are not translated into speech at all. We shall elaborate on this statement as the chapter develops.

The whole problem of spelling arises from the fact that the spoken language and the written language are two different symbolisms. The student is familiar with many words as sounds. He has listened to radio and television for years, he has been stimulated by a language environment created by professional writers and advertising men, and he has found meaning and satisfaction in this language environment. But the words he has thus grown accustomed to and perhaps uses in speech himself are sounds and not written symbols. He has developed an "ear literacy." Now when he attempts to use in writing some of the words he knows familiarly by sound, he must represent them with a different symbolism, and a new problem in learning arises. His "eye literacy" does not match his "ear literacy." Of course, the average student has been given many hours of instruction in spelling in the elementary and secondary schools, and in this way has learned to represent a good part of his spoken vocabulary with written symbols. But language development is a continuous process, and new problems in written communication require expanded resources in vocabulary. For most people the problem of spelling, like reading, is lifelong.

The purpose of this chapter is to examine the distinctive sounds in the spoken language — the phonemes — and to study the variety of ways in which these sounds are represented in the written language.

Phonemes Explained

Let us examine, first of all, certain pairs of words which contrast only in one simple sound.

pin	sail	kind	fin	stop	rubber
bin	tail	mind	fan	step	robber

In the words *pin* and *bin*, the sounds which differentiate the meanings of the two words are the *p* sound and the *b* sound. We are sensitive to these two sounds and to the slight difference between them. We respond to the two words accordingly. Similarly we are sensitive to the difference between the *s* sound in *sail* and the *t* sound in *tail*. Our response to *kind* or *mind* is the result of a distinction between the *k* sound and the *m* sound. The differentiation of meaning between *fin* and *fan* arises from the fact that we make a distinction between the *i* sound in *fin* and the *a* sound in *fan*. Similarly we distinguish between *stop* and *step* and between *rubber* and *robber*.

Linguists in their scientific study of English have found thirty-three basic and distinctive sounds which differentiate meaning: twenty-one consonant sounds, three semi-vowel sounds (the sounds of *h*, *w*, and *y*), and nine vowel sounds. These basic sounds together with four degrees of pitch, four degrees of loudness, and four kinds of juncture make up the total of forty-five phonemes of the language.

Since there are only twenty-six letters in the English alphabet and since there is not an exact correspondence between the way we ordinarily sound the letters and the distinctive sounds of the language, linguists have developed a phonemic alphabet. The phonemic alphabet is a set of thirty-three symbols which represent the basic, distinctive sounds of the language. These symbols are invariable in their representation of the basic sounds. The same symbol always represents the same sound, and no sound may be represented by more than one symbol.

A phonemic symbol is conventionally represented with diagonal bars. For example /b/ is the sound of the *b* in *bird*. The sound of the *g* in *girl* is /g/ but the sound of the *g* in *gem* is /ĵ/, the same as the sound of the *j* in *jam*. Sounds that are not truly represented by a letter of the alphabet such as the *ng* sound in *sing* or the *th* sound in *thin* are given new symbols. The symbol /ŋ/ represents the *ng* sound in *sing*, and the symbol /θ/ represents the *th* sound in *thin*.

The following table lists all the phonemic symbols and the sounds they represent. Remember that the second column identifies the *sound* and that the spelling given here for the sound is not necessarily its only spelling.

PHONEME	SOUND
/p/	the *p* sound in *parlor*
/t/	the *t* sound in *take*
/k/	the *k* sound in *kitten*
/b/	the *b* sound in *bit*
/d/	the *d* sound in *dog*
/g/	the *g* sound in *get*
/č/	the *ch* sound in *chin*
/ǰ/	the *j* sound in *jam*
/f/	the *f* sound in *fun*
/θ/	the *th* sound in *both*
/v/	the *v* sound in *van*
/ð/	the *th* sound in *this*
/s/	the *s* sound in *sat*
/š/	the *sh* sound in *show*
/z/	the *z* sound in *zeal*
/ž/	the *z* sound in *azure*
/m/	the *m* sound in *man*
/n/	the *n* sound in *never*
/ŋ/	the *ng* sound in *ring*
/l/	the *l* sound in *lake*
/r/	the *r* sound in *run*
/w/	the *w* sound in *wish*
/y/	the *y* sound in *yes*
/h/	the *h* sound in *hat*
/i/	the *i* sound in *sin*
/e/	the *e* sound in *pen*
/æ/	the *a* sound in *cat*
/ɨ/	the vowel sound in an unstressed syllable such as in *sofa*, *button*, or *system*
/ə/	the *u* sound in *bun*
/a/	the *o* sound in *hot*
/u/	the *u* sound in *put*
/o/	the *o* sound in *cone*
/ɔ/	The *au* sound in *taught*

The student will notice that certain vowel sounds which he may believe are simple vowel sounds are not included in the above table of phonemes. For example, we do not find a phoneme for the long *a* as in *cane*, the long *e* as in *scene*, the long *i* as in *mine*, and other familiar vowel sounds. These are not simple vowel sounds but combinations or diphthongs. Some of these familiar but more complex sounds are listed below.

PHONEME (DIPHTHONG)	SOUND
/ey/	the sound of *a* as in *cake*
/iy/	the sound of *e* as in *me*
/ay/	the sound of *i* as in *bite*
/uw/	the sound of *u* as in *flute*
/aw/	the sound of *ou* as in *house*
/iw/	the sound of *u* as in *cute*
/ɔy/	the sound of *oy* as in *boy*
/eh/	the sound of *a* as in *bare*
/ah/	the sound of *a* as in *far*
/əh/	the sound of *i* as in *bird*
/ks/	the sound of *x* as in *box*
/gs/	the sound of *x* as in *exist*

The thirty-three basic distinctive sounds of English and the more complex sounds listed above include most of the sounds which the writer hears in his mind when he is faced with the problem of putting the spoken word into written symbolism.

Variant Spellings of English Sounds

We have said that the sounds of English are represented by different letters and letter combinations in writing. Let us now examine each sound and note the different ways in which it may be represented in writing.

In the following list, the first column will give the sound as symbolized by the phonemic symbol. The second column will show the various ways in which this sound may be spelled in words.

SOUND	SPELLING	ILLUSTRATION
/p/	p	price, soap
	pp	slipper
/t/	t	top, pot
	tt	bottom
	tte	silhouette
	ed	stopped

Sound	Spelling	Illustration
/k/	k	kettle, peek
	c	cat, cream
	ck	stack, mackerel
	cc	accommodate
	ch	chiropractor
	que	antique
	q	quiet
	cq	acquaint
/b/	b	base, fib
	bb	rubber
/d/	d	dog, bad
	dd	sadder
	ed	killed
/g/	g	gone, dog
	gg	egg, drugged
	gue	rogue
/č/	ch	chin, touch
	tch	kitchen
	ti	question
	te	righteous
	tu	creature
/ǰ/	j	jam
	dg	judgment
	dge	ridge
	g	gem
	gg	exaggerate
	du	graduation
	di	soldier
/f/	f	farm, if
	ff	stuff
	ph	telephone
	gh	rough
/θ/	th	thick, both
/v/	v	vile, five
	vv	flivver
	f	of

Sound	Spelling	Illustration
/ð/	th	then, heathen
	the	breathe
/s/	s	soul, this
	ss	boss
	sc	science
	c	ceiling
	ce	race
/š/	sh	show, flash
	ssi	fission
	si	expansion
	ti	ratio
	ch	chute, brochure
	ce	crustacean
	ci	fallacious
	ss	issue
	se	nauseous
	sci	conscious
	su	sure
/z/	z	zinc
	zz	drizzle
	s	was
	x	xylophone
	ss	scissors
/ž/	si	collusion
	s	pleasure
	z	azure
	g	prestige
/m/	m	map, ham
	mm	swimming
/n/	n	never, on
	nn	fanning
/ŋ/	ng	sing
	n	think
	ngue	tongue
/l/	l	love, belong
	ll	ball

Sound	Spelling	Illustration
/r/	r	run, bury
	rr	hurry
/w/	w	wet
	wh	when
	u	queen
	o	choir
/y/	y	yes
	i	view
/h/	h	hat
	wh	whole
/i/	i	sin
	o	women
	u	busy
	ui	guild
	y	sympathy
	ie	sieve
	e	English
/e/	e	pen
	a	many
	u	bury
	ea	feather
	ai	said
	ei	heifer
	ie	friend
	ay	says
	eo	jeopardy
	ae	aesthetic
/æ/	a	cat
	ai	plaid
/ɨ/	a	sofa
	e	mitten
	i	hastily
	o	button
	u	hiccup
	ai	fountain
	eo	sturgeon

Sound	Spelling	Illustration
	ou	furious
	ia	parliament
	oi	tortoise
/ə/	u	but
	o	ton
	ou	country
	oe	does
	oo	blood
/a/	o	hot
	a	what
/u/	u	put
	o	woman
	oo	wood
	ou	would
/o/	o	cone
	ow	crow
	ou	soul
	oa	coal
	eau	plateau
	ew	sew
	oe	doe
	oo	brooch
/ɔ/	au	taught
	ou	brought
	a	ball
	aw	spawn
	o	often
	oa	broad
/ey/	a	cake
	ai	train
	ay	stray
	ea	break
	ei	rein
	ey	obey
	au	gauge
	et	sobriquet

SOUND	SPELLING	ILLUSTRATION
/iy/	e	me
	ee	seen
	ei	receive
	ie	believe
	ea	clean
	ae	Caesar
	ey	Ceylon
	oe	Phoenix
	eo	people
	i	ravine
	ay	quay
	y	soliloquy
/ay/	i	nice
	ie	lie
	ei	sleight
	y	fry
	ai	Kaiser
	ay	kayak
	uy	guy
	ye	bye
	ey	eye
/uw/	u	flute
	oo	room
	ew	flew
	o	prove
	ui	nuisance
	ue	blue
	ou	croup
	eu	maneuver
	oe	canoe
	ioux	Sioux
/aw/	ou	house
	ow	cow
/iw/	u	cute
	ew	few
	ewe	ewe
	you	your
	eu	eulogy
	eau	beautiful

SOUND	SPELLING	ILLUSTRATION
	iew	view
	ue	cue
	yu	Yukon
	ueue	queue
/ɔy/	oy	boy
	oi	soil
/eh/	a	bare
	ai	stair
	ea	bear
	ay	mayor
	e	ere
	ei	heir
/ah/	a	father
	e	sergeant
	ea	hearth
/əh/	e	germ
	ea	learn
	i	third
	u	burn
	o	worm
	ou	courtesy
	y	myrrh
/ks/	x	box
	cc	occidental
	ks	books
	cks	rocks
	cs	attics
/gs/	x	exact
	gs	hogs
	ggs	eggs

This list of spellings for the different sounds in English is by no means complete and may be lengthened as more unusual words such as technical terms are studied. In our present-day culture, with rapid means of communication, we often borrow words freely from other languages, sometimes using our own pronunciation with the foreign spelling. This further complicates the problem of spelling and adds "unusual" words to our vocabularies. However, the student who acquaints himself with the common spellings of the distinctive sounds and builds word lists with each of the spellings will become more sensitive to the sounds of words and more familiar with the correspondence of sound and spelling. This correspondence exists and may be mastered through study. If this correspondence did not exist, each word in the language would be a unique spelling problem.

There are exceptions, however, so that the student not only must study the correspondence of sound and spelling, but also note instances of the lack of it. The main cause of the lack of correspondence is, of course, historical, the etymology of the word itself. We find it expressed chiefly in the "silent" letters. Consonants which do not represent any sound of the spoken word often present difficulty in the spelling of a word. Following is a partial list of words with "silent" consonants.

SILENT LETTERS	ILLUSTRATIONS
d	Wednesday
g	gnat, phlegm
h	ghost, naphtha
k	knife
l	calm, solder
m	mnemonic
n	hymn
p	psychology, psalm
gh	eight
ph	phthalein

Finally, some words in English might be called the "sports" of the language, for sound and spelling appear almost entirely unrelated. Following is a short list of such words.

colonel	diarrhoea
Worcester	pyrrhic
Conchubar	sarsaparilla
schism	sovereign
phthisic	tsetse fly

Summary

Students are often needlessly embarrassed because they are made to believe that they are "poor spellers." Spelling is a real problem growing out of the relation and lack of relation of the spoken and written representations of the language. The variant spellings of the basic sounds of English, together with the presence in the language of unusually spelled words, is confusing to the student who has had little practice in writing and limited experience in reading.

Linguists have identified the basic, distinctive sounds of English and have developed a phonemic alphabet to represent these sounds. In this chapter, we have listed the thirty-three basic sounds with their phonemic symbols, together with twelve more complex sounds (diphthongs); these forty-five phonemes represent the usual language sounds which the writer must translate into written symbols. We have also listed most of the variant spellings of each sound. The student should master the variant spellings and develop word lists of his own for each one. A list of some of the more unusual words in English with "silent" consonants has also been given; these words should be memorized and the list extended from the student's general reading.

Exercise A

It is suggested that in the following exercises students check their lists of words against a dictionary for pronunciation, in order to guard against nonstandard pronunciations.

1. List twenty words in which the sound of /p/ is spelled with the letter *p;* with *pp*.
2. List twenty words in which the sound of /t/ is spelled with the letter *t;* with *tt*.
3. List ten words in which the sound of /t/ is spelled with *ed*.
4. List five words in which the sound of /t/ is spelled with *tte*.
5. List ten words in which the sound of /k/ is spelled with the letter *k*.
6. List twenty words in which the /k/ sound is spelled with the letter *c;* with *ck*.

7. List ten words in which the /k/ sound is spelled with *cc;* with *ch.*

8. List five words in which the /k/ sound is spelled with *q;* with *cq.*

9. List twenty words in which the /b/ sound is spelled with the letter *b;* with *bb.*

10. List twenty words in which the /d/ sound is spelled with the letter *d;* with *dd;* with *ed.*

11. List twenty words in which the /g/ sound is spelled with the letter *g;* with *gg.*

12. List ten words in which the /g/ sound is spelled with *gue.*

13. List twenty words in which the /č/ sound is spelled with *ch;* with *tch.*

14. List five words in which the /č/ sound is spelled with *ti;* with *te;* with *tu.*

15. List twenty words in which the /ǰ/ sound is spelled with the letter *j.*

16. List ten words in which the /ǰ/ sound is spelled with *dg;* with *dge.*

17. List twenty words in which the /ǰ/ sound is spelled with the letter *g;* list as many as you can find spelled with *gg.*

18. List five words in which the /ǰ/ sound is spelled with *du;* with *di.*

19. List twenty words in which the /f/ sound is spelled with the letter *f;* with *ff.*

20. List ten words in which the /f/ sound is spelled with *ph;* with *gh.*

21. List twenty words illustrating the /ŋ/ sound.

22. List twenty words in which the /v/ sound is spelled with the letter *v;* list as many as you can find spelled with *vv.*

23. List the words in which the /v/ sound is spelled with the letter *f.*

24. List twenty words illustrating the /θ/ sound.

25. List twenty words in which the /s/ sound is spelled with the letter *s;* with *ss.*

26. List fifteen words in which the /s/ sound is spelled with *sc;* with *c.*

27. List ten words in which the /s/ sound is spelled with *ce.*

28. List twenty words in which the /š/ sound is spelled with *sh.*

29. List as many words as you can in which the /š/ sound is spelled with *ssi.*

30. List twenty words in which the /š/ sound is spelled with *si;* with *ti.*

31. List twenty words in which the /š/ sound is spelled with *ch.*

32. List five words in which the /š/ sound is spelled with *ce;* with *ci.*

33. List as many words as you can find in which the /š/ sound is spelled with *ss; su; se.*

34. List ten words in which the /š/ sound is spelled with *sci*.

35. List ten words in which the /z/ sound is spelled with the letter *z;* with *zz*.

36. List as many words as you can find in which the /z/ sound is spelled with *x;* with *s;* with *ss*.

37. List fifteen words in which the /ž/ sound is spelled with *si*.

38. List as many words as you can find in which the /ž/ sound is spelled with *s;* with *z;* with *g*.

39. List twenty words in which the /m/ sound is spelled with the letter *m;* with *mm*.

40. List twenty words in which the /n/ sound is spelled with the letter *n;* with *nn*.

41. List twenty words in which the /ŋ/ sound is spelled with *ng;* with *n*.

42. List as many words as you can find in which the /ŋ/ sound is spelled with *ngue*.

43. List twenty words in which the /l/ sound is spelled with the letter *l;* with *ll*.

44. List twenty words in which the /r/ sound is spelled with the letter *r;* with *rr*.

45. List twenty words in which the /w/ sound is spelled with the letter *w*.

46. List twenty words in which the /y/ sound is spelled with the letter *y*.

47. List as many words as you can find in which the /y/ sound is spelled with *i*.

48. List twenty words in which the /h/ sound is spelled with the letter *h*.

Exercise B

1. List twenty words in which the /i/ sound is spelled with the letter *i*.

2. List ten words in which the /i/ sound is spelled with the letter *y*.

3. List as many words as you can find in which the /i/ sound is spelled with *o; u; ui; ie; e*.

4. List twenty words in which the /e/ sound is spelled with the letter *e*.

5. List ten words in which the /e/ sound is spelled with *ea*.

6. List as many words as you can find in which the /e/ sound is spelled with *a; u; ai; ei; ie; ay; eo; ae*.

7. List twenty words in which the /æ/ sound is spelled with the letter *a*.

8. List as many words as you can find in which the /æ/ sound is spelled with *ai*.

9. The vowel sound of an unaccented syllable of a word is usually the sound /ĭ/. In many words, the unaccented syllable ends in the letter *r*, and it may be spelled *or*, *ar*, *er*. For example, we have the words *sailor, solar, sadder*. Make up a list of as many words as you can think of ending in unaccented syllables spelled with *or;* with *ar;* with *er*.

10. In many words the unaccented syllable is spelled *able* or *ible*. For example, we have *acceptable* and *contemptible*. Make up a list of as many words as you can find ending in unaccented syllables spelled with *able;* with *ible*.

11. In many words the unaccented syllable is spelled *ant* or *ent*. For example, we have *servant* and *dependent*. Make up a list of as many words as you can find ending in unaccented syllables spelled with *ant;* with *ent*.

12. List as many words as you can find in which the spelling of the un-accented syllable is with *u;* with *ai;* with *eo;* with *ou;* with *ia;* with *oi*.

13. List twenty words in which the /ə/ sound is spelled with the letter *u*.

14. List as many words as you can find in which the /ə/ sound is spelled with *o;* with *ou;* with *oe;* with *oo*.

15. List twenty words in which the /a/ sound is spelled with the letter *o*.

16. List as many words as you can find in which the /a/ sound is spelled with *a*.

17. List twenty words in which the /u/ sound is spelled with the letter *u*.

18. List as many words as you can find in which the /u/ sound is spelled with *o;* with *oo;* with *ou*.

19. List twenty words in which the /o/ sound is spelled with the letter *o*.

20. List ten words in which the /o/ sound is spelled with *ow;* with *oa*.

21. List as many words as you can find in which the /o/ sound is spelled with *ou; eau; ew; oe; oo*.

22. List ten words in which the /ɔ/ sound is spelled with *au; ou; aw*.

23. List as many words as you can find in which the /ɔ/ sound is spelled with *a; o; oa*.

Exercise C

1. The sound /ey/ is the long *a* sound as in *cake*. It is spelled in eight different ways — *a, ai, ay, ea, ei, ey, au, et*. Given here is a list of words with the /ey/ vowel sound with the *ai* spelling:

rain	strain
main	train

brain	sprain
Cain	domain
lain	maintain

Develop similar lists, as many words as you can find, of all the differ-ent spellings of the /ey/ sound.

2. The sound /iy/ is the long e sound as in *me*. It is spelled in twelve different ways — *e, ee, ei, ie, ea, ae, ey, oe, eo, i, ay, y*. Given here is a representative list of words with the /ey/ vowel sound with the *ei* spelling:

receive	leisure
perceive	deceive
either	receipt
neither	ceiling
seize	conceit

Develop similar lists, as many words as you can find, using each of the different spellings of the /iy/ sound.

3. The sound /ay/ is the long *i* sound as in *nice*. It is spelled in nine different ways — *i, ie, ei, y, ai, ay, uy, ye, ey*. Given here is a repre-sentative list of words with the /ay/ vowel sound with the *y* spelling:

fry	pylon
sty	python
cry	style
by	nylon
my	xylophone

Develop similar lists, as many words as you can find, using each of the different spellings of the /ay/ sound.

4. The sound /uw/ is the sound of *u* as in *flute*. It is spelled in ten different ways — *u, oo, ew, o, ui, ue, ou, eu, oe, ioux*. Given here is a representative list of words with the /uw/ vowel sound with the *ew* spelling:

flew	blew
screw	crew
stew	brew
strewn	slew
dew	Lewis

Develop similar lists, as many words as you can find, using each of the different spellings of the /uw/ sound.

5. The sound /aw/ is the vowel sound of *ou* in *house*. It is spelled in two different ways — *ou, ow*. List as many words as you can find for each spelling.

6. The sound /iw/ is the sound of *u* in *cute*. It is spelled in ten different ways — *u, ew, ewe, you, eu, eau, iew, ue, yu, ueue*. Given here is a representative list of words with the /iw/ vowel sound with the *eu* spelling:

eulogy	heuristic
Beulah	euphony
eugenic	Euclid
euthanasia	euphemism
Europe	eureka

Develop similar lists, as many words as you can find, using each of the different spellings of the /iw/ sound.

7. The sound /ɔy/ is the sound of *oy* in *boy*. It is spelled in two different ways — *oy, oi*. List as many words as you can find for each spelling.

8. The sound /eh/ is the sound of *a* in *bare*. It is a sound of a vowel combined with the *r* sound in a word. It is spelled in six different ways — *a, ai, ea, ay, e, ei*. Given here is a representative list of words with the /eh/ sound with the *ai* spelling:

air	bairn
stair	cairn
lair	flair
pair	fair
laird	despair

Develop similar lists, as many words as you can find, using each of the different spellings of the /eh/ sound.

9. The sound /ah/ is the sound of *a* in *father*. It is spelled in three different ways — *a, e, ae*. List as many words as you can find for each spelling.

10. The sound /əh/ is the sound of *e* in *germ*. It is a vowel sound combined with the *r* sound in a word. It is spelled in seven different ways — *e, ea, i, u, o, ou, y*. Given here is a representative list of words with the /əh/ sound with the *u* spelling:

urn	curl
murky	churn
lurch	church
burn	curlew
turn	Burke

Develop similar lists, as many words as you can find, using each of the different spellings of the /əh/ sound.

11. The sound /ks/ is the sound of *x* in *box*. It has five different spellings
    — *x, cc, ks, cks, cs*. List as many words as you can find for each.
12. The sound /gs/ is the sound of *x* in *exact*. It has three different spell-
    ings — *x, gs, ggs*. List as many words as you can find for each.

EXERCISE D

1. One of the factors of difficulty in spelling is the "silent" letter. Given
   here is a representative list of words in which the *g* is not pronounced:

phlegm	gnaw
paradigm	gnu
gnome	gnarled
gnat	reign
align	seignior
gnostic	sign

   Develop similar lists, using as many words as you can find, with each
   of the "silent" letters listed on page 280 and as many more as you
   can think of.
2. Some words such as *colonel* seem to have almost no relation between
   sound and spelling. Develop a continually growing list of these words
   as a result of your reading.
3. If you would like to become more familiar with phonemic symbolism,
   practice changing common words to phonemic symbols. For example,
   sing would be written /siŋ/; *cough* would be written /kɔf/; *thin* would
   be written /θin/; *box* would be written /baks/; cute would be written
   /kiwt/.
4. As a final exercise, look up the spelling rules in a collegiate dictionary.
   Make up lists of words which illustrate these rules.

18

Punctuation

THE FORM of the spoken language provides many clues to meaning. We have discussed word order, structure words, inflected forms, and their importance as signals in previous chapters. One of the most important of all clues to meaning remains to be discussed — it is what linguists call intonation.

Intonation, as the term is used here, implies the changes in pitch as the voice rises and falls, the degrees of stress or volume as the voice becomes loud or soft, and the momentary pauses between words and word groups. The combination of all of these is of great significance to oral communication.

In written communication, however, the graphic symbols of language are not reinforced by these physical means. Additional graphic symbols are needed to supply in part the reinforcement which only the voice can give to language. Thus the symbols of punctuation are used to help the reader separate the written language into meaningful syntactical units. They help to determine

288

the response by differentiating statement and question. They serve as a means of identifying the one who is communicating. They may even give extra emphasis to what is being written.

Pitch and Juncture

In speech the voice, as it rises and falls in pitch, and the pauses which separate the word groups from each other supply the important clues to syntax. The linguist thinks of these in terms of pitch and juncture.

Four levels of pitch are recognized: low, normal, high, and very high. Phonemically, they are numbered in order /1, 2, 3, 4/. We will illustrate these after a brief discussion of juncture.

Juncture relates to the joint or joining that marks the division between words and word groups. Four kinds of juncture are described: plus juncture /+/, single-bar juncture /|/, double-bar juncture /‖/, and double-cross juncture /#/.

1. They /+/ raise horses.
2. Please come here /|/ Margaret.
3. Is this house for sale /‖/
4. I am going home /#/

In example 1, the slight pause separating *they* from *raise* identifies the separate words. Plus juncture is brief, is internal, and is accompanied by no change of pitch. Its importance in communication may be seen from the following sentences.

They /+/ raise horses.
They're /+/ race horses.

Jim has a car that's /+/ tops.
Jim has a car that /+/ stops.

I know that /+/ still in the house.
I know that's /+/ Till in the house.

A blood /+/ donor must be a blood /+/ owner.

In example 2, the slight pause between *here* and *Margaret* separates the word group from the person addressed. This single-bar juncture is not as brief as the plus juncture. It is a terminal juncture and is accompanied by no change in pitch.

In example 3, the pause indicates "the end of the sentence" and
in this case is accompanied by a rising pitch. The double-bar
juncture is a longer sound break than the single-bar juncture, is
accompanied by a rising pitch, and is a terminal juncture.

The pause indicated in example 4 is usually the longest of the
four junctures and is accompanied by a falling pitch. The double-
cross juncture is a terminal juncture.

The following examples illustrate pitch (the levels phonemically
numbered) and juncture.

> Where are you going tonight?
> 2   3   1
> Where are you going tonight /#/
>
> Oh, I think I'll go to a party.
> 2   3 1
> Oh /|/ I think I'll go to a party /#/
>
> You say you're going to a party?
> 2   4
> You say you're going to a party /‖/
>
> Yes, that's what I said.
> 2   1
> Yes /|/ that's what I said /#/

Relation of Intonation to Punctuation

A writer's interest in intonation as a guide to meaning in the
spoken language centers on whatever relationship exists between
intonation and punctuation. Ideally, perhaps, a system of punctuation should reproduce the intonation patterns of the voice.
But though linguists have developed phonemic symbols for the
elements of pitch, stress, and juncture, the use of these symbols to
represent speech in writing is slow in the process and extremely
complex in the result. Speed in writing and in reading is the
product of a simplified and partial representation of intonation
signals for identifying language patterns. Punctuation is the name
given to this graphic representation which, like our language, has
developed quite casually.

Since writing is, of course, a standardized dialect of English in which a graphic symbolism is used, there is bound to be some agreement between intonation and punctuation. That this agreement is by no means complete, we all know. We have several ways of asking a question in the spoken language, yet we have but one mark to indicate it in writing. We have a great variety of punctuation signals, the comma, the colon, the semicolon, the dash, the period, and others, but no exclusive, sharply defined functions for any one of them. The fact that students must learn so many "rules" of punctuation is some evidence of diversity of function; and the fact that handbooks seldom agree on all the "rules" is further evidence of shifting opinion and practice.

The informed student of writing should be familiar with the relationship between intonation and punctuation, as well as the lack of relationship. He should be sensitive to the need for punctuation, should understand the nature of the problem and be familiar with the choices he can make in solving it.

Let us examine some of the common conventions of punctuation and relate them to the corresponding intonation patterns of speech.

Words in Series

We had roast beef, mashed potatoes, apple salad, and ice cream.

1. We had roast beef /|/ mashed potatoes /|/ apple salad /|/ and ice cream /#/

2. We had roast beef /||/ mashed potatoes /||/ apple salad /||/ and ice cream /#/

3. We had roast beef /#/ mashed potatoes /#/ apple salad /#/ and ice cream /#/

In number 1, the speaker uses a level tone of voice at each juncture except at the end of the sentence, when his voice drops. In number 2, he uses a rising inflection at each juncture except at the end of the sentence. In number 3, he lets his voice fall at each juncture. The comma is the graphic convention for all three intonation patterns, and the person reading the sentence orally may use any one of them or even a combination that is not represented above.

When adjectives are in series we do not always separate each successive adjective from the preceding one by a comma.

> She wore a light, blue dress.
> She wore a light blue dress.

In the first sentence the writer means that the dress is light and the dress is also blue. In the second sentence he means that the dress is light blue in color. The changing position of the juncture makes the intonation patterns of these two sentences different.

1. She wore a light /|/ blue dress /#/
2. She wore a light blue /|/ dress /#/

On the other hand, we may very well have a situation in which an adjective apparently modifies an adjective-noun combination. In such a case there is a juncture but no punctuation.

> Harry is a cute little boy.
> Harry is a cute /|/ little boy /#/

> Mrs. Smith is a very active old lady.
> Mrs. Smith is a very active /|/ old lady /#/

In the above sentences *little boy* and *old lady* become, in terms of syntax, compounds. *Cute* is the modifier of *little boy*, and *very active* is the modifier of *old lady*.

Appositives

The use of commas with appositives was briefly discussed in Chapter 15. In the following examples we shall examine the contrasting intonation patterns of restrictive and nonrestrictive appositives (nouns).

1. The poet Wordsworth wrote about the beauties of nature.
2. Wordsworth, the poet, wrote about the beauties of nature.

1. The poet Wordsworth /|/ wrote about the beauties of nature /#/
2. Wordsworth /|/ the poet /|/ wrote about the beauties of nature /#/

The comma is not the only mark of punctuation to set off appositives in written English. The dash, as well as parentheses, is used for this purpose.

We were invited to the Press Club banquet — the occasion for the award of journalistic "Oscars."

Peter Schmaltz' German Band (two trumpets and four bass horns) livened up the Bierstuben party.

Descriptive Adjective Clauses

1. I referred the matter to the lady *who is in charge of complaints.*
2. I referred the matter to Mrs. Bliss, *who is in charge of complaints.*

In sentence 1, the adjective clause is called a restrictive modifier since it helps to identify "the lady." The adjective clause in sentence 2 does not identify the noun which it modifies, but merely adds further information. In this sense it is descriptive and is referred to as nonrestrictive.

The following illustrations show the contrasting intonation patterns of the restrictive and descriptive adjective clauses.

1. I referred the matter to the lady who is in charge of complaints /#/
2. I referred the matter to Mrs. Bliss /|/ who is in charge of complaints /#/

Interrupting Elements

1. The truth is, however, that the man is guilty.
   The truth is /|/ however /|/ that the man is guilty /#/
2. The jury, as a matter of fact, was hand-picked by the defending counsel.
   The jury /|/ as a matter of fact /|/ was hand-picked by the defending counsel /#/
3. This investigation, if it is ever completed, should reveal some startling facts.
   This investigation /|/ if it is ever completed /|/ should reveal some startling facts /#/

As we may see above, the interrupting elements or parenthetical expressions within a sentence are set off with commas. As a rule, a single-bar juncture precedes and follows such an element.

Questions

Questions in written English are punctuated with a question mark. The terminal juncture of a question may be a double-bar juncture or it may be a double-cross juncture.

1. When are you going to Boston?
   When are you going to Boston /#/

2. Are you ever going to Boston?
   Are you ever going to Boston /‖/

3. You are going to Boston?
   You are going to Boston /‖/

4. Will they be glad to see you in Boston?
   Will they be glad to see you in Boston /‖/

5. Will they be glad to see you in Boston?
   Will they be glad to see you in Boston /#/

The first three sentences illustrate the conventional question forms. In the first sentence, the pitch falls and the voice trails off at the end, just as it does in a statement. In the second and third sentences, the pitch rises at the end and the voice stops suddenly. The fourth and fifth sentences are identical in words but different in intonation. The fourth sentence is like number 2 in its intonation pattern. The fifth sentence is a rhetorical question — no answer is expected, the pitch falls at the end, and the voice trails off.

Punctuation as an Aid to Communication

Although pitch and juncture tend to mark off the significant word groups in speech, there is little correspondence between these intonational phonemes and punctuation. We cannot say exactly that this type of juncture requires a comma or a semicolon while that type requires a period or a question mark.

The ability to punctuate appropriately (not "correctly") depends on one's knowledge of grammatical syntax and the conventions of punctuation, some of which are derived from the practices of the printer. The important thing to remember is that punctuation is an aid to communication and should be used to help the reader understand what is being written.

The force of this statement may be demonstrated by the illustration below: an unpunctuated paragraph, followed by the same paragraph punctuated. A comparison of the reading difficulty of the two will show the importance of punctuation in written communication.

the summer of 1919 passed the Senate debated the Peace Treaty the House passed the Volstead Act the Suffrage Amendment passed Congress and went to the States the R–34 made the first transatlantic dirigible flight from England to Mineola Long Island and returned safely people laughed over The Young Visitors and wondered whether Daisy Ashford was really James M Barrie the newspapers denounced sugar hoarders and food profiteers as the cost of living kept on climbing the first funeral by airplane was held ministers lamented the increasing laxity of morals among the young but still the fear and hatred of Bolshevism gripped the American mind as new strikes broke out and labor became more aggressive and revolution spread like a scourge through Europe and then in September came the Boston police strike and the fear was redoubled

The summer of 1919 passed. The Senate debated the Peace Treaty. The House passed the Volstead Act. The Suffrage Amendment passed Congress and went to the States. The R–34 made the first transatlantic dirigible flight from England to Mineola, Long Island, and returned safely. People laughed over *The Young Visitors* and wondered whether Daisy Ashford was really James M. Barrie. The newspapers denounced sugar hoarders and food profiteers as the cost of living kept on climbing. The first funeral by airplane was held. Ministers lamented the increasing laxity of morals among the young. But still the fear and hatred of Bolshevism gripped the American mind as new strikes broke out and labor became more aggressive and revolution spread like a scourge through Europe. And then, in September, came the Boston police strike, and the fear was redoubled.[1]

It is not the purpose of this chapter to review and summarize all the numerous generalizations relating to problems of punctuation. It is assumed that most college students have a fair knowledge of the conventions. There are, however, situations in which the great body of beginning writers have considerable difficulty, and these seem to cluster in four main problem areas:

1. Introductory modifier word groups
2. Restrictive and nonrestrictive modifiers
3. Compound sentences
4. The use of italics and quotation marks

[1] Frederick Lewis Allen, *Only Yesterday* (Harper and Brothers).

Introductory Modifier Word Groups

In dealing with the first problem, one has to remember that not all introductory sentence elements are set off with commas. The writer usually has to make a decision: Shall I punctuate or shall I not? In deciding, he must ask himself whether the comma is necessary to make his meaning clear, whether the statement would be ambiguous to his reader if the comma were omitted. If the comma is not needed, it becomes just an extra mark for the eye to look at and, in quantity, will slow up reading. Let us examine some sentences in which there is an introductory modifying word group, a word group coming before the subject of the sentence.

1. In the afternoon we went for a long walk.

2. On the evening of a day late in September, the first heavy rain began to fall.

3. When summer comes, you will enjoy the pleasant heat of Arizona.

4. On the other hand, Father will not permit John to go on this trip.

5. In the afternoon after the rain had stopped, the men began to build the wall.

In the first sentence, the modifier word group that comes before the subject is a short prepositional phrase. There is little danger of misreading, and so the comma is not used to set it apart from the main sentence — to warn the reader that the subject is about to appear.

In the second sentence, the introductory word group is made up of three prepositional phrases and is rather long. The comma might very well have been left out, but its use can be defended on the ground that the average reader is better able to find the subject of the sentence (mentally) as he reads if it is put in. Besides, without a comma, the reader might read "September the first."

In the third sentence, the introductory modifier is a subject-predicate word group, a subordinate clause. The comma is placed after the subordinate clause as an additional signal to mark off this constituent of the sentence because of its communicative importance.

In the fourth sentence, the introductory word group is a transitional phrase. It is there to secure coherence with what has just been said. In a sense it is a link between two sentences and punctuation marks it off as a link. Transitional phrases are short introductory phrases and are conventionally followed by commas.

In the fifth sentence, the introductory word group is a long complex structure made up of a prepositional phrase with a subordinate clause modifier. Without punctuation one might read "the rain had stopped the men." Hence the comma is necessary to avoid ambiguity and secure adequate understanding of what is being said.

To summarize, the writer should recognize that when a sentence begins with an introductory modifier word group, a problem in punctuation faces him. He will set the word group off with a comma if he finds any possibility of an ambiguous reading without punctuation. If the introductory word group is a transitional phrase or if it contains a subordinate clause, he will usually use a comma to separate it from the subject of the sentence.

The following sentences, taken from published material, illustrate these points.

> When war comes, entire nations are mobilized.[2]

> As an example of the incredible reasoning processes which have created international summitomania, we cite the conclusion reached by Averell Harriman after his "terrifying, shocking" talks with Nikita Khrushchev.[3]

> To say the least, these are naive and vain hopes.[4]

> For this reason Moscow's most important task at present is to soften U.S. public opinion. . . .[5]

> In the successful art world today there is a cult of ugliness that is every bit as offensive as the old candy-box school of pretty painting.[6]

Restrictive and Nonrestrictive Modifiers

The second main problem for the beginning writer concerns the punctuation of restrictive and nonrestrictive modifiers, mostly

[2] *The Phoenix Gazette*, July 11, 1959.
[3] *Ibid.*
[4] *The Phoenix Gazette*, July 13, 1959.
[5] *Ibid.*
[6] *Ibid.*

clauses. This problem has two aspects, the recognition of such modifiers and the punctuation involved. Let us first consider the matter of recognition.

1. I called on the plumber who lives on Eighth Street.
2. I called on the plumber, who lives on Eighth Street.

In the first sentence, the modifying clause "who lives on Eighth Street" *identifies* the plumber on whom I called. In the second sentence the clause merely adds information about the plumber; we may say that it *describes* him. The identity of the plumber is not an issue in sentence 2 — perhaps there is only one plumber. In speech (as we have noted on page 293) there would be a slight pause in sentence 2, between *plumber* and *who*, which would serve as a signal to the listener. This speech signal (a single-bar juncture), to which the listener is acutely sensitive, is represented by the comma, to which the reader may be somewhat less sensitive.

The clause in sentence 1 is called a restrictive clause and is not set off by punctuation; the clause in sentence 2 is a nonrestrictive clause and is set off by a comma.

Let us consider some further illustrations of restrictive modifying clauses.

I enjoyed the book *which you gave me.*

This is the house *that Jack built.*

The picture *that Jerry painted* will be shown at the fair.

Ask the policeman *who is standing on the corner.*

There is a time *when all good citizens must work together.*

I am going to a city *where I have many old friends.*

He walked in *just as we were sitting down to dinner.*

I waited for him *until it was dark.*

I shall be glad to go *if you will come with me.*

Civilization will be destroyed *unless we can eliminate war.*

The student will notice that the first six sentences above contain adjective clauses which are restrictive modifiers. In the last four sentences, the restrictive modifying clauses are adverbial. Adverbial clauses, of course, are not identifying clauses, but their close semantic relationship to the verb modified is similar to that of the adjective clause to the noun it modifies. This relationship is revealed in speech by the intonation pattern, which is part of the structure of the utterance and an important clue to meaning.

The following sentences contain nonrestrictive modifying clauses.

We called on Mrs. Jones, *who lives on Bank Street.*

Dr. Thompson, *who has his office in the Spring Building,* will operate on Jim.

We walked through the park, *which was very beautiful in the spring sunshine.*

The *Lusitania, which was one of the most beautiful steamers ever built,* was sunk in World War I.

We are planning to go to New York, *where we will visit some friends.*

He will remain here until Christmas, *when he will leave for Los Angeles.*

Helen will attend college this fall, *although she may remain for only one term.*

Henry will return to England in September, *if the Lord is willing and the money holds out.*

The game had ended in a defeat for the University, *while Jim sat on the bench in impatient misery.*

Plumkin was the last player the coach would ever use in any game, *because the coach was never certain which way Plumkin would run with the ball.*

The following sentences taken from published sources contain restrictive clauses.

There is scarcely a city *which does not show a bright new cluster of skyscrapers at its center.*[7]

The banker *who advised caution* was quite right about financial conditions, and so were the forecasters.[8]

In the space of two short hours, dozens of stocks lost ground *which it had required many months of the bull market to gain.*[9]

With millions of people to be dealt with it was necessary to find some selective device *that could be quickly and easily used.*[10]

The cold war is confusing *because to our minds war means shot and shell, burning and murder.*[11]

[7] Frederick Lewis Allen, *Only Yesterday.*
[8] *Ibid.*
[9] *Ibid.*
[10] *The Phoenix Gazette,* July 13, 1959.
[11] *The Phoenix Gazette,* July 11, 1959.

The following sentences taken from published sources contain nonrestrictive clauses.

> Former Attorney General Francis Biddle, *who owns one of the historic houses in Wellfleet and favors the Government's acquisition of land genuinely needed to protect shore areas,* deplores the idea of taking over and eventually destroying whole communities.[12]

> One sunny summer afternoon about six years ago, *when I was twelve,* I walked around the block to see my friend Johnny McGuire.[13]

> "But it can take action when it believes its hospitality has been abused, *as it obviously did in the Remisov case.*"[14]

> So intense was the excitement over football that stadia seating fifty and sixty and seventy thousand people were filled to the last seat when the big teams met, *while scores of thousands more sat in warm living-rooms to hear the play-by-play story over the radio. . . .*[15]

> An unaccountable pain was in her knees, *as if they were broken.*[16]

Compound Sentences

A third important punctuation problem centers in the use of compound sentences. This has been discussed to some extent in Chapter 4 and will be further elaborated here.

Compound sentences in which the connective is one of the co-ordinate conjunctions *and, but, or, nor, for, so, yet,* are usually punctuated with a comma placed before the conjunction. In sentences in which the co-ordinate clauses are very short and there is little possibility of ambiguity, the comma is often omitted before the conjunction *and.* In compound sentences in which there is internal punctuation within one or both of the co-ordinate clauses, the semicolon is sometimes used to indicate the break before the conjunction; these sentences are usually long sentences.

The conventional punctuation of compound sentences, the use of the comma or semicolon before the conjunction, is illustrated in the following sentences.

[12] *The Saturday Evening Post,* July 18, 1959.
[13] *Ibid.*
[14] *Ibid.*
[15] Frederick Lewis Allen, *Only Yesterday.*
[16] Katherine Anne Porter, "Maria Concepçion."

Lights glowed in four great crystal chandeliers, *but* they were dimmed by television lights and sunlight streaming in through high windows.[17]

Through some of this ran the threads of criminal associates and shady finance, *and* by the end of the day the atmosphere of amiability and labor statesmanship had disappeared.[18]

It is sad that the most expensively educated men in America should be so badly educated in this respect, *for* their misconception of the minds of women can hardly fail to warp their dealings with half the human race. . . .[19]

She was dressed in black; *and* at once his uplifting exultation was replaced by an awed and quivering patience before her white face, before the immobility if her reposeful pose, the more amazing to him who had encountered the strength of her limbs and the indomitable spirit in her body.[20]

He probably used it more wisely at sixty-four than he would have at thirty-four, *but* he didn't get so much fun out of it; *nor* was there anything like so much of it, *for* the income tax was terrific in 1918 and unheard of in the eighties.[21]

These rules sound elementary, *and so* they are, *but* they demand a deep change of attitude in anyone who has grown used to writing in the style now fashionable.[22]

The specialization of science is an inevitable accompaniment of progress; *yet* it is full of dangers, *and* it is cruel and wasteful, since so much that is beautiful and enlightening is cut off from most of the world.[23]

Compound sentences in which no co-ordinate conjunction is used are usually punctuated with a semicolon, but if the co-ordinate clauses are short, commas are sometimes used. The following sentences are illustrative.

The Napoleonic harrow had indeed done its work; the seed was planted; and the crop would have surprised Napoleon.[24]

[17] *The Saturday Evening Post*, July 18, 1959.
[18] *Ibid.*
[19] Lynn White, Jr., *Educating Our Daughters.*
[20] Joseph Conrad, *Victory.*
[21] Elmer Davis, *But We Were Born Free.*
[22] George Orwell, *Shooting an Elephant and Other Essays.*
[23] J. Robert Oppenheimer, "Prospects in the Arts and Sciences."
[24] Lytton Strachey, *Queen Victoria.*

The road to death is a long march beset with all evils, and the heart fails little by little at each new terror, the bones rebel at each step, the mind sets up its own bitter resistance and to what end?[25]

The small waves rolled in and over unhurriedly, lapped upon the sand in silence and retreated; the grasses flurried before a breeze that made no sound.[26]

Gazelles are almost the only animals that look good to eat when they are still alive, in fact, one can hardly look at their hind-quarters without thinking of mint sauce.[27]

In seeing, therefore, our previous experience enters in; we see what we look for. When a girl comes down the street, men notice her figure, women notice her hat, and pickpockets notice her pocket-book.[28]

Sometimes conjunctive adverbs — *therefore, however, moreover, also, then,* and others — are used as connectives in compound sentences. In such sentences a semicolon is used before the conjunctive adverb. (The use of a comma after the conjunctive adverb is a matter of judgment, depending on the relation of the connective to its clause and to the whole sentence.)

Father has lost some money in the market; *however,* his financial position is still strong.

My son has been interested in your offer; *therefore* he will be glad to ask you for an interview.

The flames shot fiercely out of the windows; *then* the walls began to crumble.

Compound sentences, as a rule, are long sentences, and should therefore be broken up into significant word groups to help the reader. The use of the semicolon, however, is somewhat controversial. Many of the older writers employ it conscientiously; many of the younger writers have all but discarded it. It may serve the writer as a means of supplying a contrast between the longer pause and the shorter pause, between the more important constituents of the sentence and the less important. The student

[25] Katherine Anne Porter, "Pale Horse, Pale Rider."
[26] *Ibid.*
[27] George Orwell, *Such, Such Were the Joys.*
[28] Wolfgang Langewiesche "You Can Learn to See More."

would probably be best advised to use the semicolon between co-ordinate clauses not connected by a conjunction since most instructors in freshman English require this type of punctuation.

Use of Italics and Quotation Marks

The last problem in punctuation which we will consider in this chapter concerns the use of quotation marks and italics, particularly in the preparation of reports.

The freshman student of composition is likely to use italics mainly in naming publications and in using words as words.

Publications may be books, magazines, or newspapers. The name of each of these is written in italics. In manuscript or in typewritten work italics are indicated by underlining.

> I read this story in *The Saturday Evening Post.*
>
> He plans to subscribe to *Reader's Digest.*
>
> *The Virginian* by Owen Wister was first published in 1902.
>
> Hervey Allen's *Israfel* is a biography of Edgar Allan Poe.
>
> I read about his appointment in *The Phoenix Gazette.*

When one is referring to a word as a word rather than using it as a symbol of communication, the word is written in italics.

> In the fifth sentence above we know that *appointment* is a noun.
>
> The verb in the first sentence is *read* and the complement is *story.*

There are, of course, many other common uses of italics. Names of ships, Pullman cars, and airplanes are italicized. So are foreign words and phrases which have not yet been accepted in our language.

> Lindbergh flew to Paris in *The Spirit of St. Louis.*
>
> Columbus' voyage of discovery to America was made in the *Pinta,* the *Nina,* and the *Santa Maria.*
>
> Father ordered roast beef *au jus* for his dinner.
>
> The foreign minister was informed that he was *persona non grata* in the United States.
>
> The legisture adjourned this morning *sine die.*

The student of composition will use quotation marks principally for directly quoted material and for the titles of articles and short stories which are part of a larger publication.

Quotation marks are used for directly quoted material if it is
not too lengthy. Otherwise the quoted matter is indicated by
single spacing (in double-spaced manuscript) and indenting within
the manuscript margins.

> Every family develops its own calendar of events over the years,
> not only the conventional birthdays and anniversaries, but
> particular celebrations. One such occasion is described by
> William Allen White in his *Autobiography:* "And so on the 27th
> of April, for forty-nine and lovely years, we have had lamb on
> our dinner table, to celebrate the triumph of mind over matter."

If the quoted material contains material already enclosed in
quotation marks, single quotation marks are used to indicate
these inner marks.

> "He spat desperately into the pen, turned his wide, sweet blue
> eyes on me that were watering, and cried: 'God 'lmighty, man
> God 'lmighty!' That was as far as he could get for a moment.
> Then he added desperately: 'I don't know about these things.
> Why don't you go and talk to her ma!' "[29]

Commas and periods are always written within the quotation
marks. Question marks and exclamation points are written within
the quotation marks if they are a part of the quoted material.
This is a printer's rule.

Students accustomed to the convention of using a comma before
direct discourse sometimes make the mistake of using a comma
also before quoted material that is an integral part of the sentence,
where such usage violates the pattern of intonation. In the first
sentence below, the comma is properly inserted before the quotation; in the second sentence it is properly omitted.

> Walt Whitman said, "You shall no longer take things at second
> or third hand, nor look through the eyes of the dead, nor feed
> on the spectres in books."
> Walt Whitman admonished his countrymen not to "take things
> at second or third hand, nor look through the eyes of the dead,
> nor feed on the spectres in books."

[29] *The Autobiography of William Allen White.*

Finally, titles of articles or short stories which are included in larger publications are placed in quotation marks.

> We read W. Somerset Maugham's "Before the Party" in our literature textbook *The College Omnibus.*
>
> I am quoting from "Ladies With the Last Word" by Ralph L. Woods. This was published in the *Saturday Review* of May 30, 1959.

Summary

The purpose of punctuation is to help your reader understand what you have written. This is done by means of graphic symbols — periods, commas, semicolons, question marks and so on — which are used mainly to separate the written language into meaningful syntactical units. Punctuation accomplishes in written communication approximately what intonation does in oral communication. However, the correlation between intonation and punctuation is inexact. The same graphic symbol may be used to represent different intonation patterns and several graphic symbols may even represent approximately the same intonation pattern. Besides, punctuation is complicated by well established conventions and even with printers' rules.

The study and knowledge of intonation is important to the writer, however, since the development of sensitivity to intonation patterns may serve to increase his awareness of punctuation problems. The student proofreading his composition orally, confronted with a pause and change of pitch, has a ready signal to warn him that punctuation of some kind is necessary. A knowledge of syntax and the conventions of punctuation will help him determine what punctuation he should use.

In this chapter, we have discussed the punctuation conventions with which college students seem to be least familiar. These include the punctuation of introductory modifying word groups, restrictive and nonrestrictive modifiers, compound sentences, and the use of italics and quotation marks.

Exercise A

Write out the following sentences with appropriate punctuation where necessary to make the meaning clear.

1. In the meantime the regiment dug itself in for protection against shellfire.
2. I have decided to invest this large sum of money which is a very risky thing to do.
3. We are going to move to Albany which is the capital of New York State.
4. In the morning you will be given your physical examination.
5. When the temperature dropped the man put on his great fur coat.
6. In fact the state will have to spend over ten million dollars for this project.
7. Father ate steak and the children ate hamburgers.
8. We quickly put up the tent but it was of little protection against the wind and rain.
9. The outcome of the war was apparent after the Allied Armies had invaded Europe.
10. The President has said that we will never give up our rights in the free city of Berlin.
11. When resistance to integration developed in Little Rock it was evident that serious trouble would result subsequent events confirmed this belief.
12. The war was over the soldiers had returned home and the nation was wearily counting up the costs.
13. In many parts of the country the young folks are leaving the farms to go to the cities where they hope to rise quickly to financial success.
14. The cave-in had occurred four days ago yet the rescue party was not certain that the trapped miners were dead.
15. The senator believed the situation in Europe to be very dangerous and he advised the State Department to exercise great tact in forthcoming negotiations.
16. The army halted at the banks of the river for the great body of water offered a natural line of defense to the enemy.
17. The Queen Mary which is one of the largest ocean steamers sailed into the harbor at ten o'clock.
18. I called a doctor who came immediately to attend the injured man.

19. The prospectors had to leave their claims in October or they would have been locked in by the early snow of northern Alaska.

20. There is no possibility of your passing mathematics therefore you might as well drop the course.

21. The old man was dead the whole city mourned his passing.

22. In the early morning hours before the sun was up he liked to climb the hill and watch the light streak across the sky.

23. I read this story in Good Housekeeping.

24. This is the time when all of the people must support their leaders.

25. The residents evacuated the village when they were warned of the danger of the explosion.

26. Mr. Brown will return to Boston on Monday when he will meet with the directors of the corporation.

27. Mr. Johnson wants to buy a small place where he will have room to keep a horse.

28. I am sure you will be pleased if you buy this car.

29. If you buy this car I am sure you will be pleased.

30. Civilization will be destroyed unless we can eliminate the use of armed force.

31. He will probably make a large profit from this investment although we never can be certain about such things.

32. When the jury filed out the people in the courtroom moved anxiously in their seats but the prisoner sat calmly waiting for their verdict which would mean life or death to him.

33. The article I am referring to is entitled Divorce Is Going out of Style and was published in Reader's Digest in August 1957.

34. The subject of the sentence which you have just punctuated is article.

35. His product had been losing its appeal in the low-priced market for the time had come when people were demanding more attractive styling they were asking for beauty as well as economy and performance.

36. In 1919 there had been 6,771,000 passenger cars in service in the United States by 1929 there were no less than 23,121,000. This statement is quoted directly from Only Yesterday by Frederick Lewis Allen.

37. The old man's glance brought Henry's warning to mind and with a certain feeling of curiosity I was impelled to remain with him to determine the exact nature of his motives which I had begun to suspect.

38. It would be an easy matter to multiply such incidents as these for indeed they are a matter of common experience.

39. The most exciting adventure of the trip was meeting the admiral nevertheless we were somewhat disappointed in his attitude.

40. These cocktail parties were a modus vivendi in themselves for which a new philosophy, a new ethic, and a new etiquette had to be devised.[30]

Exercise B

Write out the following paragraph and punctuate it so that its meaning will be clear to the reader.

Jim and Irene Westcott were the kind of people who seem to strike that satisfactory average of income endeavor and respectability that is reached by statistical reports in college alumni bulletins they were the parents of two young children they had been married nine years they lived on the twelfth floor of an apartment house near Sutton Place they went to the theatre on an average of 10.3 times a year and they hoped some day to live in Westchester Irene Westcott was a pleasant rather plain girl with soft brown hair and a wide fine forehead upon which nothing at all had been written and in the cold weather she wore a coat of fitch skins dyed to resemble mink you could not say that Jim Westcott looked younger than he was but you could at least say of him that he seemed to feel younger he wore his graying hair cut very short he dressed in the kind of clothes his class had worn at Andover and his manner was earnest vehement and intentionally naive the Westcotts differed from their friends their classmates and their neighbors only in an interest they shared in serious music they went to a great many concerts although they seldom mentioned this to anyone and they spent a good deal of time listening to music on the radio

Exercise C

The passage which you punctuated in Exercise B is printed here with the author's punctuation. Compare your punctuation with his, and discuss differences in meaning and style which may result from these differences in punctuation.

Jim and Irene Westcott were the kind of people who seem to strike that satisfactory average of income, endeavor and respectability that is reached

[30] Jean Stafford, "Children Are Bored on Sunday."

by the statistical reports in college alumni bulletins. They were the
parents of two young children, they had been married nine years, they
lived on the twelfth floor of an apartment house near Sutton Place, they
went to the theatre on an average of 10.3 times a year, and they hoped
some day to live in Westchester. Irene Westcott was a pleasant, rather
plain girl with soft brown hair and a wide, fine forehead upon which
nothing at all had been written, and in the cold weather she wore a coat
of fitch skins dyed to resemble mink. You could not say that Jim Westcott looked younger than he was, but you could at least say of him that
he seemed to feel younger. He wore his graying hair cut very short, he
dressed in the kind of clothes his class had worn at Andover, and his
manner was earnest, vehement, and intentionally naive. The Westcotts
differed from their friends, their classmates, and their neighbors only in
an interest they shared in serious music. They went to a great many
concerts — although they seldom mentioned this to anyone — and they
spent a good deal of time listening to music on the radio.[31]

[31] John Cheever, "The Enormous Radio," from *The Enormous Radio and
Other Stories* (Funk & Wagnalls Company).

19

Using Grammatical Resources

THIS FINAL CHAPTER will describe two kinds of practice exercises through which the student can develop skill in the use of grammatical resources to construct more effective sentences. It will also include a discussion of sentence patterns, their conventions and restrictions, and will explain how these structural patterns may lead an uninformed, inexperienced writer into ambiguous statements.

Practice Exercises I: Sentence Patterns

The first type of exercise explained here is a problem in sentence building from specifications. Its purpose is to check the student's knowledge of specific grammatical structures and to give him practice in using them. Ten sample problems are worked out.

PROBLEM NO. 1

Construct a meaningful sentence using the pattern N V, with an adverbial subordinate clause modifier and a verbal phrase modifying the noun subject.

SOLUTION

Mr. Simpson *seeing the storm clouds* ran quickly to cover *when he heard the lightning roll.*

N V pattern: *Mr. Simpson ran*
Adverbial clause modifier: "when he heard the lightning roll"
Verbal phrase modifying the subject "Mr. Simpson": "seeing the storm clouds"

PROBLEM NO. 2

Construct a meaningful sentence using the pattern N V N, with a noun in apposition with the noun complement and an adjective clause modifying this noun.

SOLUTION

The public condemned the reporter *Jack Hennessy, who had written up the story in all its lurid details.*

N V N pattern: *public condemned reporter*
Noun in apposition with noun complement: "Jack Hennessy"
Adjective clause modifying this noun: "who had written up the story in all its lurid details"

PROBLEM NO. 3

Construct a meaningful sentence of the pattern N V N, with an infinitive phrase as the complement. Use a transitive verb in the infinitive with an object modified by a prepositional phrase.

SOLUTION

I do not want *to accept a reward for this small act of kindness.*

N V N pattern: *I do not want to accept*
Transitive verb as infinitive: "*to accept*"
Prepositional phrase modifying the object of the infinitive: "for this small act of kindness"

Problem No. 4

Construct a meaningful sentence of the pattern N V N N with two single-word adjectival modifiers of the inner complement.

Solution

The committee selected the *kind, willing* Mr. Brown chairman.

N V N N pattern: *committee selected Mr. Brown chairman*
Inner complement: "Mr. Brown"
Two adjectival modifiers (single-word): "kind" "willing"

Problem No. 5

Construct a meaningful sentence consisting of two subject-predicate word groups connected by the co-ordinate conjunction *but*. Construct each subject-predicate word group in the pattern N V (linking) Adj.

Solution

The picture was beautiful, *but* the subject was difficult to understand.

N V (linking) Adj pattern: *picture was beautiful*
                              subject was difficult
The two subject-predicate word groups are connected by *but* forming a compound sentence.

Problem No. 6

Construct a meaningful sentence using the pattern N V, with an introductory subordinate clause used as a modifier of the main clause.

Solution

After the war had ended, the soldiers returned to their homes.

N V pattern: *soldiers returned*
Subordinate clause modifying the main clause: "After the war had ended"

Problem No. 7

Construct a meaningful sentence using the pattern N V N, with the noun complement a gerund phrase in which there is a subordinate clause modifier.

SOLUTION

Mr. Wilson liked *living in the country where he could enjoy the green trees and the colorful flowers.*

N V N pattern: *Mr. Wilson liked living in the country*
Gerund phrase complement: "Living in the country . . ."
Subordinate clause modifier: "where he could enjoy the green trees and the colorful flowers"

PROBLEM NO. 8

Construct a meaningful compound sentence with co-ordinate clauses connected by *and*, with each clause in the pattern N V and with an adverbial clause modifier included in the second clause.

SOLUTION

The children hurried quickly to school, *and* there they worked hard all day *because they wanted to please their teacher.*

N V pattern: *children hurried*
 they worked
The two subject-predicate word groups are connected by *and* forming a compound sentence.
Adverbial clause modifier: "because they wanted to please their teacher"

PROBLEM NO. 9

Construct a meaningful sentence in the question pattern, beginning with *how*, *why*, or other structure words of this kind. Have it contain an adjective clause modifier and an adverbial clause modifier.

SOLUTION

How would you feel *if a mechanic started to work on your car who had no experience on this particular model?*

Question pattern: "How would you feel . . ."
Adjective clause modifier: "who had no experience on this particular model"
Adverbial clause modifier: "if a mechanic started to work on your car . . ."

PROBLEM No. 10

Construct a meaningful sentence using the pattern N V (linking) N, with a noun clause used as an appositive, and with an adverbial clause modifying the verb in the noun clause.

SOLUTION

It is no secret *that many men are rejected from the armed services because they are not physically fit.*

N V (linking) N pattern: *It is* no *secret*
Noun clause used as an appositive: "that many men are rejected from the armed services . . ."
Adverbial clause modifying "are rejected": "because they are not physically fit"

The possibilities of sentence building are, of course, almost endless. The ten examples given here, however, show how this type of problem can encourage the student to draw on his knowledge of language resources, sentence patterns, and modifying elements. Although the terms of each problem are fairly specific, the solutions may be of great variety, and it is interesting and profitable to compare different solutions and discuss their accuracy and relative value. The student should be careful not to construct sentences which are trite and commonplace; he will benefit by using this opportunity to draw on his experience and enlarge his vocabulary.

Structural Ambiguity

The structures of the English sentence cannot be combined casually. They must be arranged according to conventional and time-fixed patterns. We have discussed the word order of the essential elements of a sentence — subject, verb, complement. But there are other regularities of pattern which should be considered. Ambiguity of statement often occurs in writing because of the writer's ignorance of restrictions imposed by structural pattern.

One of the most common of these patterns is observed in a sentence in which a prepositional phrase and a subordinate clause follow a word which they both modify. The phrase always precedes the clause.

Mr. Thompson lives in the *house* on First Street which has just been painted.

The men *ran* into the barn when the storm came.

Joe has a *friend* at school who comes from Flagstaff.

The *books* on the table which are bound in leather belong to Henrietta.

This fixed pattern of phrase and clause modifiers, as illustrated above, may be the source of ambiguity.

I read the end of the story, which is interesting.

This is the new wing of the house that George built.

He examined the papers of the prisoners which had been brought to him.

He looked through the glasses at the top of the house which could be seen through the trees.

He had a sweater around his neck which was tied in a knot at the arms.

The ambiguity of the above sentences arises from two elements of form. First, we tend to associate the modifier with the noun or verb nearest it. This accounts for the ridiculous interpretation of the last sentence. Second, the relative pronoun may have two referents. In the first sentence the signal *which* may indicate *end* or *story*. Consider the following sentences.

He brought in the body of the man *which* had been seen in the desert.

He brought in the body of the man *who* had been seen in the desert.

In the above sentences *which* and *who* are structural clues to meaning. The referents are certain. Consider also the two sentences which follow.

He knows the friends of Mr. Wilson, who *live* in Tempe.

He knows the friends of Mr. Wilson, who *lives* in Tempe.

Here the structural clues to the referents are *live* and *lives*. In the first sentence, *live* is the plural form of the verb and *who* is therefore substituted for *friends*. In the second sentence, *lives* is the singular form of the verb, so *who* is substituting for Mr. Wilson.

To avoid ambiguity, then, in a construction in which a prepositional phrase precedes a subordinate clause modifier, the writer must be certain that structural clues are present which will indicate to the reader the syntax of the clause.

One structure frequently used in writing sometimes gives even the careful writer some difficulty with referents. The problem arises in the following sentence.

> He is one of those people who always (has, have) the courage to tell the truth.

The use of *has* would make the referent of *who* the singular word *one*. The use of *have* makes the referent of *who* the plural word *people*. The writer, however, does not have a choice in this situation since conventional usage requires the plural form *have*. There is an exception to this usage if a positive clue is given in the main clause as in the following sentence.

> He is the *only* one of those people who has the courage to tell the truth.

Another common structural pattern that may lead to ambiguity is a verbal phrase followed by a subordinate clause. The following sentences are clear in meaning.

> He saw a *man* running down the street who had just held up the store.
>
> We found a *woman* cooking the supper who had just been hired as the cook.

The following, on the other hand, are ambiguous.

> There is a book lying on the table which belongs to my mother.
>
> We observed a man talking to a woman who had red hair.

We do not know whether it is the table or the book which "belongs to my mother," whether it is the man or the woman "who had red hair."

Still another type of ambiguity which arises from a structural pattern is the occasional confusion resulting from the fact that both a predicate adjective and an adverb may immediately follow the verb.

> The boy looked *serious* when I told him the news.
>
> The boy looked *seriously* at the picture.

In the first of the above sentences, *serious* is used as a predicate adjective after the verb *looked*, which is a linking or copulative verb in this sentence. In the second sentence, *seriously* is used as an adverbial modifier of the verb *looked*. The structural signal is clear to the reader, the *-ly* suffix which is characteristic of the adverb. If the structural signal is not there or is not clear, ambiguity may result. The following sentences illustrate this.

1. The Ford appeared *faster* than the Maxwell.
2. Sara appeared *quicker* than her mother.
3. The first dog looked *longer* than the second.
4. The Jones boy looked *hardest* of them all.
5. That young man walks *straighter* than he used to.[1]

In each of these five sentences the uncertainty of meaning is caused by two structural factors: the lack of definite signals to differentiate the adjective from the adverb, and the fact that the comparison of both the adjectives and the adverbs is effected by adding the endings *-er* and *-est*. Any one of these sentences may be clarified by supplying the proper structural signals.

1. The Ford appeared to be faster than the Maxwell.
   The Ford appeared in our block faster than the Maxwell.
2. Sara appeared to be quicker than her mother.
   Sara appeared more quickly than her mother.
3. The first dog looked longer to me than the second.
   The first dog looked longer at the food than the second.
4. The Jones boy looked hardest and cruelest of them all.
   The Jones boy looked hardest of them all for his books.
5. That young man walks straighter and more erect than he used to.
   That young man walks straighter along the path than he used to.

The pattern of single-word adjectival modifiers of a noun is fairly well fixed by usage and must be observed. The adjectives may not be arranged casually, for confusing and un-English utterances would result. The following examples illustrate the conventions of adjective pattern or sequence.

[1] Adapted from Charles C. Fries, *The Structure of English.*

The very kind old gentleman
The coming 1954 class reunion
The first annual classroom teachers' convention
The only new through campus bus
Almost all the twenty-five very famous Army officers . . .[2]

The student will notice, without resorting to a thorough analysis of the word groups, that when there is a noun modifier used adjectivally, it comes immediately before the noun it modifies. There are times when this pattern can be a source of ambiguity. The following constructions are fairly common and therefore quite clear.

Young men's suits
An old ladies' home
Fast navy planes
A portable ice chest
The noncommissioned officers' club

In the following constructions, however, the reader may not be certain of the writer's meaning. Ambiguity results from the fixed pattern.

A good-looking girl's hat
A new baby's crib
Smart women's shoes
A cool morning dip
A German silver medal

The fact that adverbs may be moved about within a sentence is sometimes the cause of ambiguity. The adverb is unique in this flexibility of position.

Silently Captain Johnson walked away from the men.
Captain Johnson walked *silently* away from the men.
Captain Johnson walked away from the men *silently*.

In the above sentences, the position of the adverb does not affect the meaning; it affects only the emphasis. But with certain adverbs, the meaning of the statement changes with the position of the adverb.

[2] Charles C. Fries, *The Structure of English.*

He *only* loaned me ten dollars.
He loaned me *only* ten dollars.

He *simply* could not talk about the matter.
He could not talk about the matter *simply*.

I *merely* wanted to ask one question.
I wanted to ask *merely* one question.

That perennial difficulty of the young writer — the misplaced modifier — is a case of ambiguity resulting from a violation of conventional form. Modifiers in English have a strong affinity for whatever word they are closest to. Having long placed our modifiers next to the word which they modify, we have come to associate the word relationships in this manner. This is particularly true of adjectival modifiers and most particularly of word group modifiers. The ambiguities of the following sentences result from careless construction by a writer who has not used his modifying elements according to convention.

The inventory was taken by an extra clerk with tabulating machines.

He stood there pointing to the boat which could be seen far out on the rough water coming into the harbor.

He had heard of the accident which befell his cousin before he returned to the city.

He plans when he goes to Chicago to visit his sister.

He met his girl friend in San Francisco in the Cow Palace where they started going around together.

Two weeks ago Joe Kelly came to the church that I was attending with his grandmother.

Mrs. Crimpy hung a beautiful picture on the wall which had been painted by Picasso.

The careless waitress spilled the coffee down Mrs. Twimby's back, which was fortunately ice cold.

No attempt has been made here to elaborate on all types of structural ambiguity. The student will find examples of ambiguous statements in his reading and should copy them down for study and discussion. However, some of the ambiguity he thus encounters will arise out of the multiple meanings of certain words, as a pun is ambiguous. This is called "lexical ambiguity," as distinguished from the "structural ambiguity" which has been the subject of this discussion.

Practice Exercises II: Synthesis and Coherence

Our second type of practice in the use of language structures is an exercise in synthesis. It consists in building sentences from a number of separate but related statements of fact or idea. The object is to use the language resources of English to express the given facts and ideas most effectively in one or more coherent sentences. To illustrate this exercise, a number of problems are given here with suggested solutions.

PROBLEM NO. 1

> A heavy rainstorm occurred on Tuesday.
> The storm was in Globe, Arizona.
> The property damage amounted to $100,000.

SOLUTIONS

1. There was a heavy rainstorm in Globe, Arizona, on Tuesday. It caused property damage amounting to $100,000.
2. A heavy rainstorm occurred in Globe, Arizona, on Tuesday and caused property damage amounting to $100,000.
3. Property damage in Globe, Arizona, amounting to $100,000 was caused by a heavy rainstorm on Tuesday.
4. The heavy rainstorm in Globe, Arizona, on Tuesday caused $100,000 property damage.

(The student should decide which statement expresses the facts most effectively and why.)

PROBLEM NO. 2

> Dwight D. Eisenhower was elected President in 1952.
> Mr. Eisenhower had been a successful general during World War II.
> Mr. Eisenhower was the candidate of the Republican Party.

SOLUTIONS

1. Dwight D. Eisenhower had been a successful general in World War II, and in 1952 he was elected President. He was the candidate of the Republican Party.

2. Dwight D. Eisenhower, who had been a successful general of World War II, was elected President in 1952. He was the candidate of the Republican Party.

3. Dwight D. Eisenhower, who had been a successful general in World War II, was elected President in 1952 as the candidate of the Republican Party.

4. A successful general of World War II, Dwight D. Eisenhower was elected President in 1952 as the candidate of the Republican Party.

PROBLEM NO. 3

Friedrich Wilhelm Nietzsche was born in Germany in 1844.

He died in 1900.

He is famous as a philosopher.

He believed in the doctrine of the superman and the superstate.

SOLUTIONS

1. Friedrich Wilhelm Nietzsche was born in Germany in 1844 and died in 1900. He was a famous philosopher who believed in the doctrine of the superman and the superstate.

2. Friedrich Wilhelm Nietzsche, the famous German philosopher, was born in 1844 and died in 1900. He believed in the doctrine of the superman and the superstate.

3. Friedrich Wilhelm Nietzsche, the famous German philosopher who believed in the doctrine of the superman and the superstate, was born in 1844 and died in 1900.

4. Friedrich Wilhelm Nietzsche, 1844-1900, was the famous German philosopher who believed in the doctrine of the superman and the superstate.

PROBLEM NO. 4

The Madison Boy Scout Troop has twenty-five members.

They plan to go to summer camp in August.

They will camp at North Lake.

There are ten log cabins in the camp.

SOLUTIONS

1. In August when they are planning to go to camp, the Madison Boy Scout Troop, which has twenty-five members, will go to North Lake, where they have ten log cabins.

2. The Madison Boy Scout Troop is planning to go to summer camp in August. The twenty-five members will go to North Lake, where they have ten log cabins.

3. The twenty-five members of the Madison Boy Scout Troop are planning to go to summer camp in August at North Lake, where they have ten log cabins.

4. The summer camp of the Madison Boy Scout Troop will be held in August at North Lake. The troop of twenty-five members will be housed in ten log cabins.

PROBLEM No. 5

The road was narrow and wet.

Bob had to drive carefully.

He arrived at Helen's house at ten.

It was too late to go to the movies.

SOLUTIONS

1. Bob did not arrive at Helen's house until ten, which was too late to go to the movies. He had to drive carefully because the road was narrow and wet.

2. Because the road was narrow and wet, Bob had to drive carefully, and he did not arrive at Helen's house until ten. This was too late to go to the movies.

3. The road was narrow and wet, and Bob had to drive carefully. He arrived at Helen's house at ten, too late to go to the movies.

4. Since the road was narrow and wet, Bob had to drive carefully. When he arrived at Helen's house at ten, it was too late to go to the movies.

PROBLEM No. 6

Thomas Hardy was born in Dorchester, England, in 1840.

As a young man he trained for the profession of architecture.

He became later one of England's novelists.

Many of his novels deal with the southern English countryside.
They are filled with fatalism and a deep-rooted pessimism.

SOLUTIONS

1. When Thomas Hardy, who was born in Dorchester, England,
   in 1840, was a young man he trained for the profession of
   architecture. He later became one of England's great novelists who wrote of the southern English countryside. His
   novels are filled with fatalism and a deep-rooted pessimism.

2. Thomas Hardy, who was born in Dorchester, England, in 1840,
   trained as a young man for the profession of architecture.
   However, he became one of England's great novelists, writing
   novels of the southern English countryside which are filled
   with fatalism and a deep-rooted pessimism.

3. Thomas Hardy, one of England's great novelists, wrote novels
   dealing with the southern English countryside which are
   filled with fatalism and a deep-rooted pessimism. He was
   born in Dorchester in 1840, and when he was a young man,
   he trained for the profession of architecture.

4. Although Thomas Hardy, who was born in 1840, trained as a
   young man for the profession of architecture, he became one
   of England's great novelists. His novels deal with the southern
   English countryside and are filled with fatalism and a deep-
   rooted pessimism.

PROBLEM No. 7

Dad was recalling the roaring 1920's for us last night.

Many women began to smoke cigarettes.

Bobbed hair became stylish.

Women wore short skirts.

The vogue of rouge and lipstick spread over the country.

Beauty shops sprang up on every street to give facials and other
youth-saving treatments.

SOLUTIONS

1. Dad recalled for us last night that in the roaring 1920's many
   women began to smoke and bob their hair and wear short
   skirts and use rouge and lipstick. He said that beauty shops,
   which gave facials and other youth-saving treatments, sprang
   up on every street.

2. The roaring 1920's were recalled for us by Dad last night, who said that at this time many women began to smoke. Bobbed hair became stylish, as well as short skirts. Beauty shops, where facials and other youth-saving treatments were given, sprang up on every street.

3. Dad was recalling the roaring 1920's for us last night. He told us that not only did many women begin to smoke cigarettes, but that they also bobbed their hair and wore short skirts. As the vogue for rouge and lipstick spread over the country, beauty shops sprang up on every street to give facials and other youth-saving treatments.

4. Recalling the roaring 1920's for us last night, Dad said that many women began to smoke cigarettes, bob their hair, and wear short skirts. The vogue of rouge and lipstick spread over the country, and beauty shops sprang up on every street to give facials and other youth-saving treatments.

PROBLEM No. 8

The nations of the world face the problem of peace and war.

The development of scientific study of the atom has created a new means of destruction.

This threatens our civilization.

SOLUTIONS

1. The development of scientific study of the atom has created a new means of destruction. For this reason, the nations of the world face the problem of peace and war, since our civilization is threatened.

2. Our civilization is threatened by the new means of destruction developed by the scientific study of the atom. The nations of the world now face the problem of peace and war.

3. Because our civilization is threatened by the new means of destruction developed by the scientific study of the atom, the nations of the world face the problem of peace and war.

4. The nations of the world face the problem of peace and war, for the development of scientific study of the atom has created a new means of destruction which threatens our civilization.

The value of the type of exercise which has been elaborated here depends on a number of factors. First, of course, the student should be familiar with the structures of the English language. Second, a number of different solutions to the problem, using a variety of structures, should be developed. Third, the student should evaluate his solutions in terms of their effectiveness of communication and select the one he believes to be the best. Finally, analyses of "best" solutions of different members of the class should take into careful consideration such matters as style, coherence, economy of statement, faithfulness to given data, and shades of meaning. In class discussions, the instructor should insist on the use of grammatical terminology and nomenclature.

Summary

Improvement in written composition may be accomplished by means of developing more effective sentence structures. The knowledge of grammatical resources alone is insufficient to guarantee improvement in sentence construction. One must learn to *use* these resources through practice, directed practice.

In this chapter two types of practice exercises have been discussed and illustrated. One type is the building of sentences on basic patterns according to given specifications. The other is an exercise in synthesizing sentences from related facts or ideas stated separately and evaluating the results in terms of effectiveness of communication.

Because the structures of English cannot be combined casually, the attention of the student has been called once again to certain restrictions of pattern. A number of types of structural ambiguity have been discussed and illustrated.

This last chapter of the book has been developed both as a test of grammatical knowledge and as a means of improving skill in sentence construction. The emphasis, as it has been throughout the text, is on use. The failure to make grammar functional in the past, it seems to the writer, has been largely because the student has not been directed to use a mastery of the knowledge of language structure in developing technical skill in sentence construction.

EXERCISE A

The following are problems in sentence building from speci-fications. In each case, the problem is to build a meaningful sentence according to the given basic pattern and fulfilling the stated requirements.

1. Use the pattern N V to build a sentence with an adjective subordinate clause containing a prepositional phrase modifier.

2. Use the pattern N V N to build a sentence with an adverbial clause modifier and a participial phrase modifying the subject of the sentence.

3. Use a question pattern introduced by the structure word *which* to build a sentence containing an infinitive phrase modifying a direct object.

4. Use the pattern N V N N with a participial phrase modifying the subject and an adjective clause modifying the inner complement.

5. Use the pattern N V with three single-word adjectival modifiers of the subject.

6. Use the pattern N V with three single-word adverbial modifiers of the verb.

7. Use the pattern N V N with an infinitive phrase as the direct object that has an adverbial modifier.

8. Use the pattern N V N with a noun clause as the direct object.

9. Use the pattern N V N with a noun clause as the subject of the sentence.

10. Use the pattern N V N N with an infinitive phrase as the outer complement.

11. Use the pattern N V N with a noun clause in apposition with the subject.

12. Use the pattern N V N with a noun clause in apposition with the direct object.

13. Use the pattern N V N N with an adverbial clause modifying the verb.

14. Use the pattern N V N with an infinitive phrase as the direct object. In the infinitive phrase use a noun clause as the object of the infinitive.

15. Use a question pattern beginning with an auxiliary verb to build a sentence in which there is an adverbial clause modifier.

16. Use the pattern N V N to build a sentence in which the subject is compound and in which an adjective clause modifies the direct object.

17. Use the pattern N V N to build a sentence in which the verb is compound and in which an adjective clause modifies the subject.

18. Use the pattern N V with a noun in apposition with the subject.

19. Use the pattern N V with a verb in apposition with the verb.

20. Use the pattern N V with an adverb in apposition with a single-word modifier of the verb.

21. Build a compound sentence in which the pattern of each subject-predicate word group is N V, using single-word modifiers of each of the nouns and verbs.

22. Use an introductory adverbial clause in a sentence with the pattern N V.

23. Use the pattern N V N with a gerund phrase as the subject.

24. Use the pattern N V N with a gerund phrase as the object.

25. Use the pattern N V N with a gerund phrase as the subject. In the gerund phrase use a noun clause as the object of the gerund.

26. Build a compound sentence in which the pattern of the first subject-predicate word group is N V and the second is N V N. In the second main clause use an adverbial clause to modify the verb.

27. Using the co-ordinate conjunction *for*, build a compound sentence in which the pattern of each subject-predicate word group is N V, with an adjective clause modifying the subject of the second main clause.

28. Using no connectives, build a compound sentence with three main clauses arranged in order of increasing importance. Use N V N as the basic pattern of each clause.

29. Use the pattern N V to build a sentence with a compound verb of three parts, each part having an adverbial clause modifier.

30. Use the pattern N V (linking) N to build a sentence in which an infinitive phrase modifies the complement.

31. Use the pattern N V (linking) N to build a sentence in which a prepositional phrase modifies the subject and a verbal participial phrase modifies the complement.

32. Use the pattern N V (linking) N to build a sentence in which a noun clause is used as the complement.

33. Use the pattern N V (linking) Adj to build a sentence in which an infinitive phrase modifies the adjective.

34. Use the pattern N V (linking) Adj to build a sentence in which an adverbial clause modifies the adjective.

35. Use the pattern N V (linking) Adj to build a sentence in which an adjective clause modifies the noun.

36. Use an inverted sentence pattern beginning with the structure word *there* to build a sentence containing an adverbial clause which has an infinitive phrase as its complement.

Exercise B

In each of the following problems, the student is to combine the given facts in one or more coherent sentences. He should develop at least four solutions to each problem, then check the solution which he considers the most effective. The student should retain the language of the problem as far as possible.

1. Willie Smith is a second baseman.
   He plays on the Portsmouth Giants.
   He batted .350 last year.

2. The Klondike is in Northwest Canada.
   It was the scene of a gold rush in 1897.
   The gold rush lasted two years.

3. In 1910 the population was 92,000,000.
   There were 2,600 daily newspapers.
   In 1958 the population was 175,000,000.
   There were only 1,751 daily newspapers.

4. Gamal Abdel Nasser led the revolution in Egypt.
   The revolution took place on July 22, 1952.
   King Farouk was overthrown.
   The course of history in the Middle East was changed.

5. Sir Alexander Fleming discovered penicillin.
   The discovery was made in 1928.
   Fleming was a bacteriologist working on germ cultures.
   The discovery was accidental.

6. Reardon Conner is the author of *Shake Hands With the Devil*.
   The book was first published in 1938.
   It is the story of an Irish surgeon.
   It tells of his struggle against the Black and Tans.
   The time is during the Irish War for Independence.

7. The car was old and dilapidated.
   The engine was in need of repairs.
   The family was acquainted with these facts.
   Jimmy drove the car every night.
   The car left the road one night.
   Jimmy was seriously hurt.

8. It rained all afternoon.
   The game was called off.
   It will be played on Thursday.
   Jack Combs is expected to pitch.

9. Iceland is a large island.
   It is located in the North Atlantic.
   It is between Greenland and Denmark.
   It was originally a Danish possession.
   It became an independent republic in 1944.

10. The new ship steamed into the harbor.
    Friendly whistles began to blow.
    The welcoming launch moved quickly toward the ship.
    City officials and relatives of the passengers were on the launch.
    The passengers waved at the launch as it approached.

11. The storm came up late in the night.
    Heavy rain began to fall.
    A strong wind blew with considerable violence.
    No damage was done to the house or barn.

12. The President may attend a top-level conference.
    There are conditions.
    Some preliminary agreement must be made by the foreign ministers.
    Russia will have to show some evidence of good faith.

13. The manager expressed his opinion.
    The salesmen would need to work longer hours.
    More advertising would be necessary.
    A public relations campaign would have to be instituted.
    Sales would then increase.

14. Several letters have come to the editor.
    They assert that Samuel Winters did not get a fair deal.
    He was fired without a hearing.
    They demand his reinstatement.

15. Joe Smith drives his car at high speed.
    He often drives through the suburbs.
    This is very dangerous.
    He may injure himself and others.

16. Thomas Carlyle was born in Ecclefechan in Scotland.
    He was the eldest of nine children.
    He attended Edinburgh University.
    He completed his history of the French Revolution in 1837.
    This work is considered more as a literary document than as a great
    historical work.

17. Carol Brown will attend college in the fall.
    She plans to major in English.
    She has a growing interest in language and literature.
    She will specialize in the study of modern poetry.

18. Plumkin gave two reasons for his bankruptcy.
    He was unable to raise sufficient capital.
    His production methods were obsolete.
    He gave this testimony at the preliminary hearing.

19. The property tax rate is $1.70 per $100 of assessed valuation in the
    State of Arizona.
    The Maricopa tax rate is 90 cents per $100.
    These rates were adopted today.
    These rates were adopted for fiscal 1959–60.

20. Two men robbed the Jonesville State Bank.
    They were armed with shotguns.
    They wore straw hats, dark glasses, and handkerchief masks.
    They took about 50,000 dollars in cash.

21. Oliver Goldsmith wrote the poem, *The Deserted Village.*
    He was homsesick for his native County of Westmeath in Ireland.
    He had lived in the beautiful pastoral region near Lough Rea.
    Here one may still see "the never failing brook" and the "decent
    church that topped the neighboring hill."

22. The house became very quiet.
    The children had gone to bed.
    Outside the wind was blowing.
    It was very cold.

EXERCISE C

*The following sentences are ambiguous. Discuss the struc-
tural factors involved in each case and rewrite the sentence so
that the meaning is clear.*

1. Their business is sound.
2. He lives in a home on 10th Street which has just been opened up.
3. He is a friend of the plumber who is going to get married.
4. Grandma looked long in the mirror.
5. Plant flowers in April.
6. He thought of his mother looking at the old homsestead.
7. They sell only good-looking boys' clothing.

8. He eats when he travels to the city in the dining car.

9. There is a fireplace in the house, which is built of stone.

10. She offered me a dish of fresh bread pudding.

11. The foreign student learned to watch carefully printed directions.

12. Buddy Hassett sung "The Star-Spangled Banner" — one of the finest ball players.[3]

13. The teacher slapped the girl with the high-heeled shoes.

14. A large bottle costs no more.

15. He worked quickly to solve the problem.

[3] Dizzy Dean on television, August 9, 1959.

Index